# The Essence of
# Adam Smith's
# *Wealth of Nations*

# The Essence of
# Adam Smith's
## *Wealth of Nations*

Edited with an Introduction by
## Hunter Lewis

*The Essence of* . . . series of books are edited versions of great works of moral philosophy, distilled to reveal the essence of their authors' thought and argument. To read the complete, unedited version of this work, and see the excised passages, please visit our website at www.AxiosPress.com.

Axios Press
P.O. Box 118
Mount Jackson, VA 22842
888.542.9467    info@axiospress.com

**Library of Congress Cataloging-in-Publication Data**

Smith, Adam, 1723–1790.
[Inquiry into the nature and causes of the wealth of nations. Selections]
The essence of Adam Smith's Wealth of Nations / edited with an introduction by Hunter Lewis.
p. cm.
Includes bibliographical references and index.
ISBN 978-1-60419-041-0 (pbk.)
1. Economics. I. Lewis, Hunter. II. Title.

HB161.S6522 2011

330.15'3–dc22

2011009724

# Contents

## Book Two: Of the Nature, Accumulation, and Employment of Stock

## Book Three: Of the Different Progress of Opulence in Different Nations

## Book Four: Of Systems of Political Economy

## Book Five: Of the Revenue of the Sovereign or Commonwealth

*Introduction*

# Why We All Need to Read Adam Smith

T HERE ARE MANY myths about Adam Smith. Best selling economist John Kenneth Galbraith claimed that Smith was "the first economist,"[1] and thus in effect the inventor of economics. This is certainly wrong. Smith was not even the inventor of modern free market economics. That accolade would be shared by Richard Cantillon,[2] Anne-Robert-Jacques Turgot,[3] David Hume,[4] and to a lesser degree François Quesnay,[5] among others.

Famed economist Joseph Schumpeter concluded rightly that "*The Wealth of Nations* does not contain a single analytic idea, principle, or method that was entirely new in 1776."[6] A journal article has even been devoted to the question of whether Smith was a plagiarist,[7] although the charge remains unproven, and probably applies today's standard to the past in an inappropriate way.

It is closer to the truth, but still incorrect, to say that *The Wealth of Nations* is the "bible" of free market capitalism. As we shall see, Smith made too many errors for this to be the case. A very prominent free market economist, Murray Rothbard, regarded Smith, in Rothbard colleague David Gordon's telling phrase, as almost the "gravedigger," not the founder of free market economics.[8]

If Rothbard were entirely right, we could stop right here, close this introduction, and not bother to read Smith himself. To reach this conclusion, however, would be an error. There are reasons not only to read Smith, but also to study and value his work highly. In this introduction at least, we have come not to bury Smith for his undeniable faults but to praise him.

No one disputes that Smith is one of the most influential economists, and indeed thinkers, of world history. Economist Mark Skousen wrote a book describing the "big three" of economics as Smith, Marx, and Keynes. These three have clearly been the most influential, and Smith the most lastingly influential of the three. Has any single book had a greater impact on world history than *The Wealth of Nations*? The only possible competitor is Charles Darwin's *Origin of the Species*, which ignited the evolution controversy.

Is then Smith, the uber-famous economist, simply overblown, a case of earning a reputation that he does not deserve? No, not at all. Whatever his failings, he has more than earned his fame as the most profound and persuasive critic of an economic system traditionally referred to as mercantilism, but more recently (and quite appropriately) called "crony capitalism." Smith's critique is always relevant, because crony capitalism is the dominant economic system of world history. It is especially relevant today, when this type of capitalism is especially strong, both in the developed and the developing world.

What exactly is crony capitalism? In simple terms, we can think of it as state-led capitalism gone awry. In ideal terms, state-led capitalism envisions wise, unselfish, and far-sighted public servants making economic decisions for the greater good of all of us. In reality, critics of state-led capitalism say, public servants are rarely wise and far-sighted and never unselfish. They have their own interests, which in the case of politicians focus on the immediate need to get re-elected, with the true public welfare, and especially the true long-term public welfare, mostly ignored.

Public "servants" running the economy to serve their own interests are bad enough. But we get crony capitalism when the public servants reach out to ally themselves with rich people, corporations, labor unions, trial lawyers, or other powerful private interest groups. Often these alliances are formed under the fig leaf of government "regulating" the powerful private interests. But the reality is that government and special interests work out deals behind the regulatory smokescreen, in effect combine to run the economy for their mutual immediate advantage, not the long-term advantage of the general public which government is sworn to serve.

Smith's solution to this conundrum is not to try to make regulation more honest or more effective. That, he suggests, is mostly futile. It is futile because government will never be honest enough to avoid the temptations of crony capitalism or wise enough to run the economy even if it could avoid the temptations. Indeed no one can be wise enough to run the economy. Only the preferences of millions of consumers expressed through markets can successfully order and guide our economic affairs.

The correct solution is to get government out of the economy and make markets freer. Competition, encouraged by free markets, is in the final analysis the only reliable regulator of economic life. It is not surprising that powerful private economic interests hate competition and conspire with government regulators to restrict it and create government-supported monopolies.

One of the most egregious myths about Adam Smith is that he was an apologist for powerful private interests such as rich businessmen. In this account, Smith is often described as a "conservative" economist concerned with protecting the status quo. This is absurd. It ignores what Smith actually said.

Although certainly no firebrand, Smith was more of a "revolutionary" than a "conservative." His aim in writing *The Wealth of Nations* was to attack the status quo of his day, which was crony capitalist to its core. He wanted to get government out of the economy for many reasons, but especially because he thought the marriage of money and politics created an inherently corrupt system.

We can all talk endlessly about combating corruption and cleaning up the system. But, Smith infers, this will never happen under state-led capitalism. So long as government runs the economy, private economic interests will insinuate themselves into politics. Money and power will flow back and forth through ever more corrupted channels, the same channels which today run between The City and Whitehall in the UK, Wall Street and Washington in the US, among other murky streams. Average citizens always end up getting the short end of the stick, as they did during the infamous bailout of The City and Wall Street following the Crash of 2008, and during subsequent years of high unemployment.

Capitalism has been called by some a system run for the benefit business owners. If so, this is not Smith's capitalism. He wants a system run for the benefit, not of the business owner or the worker, but of the average consumer. Of course consumers are also workers; that is how they get the wherewithal to consume. But working, like organizing and owning businesses, is a means to an end: the creation of goods and services to meet the genuine needs of the people, and not just some of the people, all of the people, especially people still living in poverty.

Smith emphasizes that

> no society can surely be flourishing and happy, of which the far greater part of the members are poor and miserable.[9]

But in a crony capitalist system, not only the interests of the poor,

> [even] . . . the interest[s] of the [average] consumer [are] constantly sacrificed[10]

to those of rulers and special interests allied with the rulers.

Government ought to be impartial in its promotion of the common good:

> To hurt, in any degree, the interest of any one order of citizens, for no other reason but to promote that of some other, is evidently contrary to that justice and equality of treatment which the sovereign owes to all the different orders of his subjects.[11]

Nevertheless,

> it is the industry which is carried on for the benefit of the rich and the powerful,

that is principally encouraged by our mercantile system. That which is carried on for
the benefit of the poor and the indigent is
too often either neglected or oppressed.[12]

Proponents of state-led capitalism often point to the
selfishness and self-interested maneuvering of private
business interests. Smith agrees with them up to a point:

The clamor and sophistry of merchants and
manufacturers easily persuade them, that
the private interest of a part, and of a subordinate part, of the society, is the general
interest of the whole.

People of the same trade seldom meet together, even for merriment and diversion,
but the conversation ends in a conspiracy
against the public, or in some contrivance
to raise prices.

The interest of the dealers . . . in any particular branch of trade or manufactures,
is always in some respects different from,
and even opposite to, that of the public. To
widen the market, and to narrow the competition, is always the interest of the dealers. To widen the market may frequently
be agreeable enough to the interest of the
public; but to narrow the competition must
always be against it, and can only serve to

enable the dealers, by raising their profits above what they naturally would be, to levy, for their own benefit, an absurd tax upon the rest of their fellow citizens.

The proposal of any new law or regulation of commerce which comes from this order, ought always to be listened to with great precaution, and ought never to be adopted till after having been long and carefully examined, not only with the most scrupulous, but with the most suspicious attention. It comes from an order of men, whose interest is never exactly the same with that of the public, who have generally an interest to deceive and even to oppress the public, and who accordingly have, upon many occasions, both deceived and oppressed it.

Is state leadership and regulation possibly solving this perennial problem? No, says Smith. When private interests abuse power, they are merely doing what government itself does. And it is the takeover of government by private interests, under guise of being controlled by government, which is especially to be feared:

The capricious ambition of kings and ministers has not, during the present and the preceding century, been more fatal to the repose of Europe, than the impertinent

jealousy of merchants and manufacturers.
The violence and injustice of the rulers of
mankind is an ancient evil, for which, I am
afraid, the nature of human affairs can scarce
admit of a remedy. But the mean rapacity,
the monopolizing spirit, of merchants and
manufacturers, who neither are, nor ought
to be, the rulers of mankind, though it cannot, perhaps, be corrected, may very easily be prevented from disturbing the tranquility of anybody but themselves.

When government and private interest increasingly
merge, we have what Smith called the "mercantile
system," and much of *The Wealth of Nations* is spent
describing its features. Among them are:

## 1. A Larger-than-Necessary Military Establishment

This appeals to the vainglory of public officials and
offered many profit opportunities for well-connected
private interests.

## 2. Colonies

Although overt colonialism has fallen out of fashion
since the 18th century, imperialism has traditionally
accompanied an overly large military, and afforded
similar scope for vainglory or private profit.

### 3. Slavery

This was a notable feature of Smith's time, which he and similar-minded reformers vigorously opposed. Smith made the salient point that slavery was actually an uneconomic system which could only be maintained through government subsidy and enforcement:

> The work done by freemen comes cheaper in the end than that performed by slaves. It is found to be so even at Boston, New York, and Philadelphia, where the wages of common labor are so high.[13]

### 4. Government-Sponsored Monopoly

Everyone, governments included, pay lip service to the proposition that

> monopoly . . . is a great enemy to good management. . . . [The best management] . . . can never be universally established, but in consequence of that free and universal competition which forces everyone to have recourse to it for the sake of self defense.[14]

Business owners know from experience that monopoly is difficult to fashion and impossible to sustain in a truly free market. They therefore seek and very often receive assistance from government in erecting trade barriers. These barriers are never acknowledged for what they are—they are justified as quality or safety controls, when their real purpose is to restrict supply and increase price. Smith offers many examples:

> [Government interferes with natural supply and demand] in the three following ways. First, by restraining the competition in some employments to a smaller number than would otherwise be disposed to enter into them; secondly, by increasing it in others beyond what it naturally would be; and, thirdly, by obstructing the free circulation of labor and stock, both from employment to employment, and from place to place.

> In Sheffield, no master cutler can have more than one apprentice at a time, by a by-law of the corporation. In Norfolk and Norwich, no master weaver can have more than two apprentices, under pain of forfeiting five pounds a month to the king. No master hatter can have more than two apprentices anywhere in England or in the English plantations, under pain of forfeiting; five pounds a month, half to the king, and half to him who shall sue in any court of record. Both these regulations . . . have been confirmed by a public law of the kingdom.

> But the 5th of Elizabeth, commonly called the Statute of Apprenticeship, it was enacted that no person should, for the future, exercise any trade [or] craft at that time exercised in England, unless he had previously served to it an apprenticeship of seven years at least; and what before had been the by-law of many particular corporations, became in England the general and public law of all trades carried on in market towns.

These examples are particular to the 18th century and earlier. But government sponsored monopoly is, if anything, more prevalent in today's economy. In the United States, for example, drugs are generally regarded as the most profitable major industry. And it is not hard to see why.

Each successful new drug is a government-sanctioned monopoly, guarded first by a government granted patent and second by government approval from the Food and Drug Administration (FDA). Moreover, only government-approved drugs or equipment or procedures may be marketed as a treatment for any disease or health condition. If a food or supplement producer claims a health benefit the government will quickly shut it down under penalty of fines or even jail.

To get a drug approved, it is common knowledge that company officials must have personal relationships with those inside the government, and it is therefore essential to hire former government employees at attractive salaries. Unfortunately, this is only one example of contemporary government sponsored monopoly: they are virtually everywhere in modern economies, just as they were everywhere in Adam Smith's day.

## 5. Barriers to Free Trade

One of the many ways that private interests, working with government, attempt to create monopolies is by erecting international trade barriers. They do this under the pretense of protecting domestic jobs, but this is just a subterfuge. As Smith notes,

> [It] cannot be doubted . . . that it was the spirit of monopoly which originally both invented and propagated this doctrine [of trade protectionism] and they who first taught it were by no means such fools as they who believed it. In every country it always is, and must be, the interest of the great body of the people, to buy whatever they want of those who sell it cheapest. The proposition is so very manifest, that is seems ridiculous to take any pains to prove it; nor could it ever have been called in question, had not the interested sophistry of merchants and manufacturers confounded the common sense of mankind.

To give the monopoly of the home market to the produce of domestic industry, in any particular art or manufacture, is in some measure to direct private people in what manner they ought to employ their capitals, and must, in almost all cases, be either a useless or a hurtful regulation. If the produce of domestic [origin] can be brought there as cheap as that of foreign industry, the regulation is evidently useless. If it cannot, it must generally be hurtful.

It is the maxim of every prudent master of a family, never to attempt to make at home what it will cost him more to make than to buy. The tailor does not attempt to make his own shoes, but buys them off the shoemaker. The shoemaker does not attempt to make his own clothes, but employs a tailor. The farmer attempts to make neither the one nor the other, but employs those different artificers. All of them find it for their interest to employ their whole industry in a way in which they have some advantage over their neighbors, and to purchase with a part of its produce, or, what is the same thing, with the price of a part of it, whatever else they have occasion for.

What is prudence in the conduct of every private family can scarce be folly in that of a great kingdom. If a foreign country can supply us with a commodity cheaper than we ourselves can make it, better buy it of them with some part of the produce of our own industry, employed in a way in which we have some advantage.

The same maxim which would in this manner direct the common sense of one, or ten, or twenty individuals, should regulate the judgment of one, or ten, or twenty millions, and should make a whole nation regard the riches of its neighbors, as a probable cause and occasion for itself to acquire riches. A nation that would enrich itself by foreign trade is certainly most likely to do so, when its neighbors are all rich, industrious, and commercial nations. A great nation, surrounded on all sides by wandering savages and poor barbarians, might, no doubt, acquire riches by the cultivation of its own lands, and by its own interior commerce, but not by foreign trade.

Nothing... can be more absurd than [the] whole doctrine of the balance of trade, upon which, not only these restraints, but almost all the other regulations of commerce, are founded. When two places trade with one another, this doctrine supposes that, if the balance be even, neither of them either loses or gains; but if it leans in any degree to one side, that one of them loses, and the other gains, in proportion to its declension from the exact equilibrium. Both suppositions are false. A trade, which is forced by means of bounties and monopolies, may be, and commonly is, disadvantageous to the country in whose favor it is meant to be established, as I shall endeavor to show hereafter. But that trade which, without force or constraint, is naturally and regularly carried on between any two places, is always advantageous, though not always equally so, to both.

By advantage or gain, I understand, not the increase of the quantity of gold and silver [the money of Smith's day], but that of the exchangeable value of the annual produce of the land and labor of the country, or the increase of the annual revenue of its inhabitants.

There is another balance . . . which [is] . . . very different from the balance of trade, and which, according as it happens to be either favorable or unfavorable, necessarily occasions the prosperity or decay of every nation. This is the balance of the annual produce and consumption. If the exchangeable value of the annual produce, it has already been observed, exceeds that of the annual consumption, the capital of the society must annually increase in proportion to this excess. The society in this case lives within its revenue; and what is annually saved out of its revenue, is naturally added to its capital, and employed so as to increase still further the annual produce.

If the exchangeable value of the annual produce, on the contrary, falls short of the annual consumption, the capital of the society must annually decay in proportion to this deficiency. The expense of the society, in this case, exceeds its revenue, and necessarily encroaches upon its capital. Its capital, therefore, must necessarily decay, and, together with it, the exchangeable value of the annual produce of its industry.*

The balance of produce and consumption is entirely different from what is called the balance of trade. It might take place in a nation which had no foreign trade, but which was entirely separate from all the world. It may take place in the whole globe of the earth, of which the wealth, population, and

---

* Note that this describes the condition of the United States at the date of publication of this book.

> improvement, may be either gradually increasing or gradually decaying.
>
> The balance of produce and consumption may be constantly in favor of a nation, though what is called the balance of trade be generally against it.

There is nothing that Smith says here which does not apply with equal force to the 21st century as the 18th. Even Smith's mockery of the simple-minded mercantilist's aim of amassing gold and silver hoards reminds us of contemporary mercantilist governments (e.g. China) relentlessly pursuing the dream of bigger and bigger official reserves, this time denominated in dollar, euro, or yen bonds, mere pieces of paper even less intrinsically valuable than yesterday's gold or silver.

Today's trade protectionism, however, often takes a different form than in Smith's day. In the 18th century, the gold standard made it difficult to manipulate a nation's currency value in order to encourage exports and discourage imports. Today currency manipulation is as important as or even more important than traditional trade barriers in protectionist policy-making.

## 6. Government Subsidies

Crony capitalist alliances between private interests and government do not just restrict or eliminate foreign (or domestic) competition. They also bestow subsidies and other favors upon politically connected industries, a practice which, as Smith says, leads to malinvestment, corruption, and outright "fraud."

Such payoffs are common enough in prosperous times, but become even more prevalent during downturns. A weak economy gives government a rationale for intervening even more, allegedly in order to fix the economy. As Smith drily notes,

> it can very seldom be reasonable to tax the industry of the great body of the people, in order to support that of some particular class of manufacturers. ... In public, as well as in private expenses, great wealth, may, perhaps, frequently be admitted as an apology for great folly. But there must surely be something more than ordinary absurdity in continuing such profusion in times of general difficulty and distress.

## 7. Labor Market Interventions

In Smith's day, the British government had for centuries restricted the mobility of laborers. If you were born in a given locality, you could only move to another with official permission, which was not easy to get. The ostensible purpose of this rule was to avoid vagrancy or the dumping of indigent persons on one locality by another. Its real purpose was to ensure a local supply of labor for rich employers, no matter what the local employment conditions. A side effect of this was to hold back innovation and change in the economy and thus to thwart economic growth.

Government intervention in labor markets has certainly not abated since Smith's day. Today the black teenage unemployment rate approaches 50%, largely because legislators refuse to exempt teenagers from minimum wage laws. The US federally mandated minimum wage is a bit over $7. But Congress has just passed national medical insurance legislation that will cost employers just under $6 an hour to pay for one employee's family coverage. When this provision comes into effect, the de facto minimum wage for employees with families will almost double, resulting in massive job loss of the very poorest workers.

## 8. Unintended Consequences as a General Disorder

> Every... [government economic intervention] . . . introduces some degree of real disorder into the constitution of the state, which it will be difficult afterwards to cure without occasioning another disorder.

## 9. Misdirected Investment

> Every system which endeavors, either, by extraordinary encouragements to draw towards a particular species of industry a

greater share of the capital of the society than what would naturally go to it, or, by extraordinary restraints, to force from a particular species of industry some share of the capital which would otherwise be employed in it, is, in reality, subversive of the great purpose which it means to promote. It retards, instead of accelerating, the progress of the society towards real wealth and greatness; and diminishes, instead of increasing, the real value of the annual produce of its land and labor.

## 10. Swelling Government Payrolls

The number of public employees increases under the mercantilist (crony capitalist) system, but so does the public pay level:

The emoluments of offices are not, like those of trades and professions, regulated by the free competition of the market, and do not, therefore, always bear a just proportion to what the nature of the employment requires. They are, perhaps, in most countries, higher than it requires; the persons who have the administration of government being generally disposed to regard both themselves and their immediate dependents, rather more than enough.

### 11. Out-of-Control Government Spending

> Great nations are never impoverished by private, though they sometimes are by public prodigality and misconduct. The whole or almost the whole, public revenue is, in most countries, employed in maintaining unproductive hands. ... Such people, as they themselves produce nothing, are all maintained by the produce of other men's labor.

> It is the highest impertinence and presumption, therefore, in kings and ministers to pretend to watch over the economy of private people, and to restrain their expense, either by sumptuary laws, or by prohibiting the importation of foreign luxuries. They are themselves always, and without any exception, the greatest spendthrifts in the society. Let them look well after their own expense, and they may safely trust private people with theirs. If their own extravagance does not ruin the state, that of the subject never will.

### 12. High Taxes Contributing to Unemployment

Smith says about taxes in general: "There is no art which one government sooner learns of another, than that of draining the pockets of the people."[15] But public officials give relatively little thought to how taxes may affect employment, an oversight which ultimately hurts government revenue as well as the unemployed.

> If direct taxes upon the wages of labor have not always occasioned a proportionable rise in those wages, it is because they have generally occasioned a considerable fall in the demand of labor [i.e. unemployment]. The declension of industry, the decrease of employment for the poor, the diminution of the annual produce of the land and labor of the country, have generally been the effects of such taxes.

> In consequence of them, also, the price of labor must always be higher than it otherwise would have been in the actual state of the demand; and this enhancement of price, together with the profit of those who advance it, must always be finally paid by the landlords and consumers. Absurd and destructive as such taxes are, . . . they take place in many countries.

> The observation of Sir Matthew Decker, that certain taxes are, in the price of certain goods, sometimes repeated and accumulated four or five times, is perfectly just with regard to taxes upon the necessaries

of life. In the price of leather, for example, you must pay not only for the tax upon the leather of your own shoes, but for a part of that upon those of the shoemaker and the tanner. You must pay, too, for the tax upon the salt, upon the soap, and upon the candles which those workmen consume while employed in your service; and for the tax upon the leather, which the salt maker, the soap maker, and the candle maker consume, while employed in their service.

In Great Britain, the principal taxes upon the necessaries of life are those upon the four commodities just now mentioned, salt, leather, soap, and candles.

As all those four commodities are real necessaries of life, such heavy taxes upon them must increase somewhat the expense of the sober and industrious poor, and must consequently raise more or less the wages of their labor. . . . [, thereby causing unemployment with no offsetting benefit to them].

The duties of customs are . . . ancient. They seem to have been called customs, as denoting customary payments, [and] . . . appear to have been originally considered as taxes upon the profits of merchants. In those ignorant times, it was not understood, that the profits of merchants are a subject not taxable directly; or that the final payment of all such taxes must fall, with a considerable overcharge, upon the consumers.

## 13. Debasement of the Currency

In earlier times, impecunious governments often simply seized private property. As Smith noted, this had a particularly chilling effect on economic activity:

> In those unfortunate countries, indeed, where men are continually afraid of the violence of their superiors, they frequently bury or conceal a great part of their stock, in order to have it always at hand to carry with them to some place of safety, in case of their being threatened with any of those disasters to which they consider themselves at all times exposed. This is said to be a common practice in Turkey, in Indostan, and, I believe, in most other governments of Asia.

> It seems to have been a common practice among our ancestors during the violence of the feudal government. Treasure-trove was, in these times, considered, as no contemptible part of the revenue of the greatest sovereigns in Europe. It consisted in

such treasure as was found concealed in the earth.

Modern governments have adopted more sophisticated means of raising revenue in addition to what can be collected in taxes. If they can find creditors, they borrow. Often the funds are repaid; sometimes they are not.

> When national debts have once been accumulated to a certain degree, there is scarce, I believe, a single instance of their having been fairly and completely paid. The liberation of the public revenue, if it has ever been brought about at all, has always been brought about by a bankruptcy; sometimes by an avowed one, through frequently by a pretended payment.

"Pretended payment" refers to debasing the currency:

> In every country of the world, I believe, the avarice and injustice of princes and sovereign states, abusing the confidence of their subjects, have by degrees diminished the real quantity of metal, which had been originally contained in their coins. The Roman As, in the latter ages of the Republic, was reduced to the twenty-fourth part of its original value, and, instead of weighing a pound, came to weigh only half an ounce.

The English pound and penny contain at present about a third only; the Scots pound and penny about a thirty-sixth; and the French pound and penny about a sixty-sixth part of their original value.

By means of those operations, the princes and sovereign states which performed them were enabled, in appearance, to pay their debts and fulfill their engagements with a smaller quantity of silver than would otherwise have been requisite. It was indeed in appearance only; for their creditors were really defrauded of a part of what was due to them. All other debtors in the state were allowed the same privilege, and might pay with the same nominal sum of the new and debased coin whatever they had borrowed in the old. Such operations, therefore, have always proved favorable to the debtor, and ruinous to the creditor.

The raising of the denomination of the coin has been [another] expedient by which a real public bankruptcy has been disguised under the appearance of a pretended payment. If a sixpence, for example, should, either by act of parliament or royal proclamation, be raised to the denomination of a shilling, and twenty sixpences to that of a pound sterling;

the person who, under the old denomination, had borrowed twenty shillings, or near four ounces of silver, would, under the new, pay with twenty sixpences, or with something less than two ounces.

A national debt of about a hundred and twenty-eight millions, near the capital of the funded and unfunded debt of Great Britain, might, in this manner, be paid with about sixty-four millions of our present money. It would, indeed, be a pretended payment only, and the creditors of the public would really be defrauded of ten shillings in the pound of what was due to them.

In some later instances, governments dispensed with metal money entirely, and financed themselves with paper. Both the US and confederate governments did this during the US Civil War, and it led directly to runaway inflation. The German government famously did the same in the 1920s, with even greater inflation. Many other governments have done the same since, including the government of the Soviet Union in its final days, and most infamously the government of Zimbabwe.

During the 1920s, government central bankers learned how to create new money without even printing bills through so-called open market operations,[16] and this has become the preferred method in developed nations. Since the 1990s, larger and larger amounts of new money have been surreptitiously "printed" by world governments, partly to pay expenses, but more often to manipulate currency values. The new money led directly to bubbles, thence to the global Crash of 2008, which in turn led to truly unprecedented levels on money "printing," now euphemistically called "quantitative easing," followed by subsequent rounds of more money "printing" when the first rounds failed to get the world borrowing and spending machine going again.

Smith would not have been entirely surprised by these events, but also not have been able to predict them. No one in his day ever imagined that governments could succeed in dispensing entirely with gold and silver backing of a currency, and thus making it possible to run what are now electronic "printing presses" continually.

## 14. Government Failure to Perform Its Essential Duties

As state control of the economy grows, government becomes even less able to perform its essential duties. Smith enumerates these duties as follows:

> According to the system of natural liberty, the sovereign has only three duties to attend to; three duties of great importance, indeed, but plain and intelligible to common understandings: first, the duty of protecting the society from the violence and invasion

of other independent societies; secondly, the duty of protecting, as far as possible, every member of the society from the injustice or oppression of every other member of it, or the duty of establishing an exact administration of justice; and, thirdly, the duty of erecting and maintaining certain public works, and certain public institutions, which it can never be for the interest of any individual, or small number of individuals to erect and maintain.

Commerce and manufactures can seldom flourish long in any state which does not enjoy a regular administration of justice; in which the people do not feel themselves secure in the possession of their property; in which the faith of contracts is not supported by law; and in which the authority of the state is not supposed to be regularly employed in enforcing the payment of debts from all those who are able to pay. Commerce and manufactures, in short, can seldom flourish in any state, in which there is not a certain degree of confidence in the justice of government.

Unfortunately government entry into the economy inevitably leads to alliances between powerful special interests and public officials. The resulting corruption utterly undermines our faith in government justice, much less government efficiency.

Smith put his view of the proper role of government even more succinctly in one of his early university lectures:

> Little else is requisite to carry a state to the highest degree of opulence from the lowest barbarism, but peace, easy taxes, and a tolerable administration of justice: all the rest being brought about by the natural course of things.[17]

## 15. Muddling through (at Unnecessary Cost to the Poor and Struggling)

Throughout most of human history, the efforts of individuals to better their condition went nowhere. There was little or no economic growth from generation to generation. This fact testified to just how bad governments were, because, in Smith's view, it is difficult to render completely futile the efforts of human enterprise. As he says,

> the natural effort which every man is continually making to better his own condition is a principle of preservation capable of preventing and correcting, in many respects, the bad effects of a political economy, in some degree both partial and oppressive. Such a

political economy, though it no doubt retards more or less, is not always capable of stopping altogether, the natural progress of a nation towards wealth and prosperity, and still less of making it go backwards. If a nation could not prosper without the enjoyment of perfect liberty and perfect justice, there is not in the world a nation which could ever have prospered.

The natural effort of every individual to better his own condition, when suffered to exert itself with freedom and security is so powerful a principle that it is alone, and without any assistance, not only capable of carrying on the society to wealth and prosperity, but of surmounting a hundred impertinent obstructions with which the folly of human laws too often encumbers its operations; though the effect of these obstructions is always more or less either to encroach upon its freedom, or to diminish its security. In Great Britain industry is perfectly secure; and though it is far from being perfectly free, it is as free as or freer than in any other part of Europe.[18]

The signal achievement of *The Wealth of Nations* is to describe mercantilism/crony capitalism both as a whole and in telling detail. As explained earlier, Smith is first and foremost a reformer, and his principal job is to explain the true costs of a corrupt system. But as a reformer, he is also concerned with providing a remedy, which he calls the System of Liberty, and which, we today call free markets:

> [When government relinquishes control of the economy, with all its unintended and damaging consequences], the obvious and simple system of natural liberty establishes itself of its own accord. Every man, as long as he does not violate the laws of justice, is left perfectly free to pursue his own interest his own way, and to bring both his industry and capital into competition with those of any other man, or order of men.

> The sovereign is completely discharged from a duty, in the attempting to perform which he must always be exposed to innumerable delusions, and for the proper performance of which, no human wisdom or knowledge could ever be sufficient; the duty of superintending the industry of private people, and of directing it towards the employments most suitable to the interests of the society.

Smith's System of Liberty also has its central characteristics.

## A. Reliance on Free Prices

Free markets are often described by their critics as both chaotic and wasteful. They are actually both orderly and productive, but only if prices are allowed to be free. Prices are an indispensable signaling device that tells all the economic players what they need to know in order to make rational (and useful) choices.

It has often been observed that the Soviet Union collapsed because it could not find a workable alternative to the free price system. But this is not just a problem for Communist systems. In the so-called market economics of today, all the biggest prices (e.g. currencies, interest rates, mortgage rates) are controlled by government and many of the lesser ones as well.

## B. Reliance on Profits

Profits are a corollary of free prices, and are indispensable regulating as well as signaling devices. Of course, we must be careful to describe the profit system accurately as the profit and loss system. The fear and pain of loss counts for as much as or more than the hope for gain.

It is sometimes alleged that the profit system makes goods more expensive, because profit is an "avoidable cost" that is simply tacked on to unavoidable costs such as labor. The truth is that profits are the whip that continually drives prices down, because high prices quickly attract new investment which increases supply relative to demand.

Even Karl Marx acknowledged (in *The Communist Manifesto*) the power of market forces to bring down prices. Marx was a close student of Smith and would have read this from *The Wealth of Nations*:

> When, by an increase in the effectual demand, the market price of some particular commodity happens to rise a good deal above the natural price, those who employ their stocks in supplying that market, are generally careful to conceal this change. If it was commonly known, their great profit would tempt so many new rivals to employ their stocks in the same way, that, the effectual demand being fully supplied, the market price would soon be reduced to the natural price, and, perhaps, for some time even below it. Secrets of this, however, it must be acknowledged, can seldom be long kept; and the extraordinary profit can last very little longer than they are kept.

Smith also notes that average profits tend to fall, not rise, in a truly free market:

> The rate of profit does not, like rent and wages, rise with the prosperity, and fall with the declension of the society. On the contrary, it is naturally low in rich, and high in poor countries.

### C. Expanding Employment and Wage Rates

Profits are also that portion of the economic pie which is most easily saved. Savings in a secure and free environment are generally invested in the pursuit of further profits, which requires hiring more workers. Demand for more workers also raises wages, which in turn may further increase productivity, because

> Where wages are high . . . we shall always find the workmen more active, diligent, and expeditious, than where they are low.

Smith further notes that high wages encourage investment in new equipment, which both raises productivity and, eventually, wages.

### D. Reliance on Personal and Business Saving

> The capitals of industry are increased by parsimony, and diminished by prodigality and misconduct.

> Whatever a person saves from his revenue he adds to his capital, and either employs it himself in maintaining an additional number of productive hands, or enables some other person to do so, by lending it to him for an interest, that is, for a share of the profits. As the capital of an individual can be increased only by what he saves from his annual revenue or his annual gains, so the capital of a society,

which is the same with that of all the individuals who compose it, can be increased only in the same manner.*

What is annually saved is as regularly consumed as what is annually spent and nearly in the same time too: but it is consumed by a different set of people. That portion of his revenue which a rich man annually spends is, in most cases, consumed by idle guests and menial servants, who leave nothing behind them in return for their consumption. That portion, which he annually saves, as, for the sake of the profit, is immediately employed as a capital, is consumed in the same manner and nearly in the same time too, but by a different set of people: by laborers, manufacturers, and artificers, who reproduce, with a profit, the value of their annual consumption.†

---

* Smith was living before the fully global economy but his point still remains valid, that saving is needed to fund investment. Some economists, most notably John Maynard Keynes, have assumed that government-printed money could be substituted for savings, but both logic and economic history argue against this.

† It is often argued by politicians and those not schooled in economics that the rich only benefit the economy by spending on luxuries, and that their tendency to save will depress rather than stimulate the economy. This argument is then translated into a call for very high tax levels for the rich. Smith shows that this is quite false. Saving is also a form of spending, and when channeled into well-considered investments, the most valuable kind of spending for an economy.

By what a frugal man annually saves, he not only affords maintenance to an additional number of productive hands, for that of the ensuing year, but like the founder of a public workhouse he establishes, as it were, a perpetual fund for the maintenance of an equal number in all times to come. The perpetual allotment and destination of this fund, indeed, is not always guarded by any positive law, by any trust-right or deed of mortmain. It is always guarded, however, by a very powerful principle, the plain and evident interest of every individual to whom any share of it shall ever belong. No part of it can ever afterwards be employed to maintain any but productive hands, without an evident loss to the person who thus perverts it from its proper destination.

If the prodigality of some were not compensated by the frugality of others, the conduct of every prodigal, by feeding the idle with the bread of the industrious, would tend not only to beggar himself, but to impoverish his country.

### E. An Equivocal View of the Rich

Smith generally takes a jaundiced and critical view of the rich. He says that

> with the greater part of rich people, the chief enjoyment of riches consists in the parade of riches; which, in their eye, is never so complete as when they appear to possess those decisive marks of opulence which nobody can possess but themselves.

But he does recognize that they have a special role to play as savers, because unlike most people, the truly rich simply cannot spend all their income, and thus must save. And insofar as they are business owners, their

> natural selfishness and rapacity[19]

is regulated by their very desire for profit:

> The real and effectual discipline which is exercised over [an employer or other economic actor] is not that of [outside parties including government], but that of his customers. It is the fear of losing their employment which restrains his frauds and corrects his negligence.

## F. Reliance on Enlightened Self-Interest as the Chief Economic Motivator

Not surprisingly, the following are some of the most frequently cited passages of *The Wealth of Nations*:

> [The] division of labor, from which so many advantages are derived, is not originally the effect of any human wisdom, which foresees and intends that general opulence to which it gives occasion. It is the necessary, though very slow and gradual, consequence of a certain propensity in human nature to truck, barter, and exchange one thing for another.

> In civilized society [an individual] stands at all times in need of the cooperation and assistance of great multitudes, while his whole life is scarce sufficient to gain the friendship of a few persons. It is in vain for him to expect . . . [assistance] . . . from [the] benevolence [of others] only. He will be more likely to prevail if he can interest their self-love in his favor, and show them that it is for their own advantage to do for him what he requires of them.

> It is not from the benevolence of the butcher, the brewer, or the baker, that we expect our dinner, but from their regard to their own interest. We address ourselves, not to their

humanity, but to their self-love, and never talk to them of our own necessities, but of their advantages.

Every individual is continually exerting himself to find out the most advantageous employment for whatever capital he can command. It is his own advantage, indeed, and not that of the society, which he has in view. But the study of his own advantage naturally, or rather necessarily, leads him to prefer that employment which is most advantageous to the society.

As every individual, therefore, endeavors as much as he can, both to employ his capital in the support of domestic industry, and so to direct that industry that its produce may be of the greatest value; every individual necessarily labors to render the annual revenue of the society as great as he can. He generally, indeed, neither intends to promote the public interest, nor knows how much he is promoting it.

By preferring the support of domestic to that of foreign industry, he intends only his own security; and by directing that industry in such a manner as its produce may be of the greatest value, he intends only his own gain; and he is in this, as in many other cases, led by an invisible hand to promote an end which was no part of his intention.

Nor is it always the worse for the society that it was no part of it. By pursuing his own interest, he frequently promotes that of the society more effectually than when he really intends to promote it. I have never known much good done by those who affected to trade for the public good. It is an affectation, indeed, not very common among merchants, and very few words need be employed in dissuading them from it.

The species of domestic industry which his capital can employ, and of which the produce is likely to be of the greatest value, every individual, it is evident, can in his local situation judge much better than any statesman or lawgiver can do for him. The statesman, who should attempt to direct private people in what manner they ought to employ their capitals, would not only load himself with a most unnecessary attention, but assume an authority which could safely be trusted, not only to no single person, but to no council or senate whatever, and which would nowhere be so dangerous as in the hands of a man who had folly

and presumption enough to fancy himself
fit to exercise it.

Smith has sometimes been dismissed as a propo-
nent, even a salesman, of selfishness. This is false. In
his first book, *The Theory of Moral Sympathy*, Smith
says that human beings are often moved to altruism
by what he calls sympathy (we might call it empathy),
which he clearly regards in a very positive light.

At the very last Smith wants our self-interest to be
rational and enlightened. He is well aware of how irra-
tional self-interest can be and how it has torn societies asunder and kept them poor. The main point here
is that no amount of human goodwill or altruism will
create the orderly webs of cooperation that we all need
in order to survive. Nor will a command and control
system led from the top by government, even a more
honest government than we actually get, succeed.

It is only free markets, pitifully hampered and con-
strained as they have been by misguided government
interventions, which have got us as far as we have
come, by channeling our aggressions away from violence and theft and toward constructive enterprise.
And it is free markets alone which offer any hope of
eliminating poverty in an environmentally and eco-
nomically sustainable way.

By emphasizing enlightened self-interest, Smith
was no doubt being a realist, and no doubt making an
important point. But as this author argued in *Are the*

*Rich Necessary?*, self-interest—even enlightened self-interest—is over-emphasized. The gist of the argument is that the private market system is not fundamentally grounded in self-interest:

> Adam Smith seriously erred in suggesting that it was, and his authority has misled us for centuries. The market system teaches naturally selfish people to put aside their selfishness and practice some of the "highest" values of social cooperation that human beings have ever achieved.
>
> "Market values" are the diametrical opposite of "every man for himself." The "self-interest model" so beloved of economists is completely illusory. A young person may proclaim: "I will start my own business in order to be my own boss." But if he or she persists in this illusion, the new business will fail, as most do. In order to start and run a successful business, one must be willing, above all, to subordinate oneself in the service of others. One must serve one's customers and one must also serve and respect and nurture one's employees.
>
> Sometimes "bosses" are so talented or lucky that they do well without fully learning these lessons. Even then, they do not do nearly as well as they might have. The iron rule is: everything else being equal, the better you serve, the better you do. Predation, exploitation, parasitism, or greed may make this transaction, or even this year's profits, fatter. But a business is defined as the

present value of all future profits, and these true profits are ruined by selfishness, even so-called "rational" selfishness.

"Market" values are not easy. They are extremely demanding, and in many cases take generations to learn. Nor are they "lower than" or "separate from" religious values. It is true that they are not identical to religious values, but they are rather "complementary" to religion and have arguably done as much as religion to "civilize" us, especially given the dark side of religion exemplified by religious wars. It is no coincidence that it was defenders of free markets who led the battle against world slavery and finally won it, against large odds, in the nineteenth century. As economist George Stigler writes:

> Important as the moral influences of the market place are, they have not been subjected to any real study. The immense proliferation of general education, of scientific progress, and of democracy are all coincidental in time and place with the emergence of the free enterprise system of organizing the market place. I believe this coincidence was not accidental.[20]

A critic of free markets, Liah Greenfield, has asserted in her book, *The Spirit of Capitalism: Nationalism and Economic Growth*, that nationalism promotes free-market growth. The truth is just the opposite. "Market values" are at odds with nationalism, tribalism, racism, and sectarianism of all kinds, and continually teach us to tolerate, work with, and ultimately appreciate people wherever and however we find them.

The hostile attitude of most economists toward the idea of the market as a source of moral values is hard to fathom, although it may simply reflect a lack of personal familiarity with business. Listen to Geoffrey Martin Hodgson:

> The firm has to compete not simply for profit but for our confidence and trust. To achieve this, it has to abandon profit-maximization, or even shareholder satisfaction, as the exclusive objectives of the organization.[21]

This is quite wrong. In truth, confidence and trust do not in the least conflict with profits. On the contrary, one cannot have the latter without the former, as great businesses have shown throughout history.

Perhaps the ultimate wrong note of this kind was sounded by economist John Kenneth Galbraith, past president of the American Economics Association, when he wrote that

> there is nothing reliable to be learned about making money. If there were, study would be intense and everyone with a positive IQ would be rich.[22]

What Galbraith, like others, failed to see is that one does not necessarily need a high IQ to make money, but rather the right personal values, in particular an ardor to serve others and a degree of realism about how to do it (since in markets, as in life generally, good intentions alone do not suffice).[23]

US president Calvin Coolidge, like Smith a free market icon noted for a certain stringency of tone, got it right when he said that the business of America was business but that business "rest[ed] squarely on the law of service [which had its] main reliance on truth, faith, and justice."[24]

### G. Honest Money

It may be debated whether Smith over-emphasized rational self-interest. It may also be debated whether he got government monetary policy right. This author for one thinks he got it mostly wrong. Given that monetary policy has had such a large impact on economic affairs since his day, and also given Smith's immense authority, it is worth taking a moment to consider what exactly *The Wealth of Nations* said about this subject.

In the first place, Smith objects to government issued paper money. His argument is sensible:

> The paper currencies of North America consisted, not in bank notes payable to the bearer on demand, but in a government paper, of which the payment was

not eligible till several years after it was issued; and though the colony governments paid no interest to the holders of this paper, they declared it to be, and in fact rendered it, a legal tender of payment for the full value for which it was issued.

Allowing the colony security to be perfectly good, a hundred pounds payable fifteen years hence, for example, in a country where interest is at six per cent, is worth little more than forty pounds ready money. To oblige a creditor, therefore, to accept of this as full payment for a debt of hundred pounds actually paid down in ready money, was an act of such violent injustice, as has scarce, perhaps, been attempted by the government of any other country which pretended to be free. It bears the evident marks of having originally been, what the honest and downright Doctor Douglas assures us it was, a scheme of fraudulent debtors to cheat their creditors.

As suggested above, Smith does not object to paper money issued by banks, assuming it is backed by gold or silver, and that it is restricted and regulated by government:

If bankers are restrained from issuing any circulating bank notes, or notes payable to

the bearer, for less than a certain sum; and
if they are subjected to the obligation of an
immediate and unconditional payment of
such bank notes as soon as presented, their
trade may, with safety to the public, be rendered in all other respects perfectly free.

He says that these government restrictions are necessary because some banks act foolishly:

Had every particular banking company always understood and attended to its own
particular interest, the circulation never
could have been overstocked with paper
money. But every particular banking company has not always understood or attended
to its own particular interest, and the circulation has frequently been overstocked
with paper money.

It is not, however, just the bankers who are respon-
sible for this problem:

The over-trading of some bold projectors
in both parts of the United Kingdom was
the original cause of this excessive circulation of paper money.[25]

Smith is aware that calling for government intervention into banking affairs is inconsistent with the rest of
his argument:

To restrain private people, it may be said, from receiving in payment the promissory notes of a banker for any sum, whether great or small, when they themselves are willing to receive them; or, to restrain a banker from issuing such notes, when all his neighbors are willing to accept of them is a manifest violation of that natural liberty, which it is the proper business of law not to infringe, but to support. Such regulations may, no doubt, be considered as in some respect a violation of natural liberty. But those exertions of the natural liberty of a few individuals, which might endanger the security of the whole society, are, and ought to be, restrained by the laws of all governments; of the most free, as well as or the most despotical. The obligation of building party walls, in order to prevent the communication of fire, is a violation of natural liberty, exactly of the same kind with the regulations of the banking trade which are here proposed.

Smith also seems to have rejected the worry that allowing paper bank notes would lead to consumer price inflation:

The increase of paper money, it has been said, by augmenting the quantity, and consequently diminishing the value, of the whole currency, necessarily augments the money price of commodities. But as the quantity of gold and silver, which is taken from the currency, is always equal to the quantity of paper which is added to it, paper money does not necessarily increase the quantity of the whole currency.

Smith adds that it is proper for government to regulate and restrict the interest rates that banks charge:

In countries where interest is permitted, the law in order to prevent the extortion of usury generally fixes the highest rate which can be taken without incurring a penalty. . . . In a country such as Great Britain, where money is lent to government at three per cent and to private people, upon good security, at four and four-and-a-half, the present legal rate, five per cent is perhaps as proper as any.

There is an acknowledgment that ready access to cheap but fluctuating bank credit poses a special problem for the conservative business operator. If a business can earn 8% on its capital, it can earn a great deal more by augmenting that capital by borrowing at 4%. The extra profits may in turn enable this business, through borrowing, to expand faster than its competitors, cut price, or otherwise drive competitors out of business. The more conservative business may thus feel itself obliged to borrow whether or not it wishes to, and then both imprudent and prudent business may both collapse if credit is suddenly withdrawn.

Since Smith's time, we have witnessed great credit expansions and great collapses. These have become ever more dramatic and more troublesome, and have not been arrested by the creation of government central banks, indeed they appear to have become worse. In our day, banks are no longer able to print their own paper money. But they are able to issue checks, and these checks act as money. So one way or another, both banks and central banks are able to expand and contract both the supply of money in the economy and the availability and terms of credit.*

In Smith's day, there was still a debate about whether banks should be able to lend more than the money that was actually in the vault. It was not at all clear that they could. Banks began as gold and silver warehouses, and other warehouses were not (and are not) permitted to lend more than they hold or to lend at all without the depositor's explicit permission. Eventually, long after Smith's death, it was decided by courts that banks, unlike other warehouses, could do these things, even though this "fractional reserve banking system" expanded and contracted both money and credit in an unpredictable and often erratic way, which in turn contributed to economic booms and busts.

---

* For a more complete explanation of how this works see Hunter Lewis, *Are the Rich Necessary?* (Mt. Jackson, VA: Axios Press, 2009), 303.

Unaccountably, Smith is mostly silent about all this. He seems to excuse loose credit, so long as it is regulated by government, even though elsewhere he argues that government regulation cannot work, and that government, being chronically short of funds, will adopt every furtive and destructive device to fund itself. If government cannot be trusted to impose honest taxes or rein in its borrowing, how can government be entrusted with control of the entire money and lending system? No wonder that some contemporary free market economists are so critical of Smith.

*Wealth of Nations* also argued that

> the quantity of money ... must in every country naturally increase as the value of the annual produce increases. The value of the consumable goods annually circulated within the society being greater, will require a greater quantity of money to circulate them.

This proposition may seem obviously true, but actually needs a second look. There is no empirical evidence that additional money is needed as an economy expands. If an economy consists of four identical tools and four dollars, the production of four more tools does not require the production of four more dollars. In the first instance, the tools may each be worth $1. In the latter, the price falls to 50¢. In either case, the role of money, which in this case is to make it possible to trade goods, remains unaffected.

Why does Smith's lapse on this point matter? Because he himself says that

> no complaint is more common than that of a scarcity of money.[26]

He adds that

> the attention of government never was so unnecessarily employed, as when directed to watch over the preservation or increase of the quantity of money in any country.

But, this injunction notwithstanding, the idea that the money supply must continually increase has been one of the prime justifications for government control of money. It was the supposed need for an "elastic currency" that was invoked in order to pass legislation creating the US Federal Reserve Board in 1913. Of course no one at that time imagined how rapidly the new central bank would run the monetary printing presses, especially during the 1920s boom, the dot com boom of the 1990s, the housing boom that followed, or especially after the Crash of 2008, or that all the new money created would reduce the purchasing power of the dollar over a little less than a century by about 97%.

As economist Ludwig von Mises has noted,

> if one looks at the catastrophic consequences of the great paper money inflations, one

must admit that … it would be futile to re-
tort that these catastrophes were brought
about by the improper use which the governments made of the powers that credit
money and fiat money placed in their hands
and that wise governments would have adopted sounder policies. As money can never
be neutral and stable in purchasing power, a
government's plans concerning the determi-
nation of the quantity of money can never
be impartial and fair to all members of society. Whatever a government does in the
pursuit of aims to influence the height of
purchasing power depends necessarily upon
the rulers' personal value judgments. It always furthers the interests of some groups
of people at the expense of other groups. It
never serves what is called the commonweal
or the public welfare. In the field of monetary policies too there is no such thing as
a scientific ought.[27]

It must be stressed that what has been characterized
here as Smith's monetary errors are debated. This author
regards them as disastrous for subsequent economic history. If only, one wonders, Smith had got this right—
how much boom and bust and human suffering would
have been averted. But conventional opinion in contemporary economics disagrees. It is either not much

concerned with Smith's monetary policy, or agrees with it, or excuses it.

There is a consensus among economists about some of Smith's other errors. The notion that

> the most decisive mark of the prosperity of any country is the increase of the number of its inhabitants,

is not correct. The statement that

> the greatest improvements in the productive powers of labor . . . seem to have been the effects of the division of labor,

is only partly correct. Capital accumulation (which Smith embraces) and new technology arguably matter as much. It is worth noting that there is not much said about technology in *The Wealth of Nations* and nothing at all about the industrial revolution that was taking shape in Britain at the time. Also missing is the role of the entrepreneur, something mentioned by two earlier apostles of free markets, Cantillon and Turgot.

There are more lapses. No one today agrees that agriculture is inherently more productive than manufacturing, or that housing and services do not count at all as productive economic activity,[28] only as here today and gone forever tomorrow consumption. Many economists also disagree with Smith's approval of retaliatory tariffs[29] (tariffs raised to combat others). It might be added that retaliatory tariffs are the kind of loophole that crony capitalist governments and their private interest friends love. Cannot all tariffs, in the same way be characterized as retaliatory?

Smith's most notorious and generally accepted blunder was his theory of what made goods valuable and how they were priced. As we shall see, this blunder mattered a great deal, but first we should let Smith speak for himself on this important subject of economic valuation:

> What are the rules which men naturally observe, in exchanging either money, or [goods]? These rules determine what may be called the exchangeable value of goods.
>
> The word VALUE, it is to be observed, has two different meanings, one may be called "value in use"; the other, "value in exchange." The things which have the greatest value in use have frequently little or no value in exchange; and, on the contrary, those which have the greatest value in exchange have frequently little or no value in use. Nothing is more useful than water; but it will purchase scarce anything; scarce anything can be had in exchange for it. A diamond, on the contrary, has scarce any value in use; but a very great quantity of other goods may frequently be had in exchange for it.

Every man is rich or poor according to the degree in which we can afford to enjoy the necessaries, conveniences, and amusements of human life. But after the division of labor has once thoroughly taken place, it is but a very small part of these with which a man's own labor can supply him. The far greater part of them he must derive from the labor of other people, and he must be rich or poor according to the quantity of that labor which he can command, or which he can afford to purchase.

The value of any commodity, therefore, to the person who possesses it, and who means not to use or consume it himself, but to exchange it for other commodities, is equal to the quantity of labor which it enables him to purchase or command. Labor therefore, is the real measure of the exchangeable value of all commodities.

As a corollary of this, high or low wages and profit are the causes of high or low price. It is because high or low wages and profit must be paid, in order to bring a particular commodity to market, that its price is high or low.

At all times and places, that is dear which it is difficult to come at, or which it costs much labor to acquire; and that cheap which is to be had easily, or with very little labor. Labor alone, therefore, never varying in its own value, is the ultimate and real standard by which the value of all commodities can at all times and places be estimated and compared. It is their real price; money is their nominal price only.

When the price of any commodity is neither more nor less than what is sufficient to pay the rent of the land, the wages of the labor, and the profits of the stock employed in raising, preparing, and bringing it to market, according to their natural rates, the commodity is then sold for what may be called it natural price.

The actual price, at which any commodity is commonly sold, is called its market price. It may either be above, or below, or exactly the same with its natural price.

The market price of every particular commodity is regulated by the proportion between the quantity which is actually brought to market, and the demand of those who are willing to pay the natural price of the commodity, or the whole value of the rent, labor, and profit, which must be paid in order to bring it thither.

> Such people [who pay the price] may be
> called the effectual demanders, and their
> demand the effectual demand; since it
> maybe sufficient to effectuate the bring-
> ing of the commodity to market. It is dif-
> ferent from the absolute demand. A very
> poor man may be said, in some sense, to
> have a demand for a coach and six horses;
> he might like to have it; but his demand is
> not an effectual demand, as the commod-
> ity can never be brought to market in or-
> der to satisfy it.

The preceding makes some useful points, but is generally garbled. As economist Joseph Schumpeter and
others have noted, it seems to express several different
theories of economic pricing: usefulness; labor cost;
difficulty of acquisition; imbedded rent, labor, and
profit; supply and demand—with perhaps an overall
emphasis on labor cost.

Smith's mentor, the noted philosopher (and economist) David Hume, read *Wealth of Nations* during
his final illness. He approved highly of it, but at once
noted the error on pricing: "If you were at my fire-
side, I should dispute some of your principles. I cannot
think . . . but that price is determined altogether by the
quantity and the demand."[30]

In other words, a product is not worth the labor
in it, or even the rent, labor, and expected profit. It

is worth whatever someone is willing to pay for it. Moreover, the seller and buyer do not make an equal exchange. The seller values cash more than the product; the buyer the reverse. This is possible because valuation is subjective in nature.

By the late 19th century, approximately a century after Smith, economists had worked all this out. But in the meantime Karl Marx had seized on Smith's "labor theory of value" to justify an attack on what he called, in his own verbal coinage, capitalism. If labor is what makes goods valuable, then workers should not share that value with capitalists. Profit in this view is both unnecessary and illegitimate.

Marx agreed that capital investment and equipment entered into the equation, but these were characterized as labor from the past. He did not attempt to explain why today's laborers deserved emolument from labor of the past, or how any of this squared with the dictum "from each according to his ability, to each according to his need."[31] But insofar as Marx depended on a labor theory of value, it may be said that Marxist communism depended on Smith.

Well, we all make our mistakes. And we cannot choose what others will do with our ideas. The unmistakable truth remains that Adam Smith very much deserves his central place in the pantheon of economic thinkers, not because he got free market theory right, but because he got mercantilism/crony capitalism so unmistakable right.

In Smith's day, as in our day, it is crony capitalism that rules the roost. This is hard on all of us, but especially the poor and disadvantaged. As Smith states, this is a very sorry state of affairs, and we should not accept it. We should lay bare the flaws of the current system and demand reform, just as Smith and our 18th century forebears did. And we should take special care not to get sidetracked by false panaceas offered by "correctors" of Smith such as Marx or John Maynard Keynes, precisely because their "corrections" lead in practice to more rather than less crony capitalism.*

—Hunter Lewis

## A Biographical Sketch

Adam Smith (1723–1790) was born in Kirkcaldy Scotland where his father who died a few months before his birth, had been controller of customs. At age three he was taken to visit an uncle, where, playing alone, he was seized by a group of "tinkers." Fortunately this was noticed and after a hot pursuit, the boy was abandoned and recovered. But for this recovery, we might never have had *The Theory of Moral Sentiments*, Smith's first book, or *The Wealth of Nations*.

In 1737 Smith enrolled at the University of Glasgow, where he studied under Hutcheson, who became an

---

* For more on John Maynard Keynes and crony capitalism, see Hunter Lewis, *Where Keynes Went Wrong* (Mt. Jackson, VA: Axios Press, 2009).

important mentor and source of his ideas. In 1740 he went to Oxford, where appalled by the utter sloth and neglect of students by teachers, he nevertheless stayed seven years. This was followed by two years at home with his mother, Margaret; then a period of three years lecturing in Edinburgh, where he met and became greatly influenced by the philosopher and economist David Hume; then a move back to Glasgow as professor of logic in 1751, which led to the chair of moral philosophy (then incorporating economics) a year later.

Smith remained at Glasgow for almost twelve years. Later he described it as "by far the most useful, and therefore by far the happiest period of my life."[32] In 1763, four years after the publication of his first book established his name throughout Britain, he was asked to accompany the young Duke of Buccleuch on a continental tour. This was a very lucrative offer, involving a lifetime pension, and Smith decided to resign his professorship.

Smith and the young Duke got along very well, residence in Paris opened up a new world including the most famous economist of the day, François Quesnay, as well as Anne-Robert-Jacques Turgot, another exponent of free markets and critic of the dominant mercantilist policies of the day. Two and a half years into the tour, the Duke's younger brother was suddenly murdered in France, and the party returned to Britain.

For ten years beginning in 1766, Smith lived with his mother at Kirkcaldy, engaged in writing *The Wealth of*

*Nations.* He also described this period as one of great happiness. He was able to send the completed work to his close friend David Hume and also to visit him just prior to his death. Smith's attack on mercantilism really took up where Hume had left off in his own economic writing. Smith also published a letter (to W. Strahan, Smith's publisher) describing Hume's last days, a warm tribute to his friend that offended many churchmen, because of Hume's celebrated atheism.

After the publication of *The Wealth of Nations* in 1776, Smith spent two years in London, enjoying the success of his book and increasing fame. In 1778, his reputation and especially the efforts of the Duke of Buccleuch secured him the office of Commissioner of Customs in Scotland, a very handsomely remunerated post, and he moved back to Scotland, taking a house with his mother in Edinburgh. Between his new stipend and the continuing pension from the Duke, Smith was now fairly rich, and it is thought that he spent much of it on secret charities.

Smith's mother died in 1784, then two years later, his cousin, Tane Douglas, who also lived with him. Thereafter his health failed, he suffered, and finally died on July 17, 1790. By his will, most of his unpublished manuscripts were burned, but some survived.

## Book One

# Of the Causes of Improvement in the Productive Power of Labor and of the Order According to Which Its Produce is Naturally Distributed among the Different Ranks of the People

## Chapter One

# Of the Division of Labor

**T**HE GREATEST IMPROVEMENTS in the productive powers of labor. . . seem to have been the effects of the division of labor.

To take an example, [from] the trade of a pin maker; . . . one man draws out the wire, another straights it, a third cuts it, a fourth points it, a fifth grinds it at the top for receiving the head; to make the head requires two or three distinct operations, to put it on is a peculiar business, to whiten the pins is another, it is even a trade by itself to put them into the paper; and the important business of making a pin is, in this manner, divided into about eighteen distinct operations. . . . I have seen a small manufactory of this kind, where ten men only were employed, and where some of them consequently performed two or three distinct operations. . . . Those ten persons . . . could make among them upwards of forty-eight thousand pins in a day. Each person, therefore, making a tenth part of forty-eight thousand pins, might be considered as making four thousand eight hundred pins in a day. But if they had all wrought separately and independently, and without any of them having been educated to this peculiar business, they certainly could not each of them have made twenty, perhaps not one pin in a day. . . .

In every other art and manufacture, the effects of the division of labor are similar to what they are in this very trifling one, though, in many of them, the labor can neither be so much subdivided, nor reduced to so great a simplicity of operation. . . .

It is the great multiplication of the productions of all the different arts, in consequence of the division of labor, which occasions, in a well-governed society, that universal opulence which extends itself to the lowest ranks of the people. . . .

Observe the accommodation of the most common artificer or day laborer in a civilized and thriving country and you will perceive that the number of people whose industry has been employed in procuring him this accommodation exceeds all computation. The woolen coat, for example, which covers the day laborer, as coarse and rough as it may appear, is the produce of the joint labor of a great multitude of workmen. The shepherd, the sorter of the wool, the wool comber or carder, the dyer, the scribbler, the spinner, the weaver, the fuller, the dresser, with many others, must all join their different arts in order to complete even this homely production. How many merchants and carriers, besides, must have been employed in transporting the materials from some of those workmen to others who often live in a very distant part of the country? How much commerce and navigation in particular, how many shipbuilders, sailors, sail makers, rope makers, must have been employed in order to bring together the different drugs made use of by the dyer, which often come from the remotest corners of the world? What a variety of labor, too, is necessary in order to produce the tools of the meanest of those workmen! To say nothing of such complicated machines as the ship of the sailor, the mill of the fuller, or even the loom of the weaver, let us consider only what a variety of labor is requisite in order to form that very simple machine, the shears with which the shepherd clips the wool. The miner, the builder of the furnace for smelting the ore, the feller of the timber, the burner of the charcoal to be made use of in the smelting house, the brick maker, the bricklayer, the workmen who attend the furnace, the millwright, the forger, the smith, must all of them join their different arts in order to produce them. . . . Without the assistance and cooperation of many thousands, the very meanest person in a civilized country could not be provided, even according to, what we very falsely imagine, the easy and simple manner in which he is commonly accommodated. . . .

## Chapter Two

# Of the Principle Which Gives Occasion to the Division of Labor

THIS DIVISION OF labor, from which so many advantages are derived, is not originally the effect of any human wisdom, which foresees and intends that general opulence to which it gives occasion. It is the necessary, though very slow and gradual, consequence of a certain propensity in human nature . . . to truck, barter, and exchange one thing for another.

. . . In civilized society [an individual] stands at all times in need of the cooperation and assistance of great multitudes, while his whole life is scarce sufficient to gain the friendship of a few persons. . . . It is in vain for him to expect . . . [assistance] . . . from [the] benevolence [of others] only. He will be more likely to prevail if he can interest their self-love in his favor, and show them that it is for their own advantage to do for him what he requires of them. . . .

It is not from the benevolence of the butcher, the brewer, or the baker, that we expect our dinner, but from their regard to their own interest. We address ourselves, not to their humanity, but to their self-love, and never talk to them of our own necessities, but of their advantages. . . .

# That the Division of Labor Is Limited by the Extent of the Market

A s it is the power of exchanging that gives occasion to the division of labor, so the extent of this division must always be limited by the extent of . . . the market. When the market is very small, no person can have any encouragement to dedicate himself entirely to one employment. . . .

## Chapter Four

# Of the Origin and Use of Money

WHEN THE DIVISION of labor has been once thoroughly established, it is but a very small part of a man's wants which the produce of his own labor can supply. He supplies the far greater part of them by exchanging that surplus part of the produce of his own labor. . . .

But when the division of labor first began to take place, this power of exchanging must frequently have been very much clogged and embarrassed in its operations. One man, we shall suppose, has more of a certain commodity than he himself has occasion for, while another has less. . . . But if this latter should chance to have nothing that the former stands in need of, no exchange can be made between them. . . .

Different metals have been made use of by different nations [to solve this problem and facilitate exchange]. Iron was the common instrument of commerce among the ancient Spartans, copper among the ancient Romans, and gold and silver among all rich and commercial nations. . . .

. . . [But] in every country of the world, I believe, the avarice and injustice of princes and sovereign states, abusing the confidence of their subjects, have by degrees diminished the real quantity of metal, which had been originally contained in their coins. The Roman, as in the latter ages of the republic, was reduced to the twenty-fourth part of its original value, and, instead of weighing a pound, came to weigh only half an ounce. The English pound and penny contain at present about a third only; the Scots pound and penny about a thirty-sixth; and the French pound and penny about a sixty-sixth part of their original value. By means of those operations, the princes and sovereign states which performed them were enabled, in appearance, to pay their debts and fulfill their engagements with a smaller quantity of silver than would otherwise have been requisite. It was indeed in appearance only; for their creditors were really defrauded of a part of what was due to them. All other debtors in the state were allowed the same privilege, and might pay with the same nominal sum of the new and debased coin whatever they had borrowed in the old. Such operations, therefore, have always proved favorable to the debtor, and ruinous to the creditor. . . .

What are the rules which men naturally observe, in exchanging . . . either . . . money, or [goods]? . . . These rules determine what may be called the exchangeable value of goods.

The word VALUE, it is to be observed, has two different meanings, . . . one may be called "value in use"; the other, "value in exchange." The things which have the greatest value in use have frequently little or no value in exchange; and, on the contrary, those which have the greatest value in exchange have frequently little or no value in use. Nothing is more useful than water; but it will purchase scarce anything; scarce anything can be had in exchange for it. A diamond, on the contrary, has scarce any value in use; but a very great quantity of other goods may frequently be had in exchange for it. . . .

## Chapter Five

# Of the Real and Nominal Price of Commodities, or of Their Price in Labor, and Their Price in Money

EVERY MAN IS rich or poor according to the degree in which he can afford to enjoy the necessaries, conveniences, and amusements of human life. But after the division of labor has once thoroughly taken place, it is but a very small part of these with which a man's own labor can supply him. The far greater part of them he must derive from the labor of other people, and he must be rich or poor according to the quantity of that labor which he can command, or which he can afford to purchase. The value of any commodity, therefore, to the person who possesses it, and who means not to use or consume it himself, but to exchange it for other commodities, is equal to the quantity of labor which it enables him to purchase or command. Labor therefore, is the real measure of the exchangeable value of all commodities.

As a corollary of this high or low wages and profit, are the causes of high or low price. It is because high or low wages and profit must be paid, in order to bring a particular commodity to market, that its price is high or low. . . .*

But though labor be the real measure of the exchangeable value of all commodities, it is not that by which their value is commonly estimated. It is often difficult to ascertain the proportion between two different quantities of labor. The time spent in two different sorts of work will not always alone determine this proportion. The different degrees of hardship endured, and of ingenuity exercised, must likewise be taken into account. There may be more labor in an hour's hard work, than in two hours easy business; or in an hour's application to a trade which it cost ten years labor to learn, than in a month's industry, at an ordinary and obvious employment. But it is not easy to find any accurate measure either of hardship or ingenuity. In exchanging, indeed, the different productions of different sorts of labor for

---

* See Introduction, page 61, for why Smith's "Labor Theory of Value" is incorrect.

one another, some allowance is commonly made for both. It is adjusted, however, not by any accurate measure, but by the haggling and bargaining of the market, according to that sort of rough equality which, though not exact, is sufficient for carrying on the business of common life. . . .

But when barter ceases, and money has become the common instrument of commerce, every particular commodity is more frequently exchanged for money than for any other commodity. The butcher seldom carries his beef or his mutton to the baker or the brewer, in order to exchange them for bread or for beer; but he carries them to the market, where he exchanges them for money, and afterwards exchanges that money for bread and for beer. . . .

At all times and places, that is dear which it is difficult to come at, or which it costs much labor to acquire; and that cheap which is to be had easily, or with very little labor. Labor alone, therefore, never varying in its own value is alone the ultimate and real standard by which the value of all commodities can at all times and places be estimated and compared. It is their real price; money is their nominal price only. . . .

In [a] popular sense . . . labor, like commodities, may be said to have a real and a nominal price. Its real price may be said to consist in the quantity of the necessaries and conveniences of life which are given for it; its nominal price, in the quantity of money. The laborer is rich or poor, is well or ill rewarded, in proportion to the real, not to the nominal price of his labor. . . .

[As noted,] princes and sovereign states have frequently fancied that they had a temporary interest to diminish the quantity of pure metal contained in their coins. . . .

The discovery of the mines of America [also] diminished the value of gold and silver in Europe. . . .

The rents which have been reserved in corn* have preserved their value much better than those which have been reserved in money, even where the denomination of the coin has not been altered. By the 18th of Elizabeth, it was enacted, that a third of the rent of all college leases should be reserved in corn, to be paid either in kind, or according to the current prices at the nearest public market. The money arising from this corn rent, though originally but a third of the whole, is, in the present times, according to Dr. Blackstone, commonly near double of what arises from the other two-thirds. The old money rents of colleges must, according to this account, have sunk almost to a fourth part of their ancient value, or are worth little more than a fourth part of the corn which they were formerly worth. . . .

Though the real value of a corn rent . . . varies much less from century to century than that of a money rent, it varies much more from year to year. . . .

---

* American language: wheat.

Labor, therefore, it appears evidently, is the only universal, as well as the only accurate, measure of value, or the only standard by which we can compare the values of different commodities, at all times, and at all places. We cannot estimate, it is allowed, the real value of different commodities from century to century by the quantities of silver which were given for them. We cannot estimate it from year to year by the quantities of corn. By the quantities of labor, we can, with the greatest accuracy, estimate it, both from century to century, and from year to year. From century to century, corn is a better measure than silver, because, from century to century, equal quantities of corn will command the same quantity of labor more nearly than equal quantities of silver. From year to year, on the contrary, silver is a better measure than corn, because equal quantities of it will more nearly command the same quantity of labor. . . .

The northern nations who established themselves upon the ruins of the Roman empire seem to have had silver money from the first beginning of their settlements, and not to have known either gold or copper coins for several ages thereafter. There were silver coins in England in the time of the Saxons; but there was little gold coined till the time of Edward III nor any copper till that of James I of Great Britain. In England, therefore, and for the same reason, I believe, in all other modern nations of Europe, all accounts are kept, and the value of all goods and of all estates is generally computed, in silver: and when we mean to express the amount of a person's fortune, we seldom mention the number of [gold] guineas, but the number of pounds sterling which we suppose would be given for it.

Originally, in all countries, I believe, a legal tender of payment could be made only in the coin of that metal which was peculiarly considered as the standard or measure of value. In England, gold was not considered as a legal tender for a long time after it was coined into money. The proportion between the values of gold and silver money was not fixed by any public law or proclamation, but was left to be settled by the market. If a debtor offered payment in gold, the creditor might either reject such payment altogether, or accept of it at such a valuation of the gold as he and his debtor could agree upon. . . .

In process of time, and as people became gradually more familiar with the use of the different metals in coin . . . it has, in most countries, I believe, been found convenient to . . . declare by a public law, that a [gold] guinea, for example, of such a weight and fineness, should exchange for one-and-twenty [silver] shillings, or be a legal tender for a debt of that amount. . . .

. . . The late regulations have brought the gold coin as near, perhaps, to its standard weight as it is possible to bring the current coin of any nation; and the order to receive no gold at the public offices but by weight, is likely to preserve it so, as long as that order is enforced. The silver coin still continues in the same worn and degraded state as before the reformation of the gold coin. In the market, however, one-and-twenty shillings of this degraded silver coin are still considered as worth a guinea of this excellent gold coin.

The reformation of the gold coin has evidently raised the value of the silver coin which can be exchanged for it. . . .

## Chapter Six

# Of the Component Part of the Price of Commodities

WHOEVER DERIVES HIS revenue from a fund which is his own must draw it either from his labor, from his stock, or from his land. The revenue derived from labor is called wages; that derived from stock, by the person who manages or employs it, is called profit; that derived from it by the person who does not employ it himself, but lends it to another, is called the interest or the use of money. . . . The revenue which proceeds altogether from land, is called rent, and belongs to the landlord. . . .

When those three different sorts of revenue belong to different persons, they are readily distinguished; but when they belong to the same, they are sometimes confounded with one another, at least in common language. . . .

. . . In a civilized country there are but few commodities of which the exchangeable value arises from labor only, rent and profit contributing largely to that of the far greater part of them. . . .

## Chapter Seven

# Of the Natural and Market Price of Commodities

W HEN THE PRICE of any commodity is neither more nor less than what is sufficient
to pay the rent of the land, the wages of
the labor, and the profits of the stock employed in raising, preparing, and bringing it to market, according
to their natural rates, the commodity is then sold for
what may be called its natural price.

The commodity is then sold precisely for what it
is worth, or for what it really costs the person who
brings it to market; for though, in common language,
what is called the . . . cost of any commodity does not
comprehend the profit of the person who is to sell it
again, yet, if he sells it at a price which does not allow

him the ordinary rate of profit in his neighborhood, he is evidently a loser by the trade; since, by employing his stock in some other way, he might have made that profit. . . . Unless [buyers] yield him this profit, therefore, they do not repay him what [the goods] have really cost him. . . .

The actual price, at which any commodity is commonly sold, is called its market price. It may either be above, or below, or exactly the same with its natural price.

The market price of every particular commodity is regulated by the proportion between the quantity which is actually brought to market, and the demand of those who are willing to pay the natural price of the commodity, or the whole value of the rent, labor, and profit, which must be paid in order to bring it thither. Such people may be called the effectual demanders and their demand the effectual demand; since it may be sufficient to effectuate the bringing of the commodity to market. It is different from the absolute demand. A very poor man may be said, in some sense, to have a demand for a coach and six [horses]; he might like to have it; but his demand is not an effectual demand, as the commodity can never be brought to market in order to satisfy it.

When the quantity of any commodity which is brought to market falls short of the effectual demand, all those who are willing to pay the whole value of the rent, wages, and profit, which must be paid in order to bring it thither, cannot be supplied with the quantity which they want. Rather than want it altogether, some of them will be willing to give more. A competition will immediately begin among them, and the market price will rise more or less above the natural price, according to either the greatness of the deficiency, or the wealth and wanton luxury of the competitors. . . .

When the quantity brought to market exceeds the effectual demand, it cannot be all sold to those who are willing to pay the whole value of the rent, wages, and profit, which must be paid in order to bring it thither. Some part must be sold to those who are willing to pay less, and the low price which they give for it must reduce the price of the whole. The market price will sink more or less below the natural price, according as the greatness of the excess increases more or less the competition of the sellers, or according as it happens to be more or less important to them to get immediately rid of the commodity. . . .

The natural price, therefore, is, as it were, the central price, to which the prices of all commodities are continually gravitating. . . . But whatever may be the obstacles which hinder them from settling in this center of repose and continuance, they are constantly tending towards it. . . .

But though the market price of every particular commodity is in this manner continually gravitating, if one may say so, towards the natural price; yet sometimes particular accidents, sometimes natural causes, and sometimes particular regulations of policy, may, in many commodities, keep up the market price, for a long time together, a good deal above the natural price.

When, by an increase in the effectual demand, the market price of some particular commodity happens to rise a good deal above the natural price, those who employ their stocks in supplying that market, are generally careful to conceal this change. If it was commonly known, their great profit would tempt so many new rivals to employ their stocks in the same way, that, the effectual demand being fully supplied, the market price would soon be reduced to the natural price, and, perhaps, for some time even below it.... Secrets of this kind, however, it must be acknowledged, can seldom be long kept; and the extraordinary profit can last very little longer than they are kept.

Secrets in manufactures are capable of being longer kept than secrets in trade. A dyer who has found the means of producing a particular color with materials which cost only half the price of those commonly made use of, may, with good management, enjoy the advantage of his discovery as long as he lives....

A monopoly granted either to an individual or to a trading company, has the same effect as a secret in trade or manufactures. The monopolists, by keeping the market constantly understocked by never fully supplying the effectual demand, sell their commodities much above the natural price, and raise their emoluments, whether they consist in wages or profit, greatly above their natural rate.

The price of monopoly is upon every occasion the highest which can be got. The natural price, or the price of free competition, on the contrary, is the lowest which can be taken, not upon every occasion indeed, but for any considerable time together. The one is upon every occasion the highest which can be squeezed out of the buyers, or which it is supposed they will consent to give; the other is the lowest which the sellers can commonly afford to take, and at the same time continue their business.

The exclusive privileges of corporations, statutes of apprenticeship, and all those laws which restrain in particular employments, the competition to a smaller number than might otherwise go into them, have the same tendency, though in a less degree. They are a sort of enlarged monopolies, and may frequently, for ages together, and in whole classes of employments, keep up the market price of particular commodities above the natural price, and maintain both the wages of the labor and the profits of the stock employed about them somewhat above their natural rate.

Such enhancements of the market price may last as long as the regulations of policy which give occasion to them.

The market price of any particular commodity, though it may continue long above, can seldom continue long below, its natural price. Whatever part of it was paid below the natural rate, the persons whose interest it affected would immediately feel the loss, and would immediately withdraw either so much land or so much labor, or so much stock, from being employed about it, that the quantity brought to market would soon be no more than sufficient to supply the effectual demand. Its market price, therefore, would soon rise to the natural price; this at least would be the case where there was perfect liberty. . . .

## Chapter Eight

# Of the Wages of Labor

I N [THE] ORIGINAL state of things . . . the whole produce of labor belongs to the laborer. He has neither landlord nor master to share with him. . . .

But this original state of things, in which the laborer enjoyed the whole produce of his own labor, could not last beyond the first introduction of the appropriation of land and the accumulation of stock. It was at an end, therefore, long before the most considerable improvements were made in the productive powers of labor. . . .

. . . The common wages of labor depend . . . everywhere upon the contract usually made between those two parties, whose interests are by no means the same. The workmen desire to get as much, the masters to give as little, as possible. The former are disposed to combine in order to raise, the latter in order to lower, the wages of labor.

It is not, however, difficult to foresee which of the two parties must, upon all ordinary occasions, have the advantage in the dispute. . . . In all such disputes, the masters can hold out much longer. A landlord, a farmer, a master manufacturer, or merchant, though they did not employ a single workman, could generally live a year or two upon the stocks, which they have already acquired. Many workmen could not subsist a week, few could subsist a month, and scarce any a year, without employment. In the long run, the workman may be as necessary to his master as his master is to him; but the necessity is not so immediate.

We rarely hear, it has been said, of the combinations of masters, though frequently of those of workmen. But whoever imagines, upon this account, which masters rarely combine, is as ignorant of the world as of the subject. Masters are always and everywhere in a sort of tacit, but constant and uniform, combination, not to raise the wages of labor above their actual rate. To violate this combination is everywhere a most unpopular action, and a sort of reproach to a master among his neighbors and equals. . . . Masters too sometimes enter into particular combinations to sink the wages of labor even below this rate. These are always conducted with the utmost silence and secrecy. . . .

Such combinations . . . are frequently resisted by a contrary defensive combination of the workmen, who sometimes, too, without any provocation of this kind, combine, of their own accord, to raise the price of their

labor. . . . In order to bring the point to a speedy deci-
sion, they have always recourse to the loudest clamor,
and sometimes to the most shocking violence and outrage. They are desperate, and act with the folly and
extravagance of desperate men, who must either starve,
or frighten their masters into an immediate compliance
with their demands. The masters, upon these occasions,
are just as clamorous upon the other side, and never
cease to call aloud for the assistance of the civil magistrate, and the rigorous execution of those laws which
have been enacted with so much severity against the
combination of servants, laborers, and journeymen.
The workmen, accordingly, very seldom derive any
advantage from the violence of those tumultuous combinations, which, partly from the interposition of the
civil magistrate, partly from the superior steadiness of
the masters, partly from the necessity which the greater
part of the workmen are under of submitting for the
sake of present subsistence, generally end in nothing
but the punishment or ruin of the ringleaders.

But though, in disputes with their workmen, masters must generally have the advantage, there is, however, a certain rate, below which it seems impossible to
reduce, for any considerable time, the ordinary wages
even of the lowest species of labor.

A man must always live by his work, and his wages
must at least be sufficient to maintain him. They must
even upon most occasions be somewhat more, otherwise it would be impossible for him to bring up a family,

and the race of such workmen could not last beyond the first generation. Mr. Cantillon* seems, upon this account, to suppose that the lowest species of common laborers must everywhere earn at least double their own maintenance, in order that, one with another, they may be enabled to bring up two children; the labor of the wife, on account of her necessary attendance on the children, being supposed no more than sufficient to provide for herself. But one-half the children born, it is computed, die before the age of manhood. The poorest laborers, therefore, according to this account, must, one with another, attempt to rear at least four children, in order that two may have an equal chance of living to that age. But the necessary maintenance of four children, it is supposed, may be nearly equal to that of one man. The labor of an able-bodied slave, the same author adds, is computed to be worth double his maintenance; and that of the meanest laborer, he thinks, cannot be worth less than that of an able-bodied slave. Thus far at least seems certain, that, in order to bring up a family, the labor of the husband and wife together must, even in the lowest species of common labor, be able to earn something more than what is precisely necessary for their own maintenance; but in what proportion, whether in that above-mentioned, or many other, I shall not take upon me to determine.

---

* See Introduction, page 56. Richard Cantillon developed free market economics some decades before Smith and the latter seems to have relied on his work.

There are certain circumstances, however, which sometimes give the laborers an advantage, and enable them to raise their wages considerably above this rate....

When in any country the demand for those who live by wages, laborers, journeymen, servants of every kind, is continually increasing; when every year furnishes employment for a greater number than had been employed the year before, the workmen have no occasion to combine in order to raise their wages. The scarcity of hands occasions a competition among masters, who bid against one another in order to get workmen, and thus voluntarily break through the natural combination of masters not to raise wages....

The demand for those who live by wages . . . necessarily increases with the increase of the revenue and stock of every country, and cannot possibly increase without it. The increase of revenue and stock is the increase of national wealth. The demand for those who live by wages, therefore, naturally increases with the increase of national wealth, and cannot possibly increase without it.

It is not the actual greatness of national wealth, but its continual increase, which occasions a rise in the wages of labor. It is not, accordingly, in the richest countries, but in the most thriving, or in those which are growing rich the fastest, that the wages of labor are highest. England is certainly, in the present times, a much richer country than any part of North America. The wages of labor, however, are much higher in

North America than in any part of England. . . . The price of provisions is everywhere in North America much lower than in England. A dearth has never been known there. In the worst seasons they have always had a sufficiency for themselves, though less for exportation. If the money price of labor, therefore, be higher than it is anywhere in the mother country, its real price, the real command of the necessaries and conveniences of life which it conveys to the laborer, must be higher in a still greater proportion.

But though North America is not yet so rich as England, it is much more thriving and advancing with much greater rapidity to the further acquisition of riches. The most decisive mark of the prosperity of any country is the increase of the number of its inhabitants.* In Great Britain, and most other European countries, they are not supposed to double in less than five hundred years. In the British colonies in North America, it has been found that they double in twenty or five-and-twenty years. Nor in the present times is this increase principally owing to the continual importation of new inhabitants, but to the great multiplication of the species. Those who live to old age, it is said, frequently see there from fifty to a hundred, and sometimes many more, descendants from their own body. Labor is there so well rewarded, that a numerous family of children, instead of being a burden, is a source of

---

* See Introduction, page 56.

opulence and prosperity to the parents. The labor of each child, before it can leave their house, is computed to be worth a hundred pounds clear gain to them. A young widow with four or five young children, who, among the middling or inferior ranks of people in Europe, would have so little chance for a second husband, is there frequently courted as a sort of fortune. The value of children is the greatest of all encouragements to marriage. We cannot, therefore, wonder that the people in North America should generally marry very young. Notwithstanding the great increase occasioned by such early marriages, there is a continual complaint of the scarcity of hands in North America. The demand for laborers, the funds destined for maintaining them increase, it seems, still faster than they can find laborers to employ.

Though the wealth of a country should be very great, yet if it has been long stationary, we must not expect to find the wages of labor very high in it. . . . China has been long one of the richest, that is, one of the most fertile, best cultivated, most industrious, and most populous, countries in the world. It seems, however, to have been long stationary. Marco Polo, who visited it more than five hundred years ago, describes its cultivation, industry, and populousness, almost in the same terms in which they are described by travelers in the present times. . . . The accounts of all travelers, inconsistent in many other respects, agree in the low wages of labor, and in the difficulty which a laborer finds in bringing up a family in China. If by digging the ground a whole day he can get what will purchase a small quantity of rice in the evening, he is contented. The condition of artificers is, if possible, still worse. Instead of waiting indolently in their workhouses for the calls of their customers, as in Europe, they are continually running about the streets with the tools of their respective trades, offering their services, and, as it were, begging employment. The poverty of the lower ranks of people in China far surpasses that of the most beggarly nations in Europe. In the neighborhood of Canton, many hundred, it is commonly said, many thousand families, have no habitation on the land, but live constantly in little fishing boats upon the rivers and canals. The subsistence which they find there is so scanty, that they are eager to fish up the nastiest garbage thrown overboard from any European ship. Any carrion, the carcass of a dead dog or cat, for example, though half putrid and stinking, is as welcome to them as the most wholesome food to the people of other countries. Marriage is encouraged in China, not by the profitableness of children, but by the liberty of destroying them. In all great towns, several are every night exposed in the street, or drowned like puppies in the water. The performance of this horrid office is even said to be the avowed business by which some people earn their subsistence.

China, however, though it may, perhaps, stand still, does not seem to go backwards. Its towns are nowhere deserted by their inhabitants. The lands which had once been cultivated are nowhere neglected. The same, or very nearly the same, annual labor, must, therefore, continue to be performed. . . .

But it would be otherwise in a country where the funds destined for the maintenance of labor were sensibly decaying. Every year the demand for servants and laborers would, in all the different classes of employments, be less than it had been the year before. . . . This, perhaps, is nearly the present state of Bengal, and of some other of the English settlements in the East Indies. In a fertile country, which had before been much depopulated, where subsistence, consequently, should not be very difficult, and where, notwithstanding, three or four hundred thousand people die of hunger in one year, we may be assured that the funds destined for the maintenance of the laboring poor are fast decaying. The difference between the genius of the British constitution, which protects and governs North America, and that of the mercantile company which oppresses and domineers in the East Indies, cannot, perhaps, be better illustrated than by the different state of those countries.

The liberal reward of labor, therefore, as it is the necessary effect, so it is the natural symptom of increasing national wealth. The scanty maintenance of the laboring poor, on the other hand, is the natural symptom that things are at a stand, and their starving condition, that they are going fast backwards.

In Great Britain, the wages of labor seem, in the present times, to be evidently more than what is precisely necessary to enable the laborer to bring up a family....

... The price of labor ... is dearer in England than in Scotland. If the laboring poor, therefore, can maintain their families in the one part of the United Kingdom, they must be in affluence in the other. Oatmeal, indeed, supplies the common people in Scotland with the greatest and the best part of their food, which is, in general, much inferior to that of their neighbors of the same rank in England. This difference, however, in the mode of their subsistence, is not the cause, but the effect, of the difference in their wages; though, by a strange misapprehension, I have frequently heard it represented as the cause. It is not because one man keeps a coach, while his neighbor walks afoot, that the one is rich, and the other poor; but because the one is rich, he keeps a coach, and because the other is poor, he walks afoot....

It is certain, that in both parts of the United Kingdom grain was somewhat dearer in the last century than in the present, it is equally certain that labor was much cheaper. If the laboring poor, therefore, could bring up their families then, they must be much more at their ease now.... In England, the improvements of agriculture, manufactures, and commerce, began much earlier than in Scotland. The demand for labor, and consequently its price, must necessarily have increased with those improvements. In the last century, accordingly, as well as in the present, the wages of labor were higher in England than in Scotland. . . .

The real recompense of labor, the real quantity of the necessaries and conveniences of life which it can procure to the laborer, has, during the course of the present century, increased perhaps in a still greater proportion than its money price. Not only grain has become somewhat cheaper, but many other things, from which the industrious poor derive an agreeable and wholesome variety of food, have become a great deal cheaper. Potatoes, for example, do not at present, through the greater part of the kingdom, cost half the price which they used to do thirty or forty years ago. The same thing may be said of turnips, carrots, cabbages; things which were formerly never raised but by the spade, but which are now commonly raised by the plow. All sort of garden stuff, too, has become cheaper. The greater part of the apples and even of the onions consumed in Great Britain, were in the last century, imported from Flanders. The great improvements in the coarser manufactories of both linen and woolen cloth furnish the laborers with cheaper and better clothing; and those in the manufactories of the coarser metals, with cheaper and better instruments of trade, as well as with many agreeable and convenient pieces of household furniture. Soap, salt, candles, leather, and fermented liquors, have, indeed, become a good deal dearer, chiefly from the taxes which have been laid upon them. The quantity of these, however, which the laboring poor are under any necessity of consuming, is so very small, that the increase in their price does not compensate the diminution in that of so many other things. . . .

Is this improvement in the circumstances of the lower ranks of the people to be regarded as an advantage or as an inconveniency to the society? The answer seems at first abundantly plain. Servants, laborers, and workmen of different kinds, make up the far greater part of every great political society. But what improves the circumstances of the greater part can never be regarded as any inconveniency to the whole. No society can surely be flourishing and happy, of which the far greater part of the members are poor and miserable. It is but equity, besides, that they who feed, clothe, and lodge the whole body of the people, should have such a share of the produce of their own labor as to be themselves tolerably well fed, clothed, and lodged.

. . . Poverty, though it does not prevent the generation, is extremely unfavorable to the rearing of children. The tender plant is produced; but in so cold a soil, and so severe a climate, soon withers and dies. It is not uncommon, I have been frequently told, in the Highlands of Scotland, for a mother who has born twenty children not to have two alive. . . . In some places, one-half the children die before they are four years of age, in many places before they are seven, and in almost all places before they are nine or ten. This great mortality, however, will everywhere be found chiefly among the children of the common people, who cannot afford to tend them with the same care as those of better station. . . .

The liberal reward of labor enables them to provide better for their children, and consequently to bring up a greater number. . . .

The wear and tear of a slave, it has been said, is at the expense of his master; but that of a free servant is at his own expense. The wear and tear of the latter, however, is, in reality, as much at the expense of his master as that of the former. The wages paid to journeymen and servants of every kind must be such as may enable them, one with another to continue the race of journeymen and servants, according as the increasing, diminishing, or stationary demand of the society, may happen to require. But . . . the work done by freemen comes cheaper in the end than that performed by slaves. It is found to do so even at Boston, New York, and Philadelphia, where the wages of common labor are so very high. . . .

The liberal reward of labor, as it encourages the propagation, so it increases the industry of the common people. The wages of labor are the encouragement of industry, which, like every other human quality, improves in proportion to the encouragement it receives. A plentiful subsistence increases the bodily strength of the laborer, and the comfortable hope of bettering his condition, and of ending his days, perhaps, in ease and plenty, animates him to exert that strength to the utmost. Where wages are high, accordingly, we shall always find the workmen more active, diligent, and expeditious, than where they are low; in England, for example, than in Scotland; in the neighborhood of great towns, than in remote country places. . . .

. . . That a little more plenty than ordinary may render some workmen idle, cannot be well doubted; but that it should have this effect upon the greater part, or that men in general should work better when they are ill fed, than when they are well fed, when they are disheartened than when they are in good spirits, when they are frequently sick than when they are generally in good health, seems not very probable. . . .

[In addition] . . . nothing can be more absurd . . . than to imagine that men in general should work less when they work for themselves, than when they work for other people. A poor independent workman will generally be more industrious than even a journeyman who works by the piece. The one enjoys the whole produce of his own industry, the other shares it with his master. The one, in his separate independent state, is less liable to the temptations of bad company, which, in large manufactories, so frequently ruin the morals of the other. The superiority of the independent workman over those servants who are hired by the month or by the year, and whose wages and maintenance are the same, whether they do much or do little, is likely to be still greater. . . .

## Chapter Nine

# Of the Profits of Stock

I T IS NOT easy, it has already been observed, to ascertain what are the average wages of labor, even in a particular place, and at a particular time. We can, even in this case, seldom determine more than what are the most usual wages. But even this can seldom be done with regard to the profits of stock. Profit is so very fluctuating, that the person who carries on a particular trade, cannot always tell you himself what is the average of his annual profit. . . .

But . . . some notion may be formed of them from the interest of money. It may be laid down as a maxim that wherever a great deal can be made by the use of money, a great deal will commonly be given for the use of it; and that, wherever little can be made by it, less will commonly be given for it. Accordingly, therefore, as the usual market rate of interest varies in any country, we may be assured that the ordinary profits of stock must vary with it, must sink as it sinks, and rise as it rises. The progress of interest, therefore, may lead us to form some notion of the progress of profit.

By the 37th of Henry VIII all interest above ten percent was declared unlawful. More, it seems, had sometimes been taken before that. In the reign of Edward VI religious zeal prohibited all interest. This prohibition, however, like all others of the same kind, is said to have produced no effect, and probably rather increased than diminished the evil of usury. The statute of Henry VIII was revived by the 13th of Elizabeth, chap. 8, and ten percent continued to be the legal rate of interest till the 21st of James I when it was restricted to eight percent. It was reduced to six percent soon after the Restoration, and by the 12th of Queen Anne, to five percent. All these different statutory regulations seem to have been made with great propriety. They seem to have followed, and not to have gone before, the market rate of interest, or the rate at which people of good credit usually borrowed. Since the time of Queen Anne, five percent seems to have been rather above than below the market rate. Before the late war, the government borrowed at three percent; and people of good credit in the capital, and in many other parts of the kingdom, at three-and-a-half, four, and four-and-a-half percent.

. . . France is, perhaps, in the present times, not so rich a country as England; and though the legal rate of interest has in France frequently been lower than in England, the market rate has generally been higher; for there, as in other countries, they have several very safe and easy methods of evading the law. . . .

The province of Holland, on the other hand, in proportion to the extent of its territory and the number of its people, is a richer country than England. The government there borrows at two percent and private people of good credit at three. The wages of labor are said to be higher in Holland than in England, and the Dutch, it is well known, trade upon lower profits than any people in Europe. . . . When profit diminishes, merchants are very apt to complain that trade decays, though the diminution of profit is the natural effect of its prosperity, or of a greater stock being employed in it than before. . . .

. . . The great fortunes so suddenly and so easily acquired in Bengal and the other British settlements in the East Indies may satisfy us, that as the wages of labor are very low, so the profits of stock are very high in those ruined countries. The interest of money is proportionally so. In Bengal, money is frequently lent to the farmers at forty, fifty, and sixty percent and the succeeding crop is mortgaged for the payment. . . . Such enormous usury must . . . eat up the greater part of . . . profits. Before the fall of the Roman republic, a usury of the same kind seems to have been common in the provinces, under the ruinous administration of their proconsuls. The virtuous Brutus lent money in Cyprus at eight-and-forty percent as we learn from the letters of Cicero. . . .

In . . . [China] . . .the rich, or the owners of large capitals, enjoy a good deal of security, [while] the poor, or the owners of small capitals, enjoy scarce any, but are liable, under the pretence of justice, to be pillaged and plundered at any time by the inferior mandarins. . . . In every different branch, the oppression of the poor . . . establish[es] the monopoly of the rich, who, by engrossing the whole trade to themselves, [are] able to make very large profits. Twelve percent accordingly, is said to be the common interest of money in China, and the ordinary profits of stock must be sufficient to afford this large interest.

A defect in the law may sometimes raise the rate of interest considerably above what the condition of the country, as to wealth or poverty, would require. When the law does not enforce the performance of contracts, it puts all borrowers nearly upon the same footing with bankrupts, or people of doubtful credit, in better-regulated countries. The uncertainty of recovering his money makes the lender exact the same usurious interest which is usually required from bankrupts. Among the barbarous nations who overran the western provinces of the Roman Empire, the performance of contracts was left for many ages to the faith of the contracting parties. The courts of justice of their kings seldom intermeddled in it. The high rate of interest which took place in those ancient times, may, perhaps, be partly accounted for from this cause.

When the law prohibits interest altogether, it does not prevent it. Many people must borrow, and nobody will lend without such a consideration for the use of their money as is suitable, not only to what can be made by the use of it, but to the difficulty and danger of evading the law. . . .

In a country which had acquired its full complement of riches, where, in every particular branch of business, there was the greatest quantity of stock that could be employed in it, as the ordinary rate of clear profit would be very small, so the usual market rate of interest which could be afforded out of it would be so low as to render it impossible for any but the very wealthiest people to live upon the interest of their money. . . . It would be necessary that almost every man should be a man of business, or engage in some sort of trade. The province of Holland seems to be approaching near to this state. It is there unfashionable not to be a man of business. Necessity makes it usual for almost every man to be so, and custom everywhere regulates fashion. As it is ridiculous not to dress, so is it, in some measure, not to be employed like other people. As a man of a civil profession seems awkward in a camp or a garrison, and is even in some danger of being despised there, so does an idle man among men of business. . . .

The proportion which the usual market rate of interest ought to bear to the ordinary rate of clear profit necessarily varies as profit rises or falls. . . . In a country where the ordinary rate of clear profit is eight or ten percent it may be reasonable that one-half of it should go to interest, wherever business is carried on with borrowed money.... But the proportion between interest and clear profit might not be the same in countries where the ordinary rate of profit was either a good deal lower, or a good deal higher. If it were a good deal lower, one-half of it, perhaps, could not be afforded for interest; and more might be afforded if it were a good deal higher....

*Chapter Ten*

# Of Wages and Profit in the Different Employments of Labor and Stock

THE WHOLE OF the advantages and disadvantages of the different employments of labor and stock, must, in the same neighborhood, be either perfectly equal, or continually tending to equality. If, in the same neighborhood, there was any employment evidently either more or less advantageous than the rest, [taking into account risk and reward, difficulty and ease, attractiveness and unattractiveness], so many people would crowd into it in the one case, and so many would desert it in the other, that its advantages would soon return to the level of other employments. This, at least, would be the case in a society where things were left to follow their natural course, where there was perfect liberty, and where every man was perfectly free both to choose what occupation he thought proper, and to change it as often as he thought proper. . . .

Pecuniary wages and profit, indeed, are everywhere in Europe extremely different, according to the different employments of labor and stock. But this difference arises, partly . . . from the policy of Europe, which nowhere leaves things at perfect liberty. . . .

[There] are [natural] inequalities in the . . . advantages and disadvantages of the different employments of labor and stock . . . even where there is the most perfect liberty. But the policy of Europe, by not leaving things at perfect liberty, occasions other inequalities of much greater importance.

It does this chiefly in the three following ways. First, by restraining the competition in some employments to a smaller number than would otherwise be disposed to enter into them; secondly, by increasing it in others beyond what it naturally would be; and, thirdly, by obstructing the free circulation of labor and stock, both from employment to employment, and from place to place. . . .

In Sheffield, no master cutler can have more than one apprentice at a time, by a by-law of the corporation. In Norfolk and Norwich, no master weaver can have more than two apprentices, under pain of forfeiting five pounds a month to the king. No master hatter can have more than two apprentices anywhere in England, or in the English plantations, under pain of forfeiting five pounds a month, half to the king, and half to him who shall sue in any court of record. Both these regulations, though they have been confirmed by a public law of the kingdom, are evidently dictated by the same corporation-spirit which enacted the by-law of Sheffield. . . .

Seven years seem anciently to have been, all over Europe, the usual term established for the duration of apprenticeships in the greater part of incorporated trades. All such incorporations were anciently called universities, which, indeed, is the proper Latin name for any incorporation whatever. The university of smiths, the university of tailors, etc. are expressions which we commonly meet with in the old charters of ancient towns. When those particular incorporations, which are now peculiarly called universities, were first established, the term of years which it was necessary to study, in order to obtain the degree of master of arts, appears evidently to have been copied from the term of apprenticeship in common trades, of which the incorporations were much more ancient. As to have wrought seven years under a master properly qualified, was necessary, in order to entitle any person to become a master, and to have himself apprentices in a common trade; so to have studied seven years under a master properly qualified, was necessary to entitle him to become a master, teacher, or doctor (words anciently synonymous), in the liberal arts, and to have scholars or apprentices (words likewise originally synonymous) to study under him.

By the 5th of Elizabeth, commonly called the Statute of Apprenticeship, it was enacted, that no person should, for the future, exercise any trade, craft, or mystery, at that time exercised in England, unless he had previously served to it an apprenticeship of seven years at least; and what before had been the by-law of many particular corporations, became in England the general and public law of all trades carried on in market towns. For though the words of the statute are very general, and seem plainly to include the whole kingdom, by interpretation its operation has been limited to market towns; it having been held that, in country villages, a person may exercise several different trades, though he has not served a seven years apprenticeship to each, they being necessary for the conveniency of the inhabitants, and the number of people frequently not being sufficient to supply each with a particular set of hands.

By a strict interpretation of the words, too, the operation of this statute has been limited to those trades which were established in England before the 5th of Elizabeth, and has never been extended to such as have been introduced since that time. This limitation has given occasion to several distinctions, which, considered as rules of police, appear as foolish as can well be imagined. It has been adjudged, for example, that a coach maker can neither himself make nor employ journeymen to make his coach wheels, but must buy them of a master wheelwright; this latter trade having been exercised in England before the 5th of Elizabeth. But a wheelwright, though he has never served an apprenticeship to a coach maker, may either himself make or employ journeymen to make coaches; the trade of a coach maker not being within the statute, because not exercised in England at the time when it was made. The manufactures of Manchester, Birmingham, and Wolverhampton, are many of them, upon this account, not within the statute, not having been exercised in England before the 5th of Elizabeth. . . .

The property which every man has in his own labor, as it is the original foundation of all other property, so it is the most sacred and inviolable. The patrimony of a poor man lies in the strength and dexterity of his hands; and to hinder him from employing this strength and dexterity in what manner he thinks proper, without injury to his neighbor, is a plain violation of this most sacred property. It is a manifest encroachment upon the just liberty, both of the workman, and of those who might be disposed to employ him. . . . To judge whether he is fit to be employed, may surely be trusted to the discretion of the employers, whose interest it so much concerns. The affected anxiety of the lawgiver, lest they should employ an improper person, is evidently as impertinent as it is oppressive.

The institution of long apprenticeships can give no security that insufficient workmanship shall not frequently be exposed to public sale. When this is done, it is generally the effect of fraud, and not of inability; and the longest apprenticeship can give no security against fraud. Quite different regulations are necessary to prevent this abuse. The sterling mark upon plate, and the stamps upon linen and woolen cloth, give the purchaser much greater security than any statute of apprenticeship. He generally looks at these, but never thinks it worthwhile to enquire whether the workman had served a seven-year's apprenticeship.

The institution of long apprenticeships has no tendency to form young people to industry. A journeyman who works by the piece is likely to be industrious, because he derives a benefit from every exertion of his industry. An apprentice is likely to be idle, and almost always is so, because he has no immediate interest to be otherwise. . . . A young man naturally conceives an aversion to labor, when for a long time he receives no benefit from it. The boys who are put out as apprentices from public charities are generally bound for more than the usual number of years, and they generally turn out very idle and worthless. . . .

Long apprenticeships are altogether unnecessary. . . . In the common mechanic trades, those of a few days might certainly be sufficient. The dexterity of hand, indeed, even in common trades, cannot be acquired without much practice and experience. But a young man would practice with much more diligence and attention, if from the beginning he wrought as a journeyman, being paid in proportion to the little work which he could execute. . . . The master, indeed, would be a loser. He would lose all the wages of the apprentice, which he now saves, for seven years together. In the end, perhaps, the apprentice himself would be a loser. In a trade so easily learnt he would have more competitors, and his wages, when he came to be a complete workman, would be much less than at present. The same increase of competition would reduce the profits of the masters, as well as the wages of workmen. The trades, the crafts, the mysteries, would all be losers. But the public would be a gainer, the work of all artificers coming in this way much cheaper to market.

It is to prevent his reduction of price, and consequently of wages and profit, by restraining that free competition which would most certainly occasion it, that all corporations, and the greater part of corporation laws have been established. In order to erect a corporation, no other authority in ancient times was requisite, in many parts of Europe, but that of the town-corporate in which it was established. In England, indeed, a charter from the king was likewise necessary. But this prerogative of the crown seems to have been reserved rather for extorting money from the subject, than for the defense of the common liberty against such oppressive monopolies. . . .

The government of towns-corporate was altogether in the hands of traders and artificers, and it was the manifest interest of every particular class of them, to prevent the market from being overstocked, as they commonly express it, with their own particular species of industry; which is in reality to keep it always understocked. . . .

. . . Whatever regulations, tend to increase wages and profits beyond what they otherwise would be, tend to enable the town to purchase, with a smaller quantity of its labor, the produce of a greater quantity of the labor of the country. They give the traders and artificers in the town an advantage over the landlords, farmers, and laborers, in the country, and break down that natural equality which would otherwise take place in the commerce which is carried on between them. The whole annual produce of the labor of the society is annually divided between those two different sets of people. By means of those regulations, a greater share of it is given to the inhabitants of the town than would otherwise fall to them, and a less to those of the country.

The price which the town really pays for the provisions and materials annually imported into it is the quantity of manufactures and other goods annually exported from it. The dearer the latter are sold, the cheaper the former are bought. The industry of the town becomes more, and that of the country less advantageous. . . .

The inhabitants of a town being collected into one place can easily combine together. The most insignificant trades carried on in towns have, accordingly, in some place or other, been incorporated; and even where they have never been incorporated, yet the corporation-spirit, the jealousy of strangers, the aversion to take apprentices, or to communicate the secret of their trade, generally prevail in them, and often teach them, by voluntary associations and agreements, to prevent that free competition which they cannot prohibit by by-laws. The trades which employ but a small number of hands run most easily into such combinations. Half-a-dozen wool combers, perhaps, are necessary to keep a thousand spinners and weavers at work. By combining not to take apprentices, they cannot only engross the employment, but reduce the whole manufacture into a sort of slavery to themselves, and raise the price of their labor much above what is due to the nature of their work.

The inhabitants of the country, dispersed in distant places, cannot easily combine together. They have not only never been incorporated, but the incorporation spirit never has prevailed among them. No apprenticeship has ever been thought necessary to qualify for husbandry, the great trade of the country. After what are called the fine arts, and the liberal professions, however, there is perhaps no trade which requires so great a variety of knowledge and experience. . . . The direction of operations, besides, which must be varied with every change of the weather, as well as with many other accidents, requires much more judgment and discretion, than that of those which are always the same, or very nearly the same. . . .

The superiority which the industry of the towns has everywhere in Europe over that of the country is not altogether owing to corporations and corporation laws. It is supported by many other regulations. The high duties upon foreign manufactures and upon all goods imported by alien merchants all tend to the same purpose. Corporation laws enable the inhabitants of towns to raise their prices, without fearing to be undersold by the free competition of their own countrymen. Those other regulations secure them equally against that of foreigners. The enhancement of price occasioned by both is everywhere finally paid by the landlords, farmers, and laborers, of the country, who have seldom opposed the establishment of such monopolies. . . . The clamor and sophistry of merchants and manufacturers easily persuade them, that the private interest of a part, and of a subordinate part, of the society, is the general interest of the whole. . . .

People of the same trade seldom meet together, even for merriment and diversion, but the conversation ends in a conspiracy against the public, or in some contrivance to raise prices. It is impossible, indeed, to prevent such meetings, by any law which either could be executed, or would be consistent with liberty and justice. But though the law cannot hinder people of the same trade from sometimes assembling together, it ought to do nothing to facilitate such assemblies, much less to render them necessary. . . .

An incorporation not only renders them necessary, but makes the act of the majority binding upon the whole. In a free trade, an effectual combination cannot be established but by the unanimous consent of every single trader, and it cannot last longer than every single trader continues of the same mind. The majority of a corporation can enact a by-law, with proper penalties, which will limit the competition more effectually and more durably than any voluntary combination whatever.

The pretence that corporations are necessary for the better government of the trade is without any foundation. The real and effectual discipline which is exercised over a workman is not that of his corporation, but that of his customers. It is the fear of losing their employment which restrains his frauds and corrects his negligence. An exclusive corporation necessarily weakens the force of this discipline. A particular set of workmen must then be employed, let them behave well or ill. It is upon this account that, in many large incorporated towns, no tolerable workmen are to be found, even in some of the most necessary trades. If you would have your work tolerably executed, it must be done in the suburbs, where the workmen, having no exclusive privilege, have nothing but their character to depend upon, and you must then smuggle it into the town as well as you can. . . .

. . . The policy of Europe, by increasing the competition in some employments beyond what it naturally would be, occasions another inequality, of an opposite kind. . . .

. . . Sometimes the public, and sometimes the piety of private founders, have established many pensions, scholarships, exhibitions, bursaries, etc., . . . which draw many more people into trades than could otherwise pretend to follow them. In all Christian countries, I believe, the education of the greater part of churchmen is paid for in this manner. Very few of them are educated altogether at their own expense. The long, tedious, and expensive education, therefore, of those who are, will not always procure them a suitable reward, the church being crowded with people, who, in order to get employment, are willing to accept of a much smaller recompense than what such an education would otherwise have entitled them to. . . . Forty pounds a year is reckoned at present very good pay for a curate; and . . . there are many curacies under twenty pounds a year. There are journeymen shoemakers in London who earn forty pounds a year, and there is scarce an industrious workman of any kind in that metropolis who does not earn more than twenty. . . .

In professions in which there are no benefices, such as law and physic, if an equal proportion of people were educated at the public expense, the competition would soon be so great as to sink very much their pecuniary reward. . . .

That unprosperous race of men, commonly called men of letters, are pretty much in the situation which lawyers and physicians probably would be in, upon the foregoing supposition. In every part of Europe, the greater part of them have been educated for the church, but have been hindered by different reasons from entering into holy orders. They have generally, therefore, been educated at the public expense; and their numbers are everywhere so great, as commonly to reduce the price of their labor to a very paltry recompense. . . .

. . . Before the invention of the art of printing, a scholar and a beggar seem to have been terms very nearly synonymous. The different governors of the universities, before that time, appear to have often granted licenses to their scholars to beg.

In ancient times, before any charities of this kind had been established for the education of indigent people to the learned professions, the rewards of eminent teachers appear to have been much more considerable. . . . Many eminent teachers in those times appear to have acquired great fortunes. Gorgias made a present to the temple of Delphi of his own statue in solid gold. We must not, I presume, suppose that it was as large as the life. His way of living, as well as that of Hippias and Protagoras, two other eminent teachers of those times, is represented by Plato as splendid, even to ostentation. Plato himself is said to have lived with a good deal of magnificence. Aristotle, after having been tutor to Alexander, and most munificently rewarded, as it is universally agreed, both by him and his father, Philip, thought it worth-while, notwithstanding, to return to Athens, in order to resume the teaching of his school. . . .

. . . The policy of Europe, by obstructing the free circulation of labor and stock, both from employment to employment, and from place to place, occasions [other] cases [of] inequality . . . and disadvantages of their different employments. . . .

... In many different manufactures, the operations are so much alike, that the workmen could easily change trades with one another, if absurd laws did not hinder them. The arts of weaving plain linen and plain silk, for example, are almost entirely the same. That of weaving plain woolen is somewhat different; but the difference is so insignificant, that either a linen or a silk weaver might become a tolerable workman in a very few days. If any of those three capital manufactures, therefore, were decaying, the workmen might find a resource in one of the other two which was in a more prosperous condition; and their wages would neither rise too high in the thriving, nor sink too low in the decaying manufacture. ...

The obstruction which corporation laws give to the free circulation of labor is common, I believe, to every part of Europe. That which is given to it by the poor laws is, so far as I know, peculiar to England. It consists in the difficulty which a poor man finds in obtaining a settlement, or even in being allowed to exercise his industry in any parish but that to which he belongs. ... It may be worthwhile to give some account of the rise, progress, and present state of this disorder ... of England.

When, by the destruction of monasteries, the poor had been deprived of the charity of those religious houses, after some other ineffectual attempts for their relief, it was enacted, by the 43rd of Elizabeth, chap. 2, that every parish should be bound to provide for its own poor, and that overseers of the poor should be annually appointed, who, with the churchwardens, should raise, by a parish rate, competent sums for this purpose.

By this statute, the necessity of providing for their own poor was indispensably imposed upon every parish. Who were to be considered as the poor of each parish became, therefore, a question of some importance. This question, after some variation, was at last determined by the 13th and 14th of Charles II when it was enacted, that forty days undisturbed residence should gain any person a settlement in any parish; but that within that time it should be lawful for two justices of the peace, upon complaint made by the churchwardens or overseers of the poor, to remove any new inhabitant to the parish where he was last legally settled; unless he either rented a tenement of ten pounds a year, or could give such security for the discharge of the parish where he was then living, as those justices should judge sufficient.

Some frauds, it is said, were committed in consequence of this statute; parish officers sometime's bribing their own poor to go clandestinely to another parish, and, by keeping themselves concealed for forty days, to gain a settlement there, to the discharge of that to which they properly belonged. It was enacted, therefore, by the 1st of James II that the forty days undisturbed residence of any person necessary to gain a settlement, should be accounted only from the time of his delivering notice, in writing, of the place of his abode and the number of his family, to one of the churchwardens or overseers of the parish where he came to dwell. . . .

. . . It was further enacted by the 3rd of William III that the forty days residence should be accounted only from the publication of such notice in writing on Sunday in the church, immediately after divine service. . . .

The very unequal price of labor which we frequently find in England, in places at no great distance from one another, is probably owing to the obstruction which the law of settlements gives to a poor man who would carry his industry from one parish to another. . . . A single man, indeed who is healthy and industrious, may sometimes reside by sufferance; but a man with a wife and family who should attempt to do so, would, in most parishes, be sure of being removed; and, if the single man should afterwards marry, he would generally be removed likewise. The scarcity of hands in one parish, therefore, cannot always be relieved by their superabundance in another, as it is constantly in Scotland, and I believe, in all other countries where there is no difficulty of settlement. . . . In England, it is often more difficult for a poor man to pass the artificial boundary of a parish, than an arm of the sea, or a ridge of high mountains, natural boundaries which sometimes separate very distinctly different rates of wages in other countries.

To remove a man who has committed no misdemeanor, from the parish where he chooses to reside, is an evident violation of natural liberty and justice. The common people of England, however, so jealous of their liberty, but like the common people of most other countries, never rightly understanding wherein it consists, have now, for more than a century together, suffered themselves to be exposed to this oppression without a remedy. . . . There is scarce a poor man in England, of forty years of age, I will venture to say, who has not, in some part of his life, felt himself most cruelly oppressed by this ill-contrived law of settlements.

I shall conclude this long chapter with observing, that though anciently it was usual to rate wages, first by general laws extending over the whole kingdom, and afterwards by particular orders of the justices of peace in every particular county, both these practices have now gone entirely into disuse. "By the experience of above four hundred years," says Doctor Burn, "it seems time to lay aside all endeavors to bring under strict regulations, what in its own nature seems incapable of minute limitation; for if all persons in the same kind of work were to receive equal wages, there would be no emulation, and no room left for industry or ingenuity."

Particular acts of parliament, however, still attempt sometimes to regulate wages in particular trades, and in particular places. Thus the 8th of George III prohibits, under heavy penalties, all master tailors in London, and five miles round it, from giving, and their workmen from accepting, more than two shillings and seven pence halfpenny a day, except in the case of a general mourning. Whenever the legislature attempts to regulate the differences between masters and their workmen, its counselors are always the masters. . . . When masters combine together, in order to reduce the wages of their workmen, they commonly enter into a private bond or agreement, not to give more than a certain wage, under a certain penalty. Were the workmen to enter into a contrary combination of the same kind, not to accept of a certain wage, under a certain penalty, the law would punish them very severely; and, if it dealt impartially, it would treat the masters in the same manner. But the 8th of George III enforces by law that very regulation which masters sometimes attempt to establish by such combinations. The complaint of the workmen, that it puts the ablest and most industrious upon the same footing with an ordinary workman, seems perfectly well founded.

In ancient times, too, it was usual to attempt to regulate the profits of merchants and other dealers, by regulating the price of provisions and other goods. The assize* of bread is, so far as I know, the only remnant of this ancient usage. Where there is an exclusive corporation, it may, perhaps, be proper to regulate the price of the first necessary of life. But, where there is none, the competition will regulate it much better than any assize. . . .

---

* The word "assize" can mean a session or ordinance but here refers to a price control.

## Chapter Eleven

# Of the Rent of Land
[Agriculture]

GOOD ROADS, CANALS, and navigable rivers, by diminishing the expense of carriage, put the remote parts of the country more nearly upon a level with those in the neighborhood of the town. They are upon that account the greatest of all improvements. They encourage the cultivation of the remote, which must always be the most extensive circle of the country. They are advantageous to the town by breaking down the monopoly of the country in its neighborhood. They are advantageous even to that part of the country. Though they introduce some rival commodities into the old market, they open many new markets to its produce. Monopoly, besides, is a great enemy to good management, which can never be universally established, but in consequence of that free and universal competition which forces everybody to have recourse to it for the sake of self-defense. It is not more than fifty years ago, that some of the counties in the neighborhood of London petitioned the parliament against the extension of the turnpike roads into the remoter counties. Those remoter counties, they pretended, from the cheapness of labor, would be able to sell their grass and corn cheaper in the London market than themselves, and would thereby reduce their rents, and ruin their cultivation. Their rents, however, have risen, and their cultivation has been improved since that time. . . . *

. . . It is not more than a century ago, that in many parts of the Highlands of Scotland, butcher's meat was as cheap as or cheaper than even bread made of oatmeal. The Union opened the market of England to the Highland cattle. Their ordinary price, at present, is about three times greater than at the beginning of the century, and the rents of many Highland estates have been tripled and quadrupled in the same time. In almost every part of Great Britain, a pound of the best butcher's meat is, in the present times, generally worth more than two pounds of the best white bread; and in plentiful years it is sometimes worth three or four pounds. . . .

In Virginia and Maryland, the cultivation of tobacco is preferred, as most profitable, to that of corn [wheat].

---

* This an argument for global, not just regional, trade.

Tobacco might be cultivated with advantage through the greater part of Europe; but, in almost every part of Europe, it has become a principal subject of taxation; and to collect a tax from every different farm in the country where this plant might happen to be cultivated, would be more difficult, it has been supposed, than to levy one upon its importation at the customhouse. The cultivation of tobacco has, upon this account, been most absurdly prohibited through the greater part of Europe, which necessarily gives a sort of monopoly to the countries where it is allowed; and as Virginia and Maryland produce the greatest quantity of it, they share largely, though with some competitors, in the advantage of this monopoly. Our tobacco planters have shown the same fear of the superabundance of tobacco, which the proprietors of the old vineyards in France have of the superabundance of wine. By act of assembly, they have restrained its cultivation to six thousand plants, supposed to yield a thousand weight of tobacco, for every Negro between sixteen and sixty years of age. Such a Negro, over and above this quantity of tobacco, can manage, they reckon, four acres of Indian corn. To prevent the market from being overstocked, too, they have sometimes, in plentiful years, we are told by Dr. Douglas (I suspect he has been ill informed), burnt a certain quantity of tobacco for every negro, in the same manner as the Dutch are said to do of spices. If such violent methods are necessary to keep up the present price of tobacco, the superior advantage of its culture over that of corn, if it still has any, will not probably be of long continuance. . . .

In some parts of Lancashire, it is pretended, I have been told, that bread of oatmeal is a heartier food for laboring people than wheaten bread, and I have frequently heard the same doctrine held in Scotland. I am, however, somewhat doubtful of the truth of it. The common people in Scotland, who are fed with oatmeal, are in general neither so strong nor so handsome as the same rank of people in England, who are fed with wheaten bread. They neither work so well, nor look so well; and as there is not the same difference between the people of fashion in the two countries, experience would seem to show, that the food of the common people in Scotland is not so suitable to the human constitution as that of their neighbors of the same rank in England. But it seems to be otherwise with potatoes. The chairmen, porters, and coal heavers in London, and those unfortunate women who live by prostitution, the strongest men and the most beautiful women perhaps in the British dominions, are said to be, the greater part of them, from the lowest rank of people in Ireland, who are generally fed with this root.* No food can afford a more decisive proof of its nourishing quality, or of its being peculiarly suitable to the health of the human constitution.

---

* Potatoes are a more complete food than oats or wheat, although today cause a concern about spiking blood sugar because of being high on the glycemic scale, especially if eaten without skins. Ironically, this is much less true of sweet potatoes and yams.

It is difficult to preserve potatoes through the year, and impossible to store them like corn, for two or three years together. The fear of not being able to sell them before they rot, discourages their cultivation, and is, perhaps, the chief obstacle to their ever becoming in any great country, like bread, the principal vegetable food of all the different ranks of the people. . . .

After food, clothing and lodging are the two great wants of mankind. . . .

When, by the improvement and cultivation of land, the labor of one family can provide food for two, the labor of half the society becomes sufficient to provide food for the whole. The other half, therefore, or at least the greater part of them, can be employed in providing other things, or in satisfying the other wants and fancies of mankind. Clothing and lodging, household furniture, and what is called equipage, are the principal objects of the greater part of those wants and fancies. The rich man consumes no more food than his poor neighbor. In quality it may be very different, and to select and prepare it may require more labor and art; but in quantity it is very nearly the same. But compare the spacious palace and great wardrobe of the one, with the hovel and the few rags of the other, and you will be sensible that the difference between their clothing, lodging, and household furniture, is almost as great in quantity as it is in quality. The desire of food is limited in every man by the narrow capacity of the human stomach; but the desire of the conveniences and ornaments of building, dress, equipage, and household furniture, seems to have no limit or certain boundary. [These] . . . desires . . . seem to be altogether endless. . . .

. . . With the greater part of rich people, the chief enjoyment of riches consists in the parade of riches; which, in their eye, is never so complete as when they appear to possess those decisive marks of opulence which nobody can possess but themselves. In their eyes, the merit of an object, which is in any degree either useful or beautiful, is greatly enhanced by its scarcity, or by the great labor which it requires to collect any considerable quantity of it; a labor which nobody can afford to pay but themselves. Such objects they are willing to purchase at a higher price than things much more beautiful and useful, but more common. . . .

The demand for the precious stones arises altogether from their beauty. They are of no use but as ornaments; and the merit of their beauty is greatly enhanced by their scarcity, or by the difficulty and expense of getting them from the mine. . . .

The most abundant mines, either of the precious metals, or of the precious stones, could add little to the wealth of the world. A produce, of which the value is principally derived from its scarcity, is necessarily degraded by its abundance. . . .

. . . The poor inhabitants of Cuba and St. Domingo, when they were first discovered by the Spaniards, used to wear little bits of gold as ornaments in their hair and other parts of their dress. They seemed to value them as we would do any little pebbles of somewhat more than ordinary beauty, and to consider them as just worth the picking up, but not worth the refusing to anybody who asked them. They gave them to their new guests at the first request, without seeming to think that they had made them any very valuable present. They were astonished to observe the rage of the Spaniards to obtain them; and had no notion that there could anywhere be a country in which many people had the disposal of so great a superfluity of food; so scanty always among themselves, that, for a very small quantity of those glittering baubles, they would willingly give as much as might maintain a whole family for many years. . . .

# Different Effects of the Progress of Improvement upon Three Different Sorts of Rude Produce

The . . . different sorts of rude produce may be divided into three classes. . . .

### First Sort

The first sort of rude produce, of which the price rises in the progress of improvement, is that which it is scarce in the power of human industry to multiply at all. It consists in those things which nature produces only in certain quantities, and which being of a very perishable nature, it is impossible to accumulate together the produce of many different seasons. Such are the greater part of rare and singular birds and fishes, many different sorts of game, almost all wild fowl, all birds of passage in particular, as well as many other things. When wealth, and the luxury which accompanies it, increase, the demand for these is likely to increase with them, and no effort of human industry may be able to increase the supply much beyond what it was before this increase of the demand. The quantity of such commodities, therefore, remaining the same, or nearly the same, while the competition to purchase them is continually increasing, their price may rise to any degree of extravagance, and seems not to be limited by any certain boundary. . . .

## Second Sort

The second sort of rude produce . . . is that which human industry can multiply in proportion to the demand. . . .

## Third Sort

The third and last sort of rude produce . . . is that in which the efficacy of human industry, in augmenting the quantity, is either limited or uncertain. The real price of this sort of rude produce naturally tends to rise in the progress of improvement, yet, according as different accidents happen to render the efforts of human industry more or less successful in augmenting the quantity, it may happen sometimes even to fall, sometimes to continue the same . . . and sometimes to rise. . . .

In England, notwithstanding the flourishing state of its woolen manufacture, the price of English wool has fallen very considerably since the time of Edward III....

This degradation, both in the real and nominal value of wool, could never have happened in consequence of the natural course of things. It has accordingly been the effect of violence and artifice. First, of the absolute prohibition of exporting wool from England; secondly, of the permission of importing it from Spain, duty-free; thirdly, of the prohibition of exporting it from Ireland to another country but England. In consequence of these regulations, the market for English wool, instead of being somewhat extended, in consequence of the improvement of England, has been confined to the home market, where the wool of several other countries is allowed to come into competition with it, and where that of Ireland is forced into competition with it. As the woolen manufactures, too, of Ireland, are fully as much discouraged as is consistent with justice and fair dealing, the Irish can work up but a smaller part of their own wool at home, and are therefore obliged to send a greater proportion of it to Great Britain, the only market they are allowed....

Whatever regulations tend to sink the price, either of wool or of raw hides, below what it naturally would be, must, in an improved and cultivated country, have some tendency to raise the price of butcher's meat. The price both of the great and small cattle, which are fed on improved and cultivated land, must be sufficient to pay the rent which the landlord, and the profit which the farmer, has reason to expect from improved and culti-vated land. If it is not, they will soon cease to feed them. Whatever part of this price, therefore, is not paid by the wool and the hide must be paid by the carcass. The less there is paid for the one, the more must be paid for the other. In what manner this price is to be divided upon the different parts of the beast, is indifferent to the land-lords and farmers, provided it is all paid to them. . . .

The wool of Scotland fell very considerably in its price in consequence of the union with England, by which it was excluded from the great market of Europe, and confined to the narrow one of Great Britain. The value of the greater part of the lands in the southern counties of Scotland, which are chiefly a sheep coun-try, would have been very deeply affected by this event, had not the rise in the price of butcher's meat fully compensated the fall in the price of wool. . . .

In increasing the quantity of the different minerals and metals which are drawn from the bowels of the earth, that of the more precious ones particularly, the efficacy of human industry seems not to be limited, but to be altogether uncertain. . . .

The fertility or barrenness of the mines, which may happen at any particular time to supply the commercial world, is a circumstance which, it is evident, may have no sort of connection with the state of industry in a particular country. It seems even to have no very nec-essary connection with that of the world in general. As arts and commerce, indeed, gradually spread themselves over a greater and a greater part of the earth, the search for new mines, being extended over a wider surface, may have somewhat a better chance for being successful than when confined within narrower bounds. The discovery of new mines, however, as the old ones come to be gradually exhausted, is a matter of the greatest uncertainty and such as no human skill or industry can insure. . . . In the course of a century or two, it is possible that new mines may be discovered, more fertile than any that have ever yet been known; and it is just equally possible, that the most fertile mine then known may be more barren than any that was wrought before the discovery of the mines of America. Whether the one or the other of those two events may happen to take place, is of very little importance to the real wealth and prosperity of the world, to the real value of the annual produce of the land and labor of mankind. Its nominal value, the quantity of gold and silver by which this annual produce could be expressed or represented, would, no doubt, be very different; but its real value, the real quantity of labor which it could purchase or command, would be precisely the same. A shilling might, in the one case, represent no more labor than a penny does at present; and a penny, in the other, might represent as much as a shilling does now. But in the one case, he who had a shilling in his pocket would be no richer than he who has a penny at present; and in the other, he who had a penny would be just as rich as he who has a shilling now. . . .

# Effects of the Progress of Improvement upon the Real Price of Manufactures

It is the natural effect of improvement, to diminish gradually the real price of almost all manufactures. . . . In consequence of better machinery, of greater dexterity, and of a more proper division and distribution of work, all of which are the natural effects of improvement, a much smaller quantity of labor becomes requisite for executing any particular piece of work; and though, in consequence of the flourishing circumstances of the society, the real price of labor should rise very considerably, yet the great diminution of the quantity will generally much more than compensate the greatest rise which can happen in the price.

There are, indeed, a few manufactures, in which the necessary rise in the real price of the rude materials will more than compensate all the advantages which improvement can introduce into the execution of the work In carpenters' and joiners' work, and in the coarser sort of cabinet work, the necessary rise in the real price of barren timber, in consequence of the improvement of land, will more than compensate all the advantages which can be derived from the best machinery, the greatest dexterity, and the most proper division and distribution of work.

But in all cases in which the real price of the rude material either does not rise at all, or does not rise very much, that of the manufactured commodity sinks very considerably.

This diminution of price has, in the course of the present and preceding century, been most remarkable in those manufactures of which the materials are the coarser metals. A better movement of a watch, than about the middle of the last century could have been bought for twenty pounds, may now perhaps be had for twenty shillings. In the work of cutlers and locksmiths, in all the toys which are made of the coarser metals, and in all those goods which are commonly known by the name of Birmingham and Sheffield ware, there has been, during the same period, a very great reduction of price, though not altogether so great as in watch-work. It has, however, been sufficient to astonish the work-men of every other part of Europe, who in many cases acknowledge that they can produce no work of equal goodness for double or even for triple the price. . . .

In the clothing manufacture* there has, during the same period, been no such sensible reduction of price. The price of superfine cloth, I have been assured, on the contrary, has, within these five-and-twenty or

---

* The revolution in cheap cotton clothing had not yet arrived. Wool and linen manufacturers, however, had already lost their battle to ban cotton, so the groundwork had been laid for the textile products that both sparked and epitomized the British Industrial Revolution. By contrast, cotton was banned in France to protect the powerful interests in wool and linen, which meant that France fell far behind Britain in learning industrial methods. This is one of the most important, and least known, episodes in world economic history.

thirty years, risen somewhat in proportion to its quality, owing, it was said, to a considerable rise in the price
of the material, which consists altogether of Spanish wool. That of the Yorkshire cloth, which is made
altogether of English wool, is said, indeed, during the
course of the present century, to have fallen a good
deal in proportion to its quality. Quality, however, is
so very disputable a matter that I look upon all information of this kind as somewhat uncertain. . . .

In 1487, being the 4th of Henry VII, it was enacted,
that "whosoever shall sell by retail a broad yard of the
finest scarlet grained, or of other grained cloth of the
finest making, above sixteen shillings, shall forfeit
forty shillings for every yard so sold." Sixteen shillings,
therefore, containing about the same quantity of silver as four-and-twenty shillings of our present money,
was, at that time, reckoned not an unreasonable price
for a yard of the finest cloth; and as this is a sumptuary law, such cloth, it is probable, had usually been sold
somewhat dearer. A guinea may be reckoned the highest price in the present times. Even though the quality
of the cloths, therefore, should be supposed equal, and
that of the present times is most probably much superior, yet, even upon this supposition, the money price
of the finest cloth appears to have been considerably
reduced since the end of the fifteenth century. But its
real price has been much more reduced. Six shillings
and eight pence was then, and long afterwards, reckoned the average price of a quarter of wheat. Sixteen

shillings, therefore, was the price of two quarters and more than three bushels of wheat. Valuing a quarter of wheat in the present times at eight-and-twenty shillings, the real price of a yard of fine cloth must, in those times, have been equal to at least three pounds six shillings and six pence of our present money. The man who bought it must have parted with the command of a quantity of labor and subsistence equal to what that sum would purchase in the present times.

The reduction in the real price of the coarse manufacture, though considerable, has not been so great as in that of the fine.

In 1463, being the 3rd of Edward IV, it was enacted, that "no servant in husbandry nor common laborer, nor servant to any artificer inhabiting out of a city or burgh, shall use or wear in their clothing any cloth above two shillings the broad yard." In the 3rd of Edward IV, two shillings contained very nearly the same quantity of silver as four of our present money. But the Yorkshire cloth which is now sold at four shillings the yard, is probably much superior to any that was then made for the wearing of the very poorest order of common servants. Even the money price of their clothing, therefore, may, in proportion to the quality, be somewhat cheaper in the present than it was in those ancient times. The real price is certainly a good deal cheaper. Ten pence was then reckoned what is called the moderate and reasonable price of a bushel of wheat. Two shillings, therefore, was the price of two bushels and near two pecks of wheat, which in the present times, at three shillings and six pence the bushel, would be worth eight shillings and nine pence. For a yard of this cloth the poor servant must have parted with the power of purchasing a quantity of subsistence equal to what eight shillings and nine pence would purchase in the present times. This is a sumptuary law, too, restraining the luxury and extravagance of the poor. Their clothing, therefore, had commonly been much more expensive.

The same order of people are, by the same law, prohibited from wearing hose, of which the price should exceed fourteen pence the pair, equal to about eight-and-twenty pence of our present money. But fourteen pence was in those times the price of a bushel and near two pecks of wheat; which in the present times, at three and six pence the bushel, would cost five shillings and three pence. We should in the present times consider this as a very high price for a pair of stockings to a servant of the poorest and lowest order. He must however, in those times, have paid what was really equivalent to this price for them.

In the time of Edward IV the art of knitting stockings was probably not known in any part of Europe. Their hose were made of common cloth, which may have been one of the causes of their dearness. The first person that wore stockings in England is said to have been Queen Elizabeth. She received them as a present from the Spanish ambassador. . . .

Secondly, the use of several very ingenious machines, which facilitate and abridge, in a still greater proportion, the winding of the worsted and woolen yarn, or the proper arrangement of the warp and woof before they are put into the loom; an operation which, previous to the invention of those machines, must have been extremely tedious and troublesome. Thirdly, is the employment of the fulling mill for thickening the cloth, instead of treading it in water. Neither wind nor water mills of any kind were known in England so early as the beginning of the sixteenth century, nor, so far as I know, in any other part of Europe north of the Alps. They had been introduced into Italy some time before. . . .

## Conclusion of the Chapter

The whole annual produce of the land and labor of every country, or, what comes to the same thing, the whole price of that annual produce, naturally divides itself, it has already been observed, into three parts; the rent of land, the wages of labor, and the profits of stock; and constitutes a revenue to three different orders of people; to those who live by rent, to those who live by wages, and to those who live by profit. These are the three great, original, and constituent, orders of every civilized society, from whose revenue that of every other order is ultimately derived.

The interest of the first of those three great orders . . . is strictly and inseparably connected with the general interest of the society. Whatever either promotes or obstructs the one, necessarily promotes or obstructs the other. . . .

The interest of the second order, that of those who live by wages, is as strictly connected with the interest of the society as that of the first. The wages of the laborer, it has already been shown, are never so high as when the demand for labor is continually rising, or when the quantity employed is every year increasing considerably. When this real wealth of the society becomes stationary, his wages are soon reduced to what is barely enough to enable him to bring up a family, or to continue the race of laborers. . . .

His employers constitute the third order, that of those who live by profit. It is the stock that is employed for the sake of profit, which puts into motion the greater part of the useful labor of every society. The plans and projects of the employers of stock regulate and direct all the most important operation of labor and profit is the end proposed by all those plans and projects. But the rate of profit does not, like rent and wages, rise with the prosperity, and fall with the declension of the society. On the contrary, it is naturally low in rich, and high in poor countries, and it is always highest in the countries which are going fastest to ruin. The interest of this third order, therefore, has not the same connection with the general interest of the society, as that of the other two. . . . The interest of the dealers, however, in any particular branch of trade or manufactures, is always in some respects different from, and even opposite to, that of the public. To widen the market, and to narrow the competition, is always the interest of the dealers. To widen the market may frequently be agreeable enough to the interest of the public; but to narrow the competition must always be against it, and can only serve to enable the dealers, by raising their profits above what they naturally would be, to levy, for their own benefit, an absurd tax upon the rest of their fellow citizens. The proposal of any new law or regulation of commerce which comes from this order, ought always to be listened to with great precaution, and ought never to be adopted till after having been long and carefully examined, not only with the most scrupulous, but with the most suspicious attention. It comes from an order of men, whose interest is never exactly the same with that of the public, who have generally an interest to deceive and even to oppress the public, and who accordingly have, upon many occasions, both deceived and oppressed it.

*Book Two*

# Of the Nature,
# Accumulation, and
# Employment of Stock

# Introduction

I N THAT RUDE state of society, in which there is no division of labor, in which exchanges are seldom made, and in which every man provides everything for himself, it is not necessary that any stock should be accumulated, or stored up beforehand, in order to carry on the business of the society. Every man endeavors to supply, by his own industry, his own occasional wants, as they occur. When he is hungry, he goes to the forest to hunt; when his coat is worn out, he clothes himself with the skin of the first large animal he kills: and when his hut begins to go to ruin, he repairs it, as well as he can, with the trees and the turf that are nearest it.

But when the division of labor has once been thoroughly introduced, the produce of a man's own labor can supply but a very small part of his occasional wants. The far greater part of them are supplied by the produce of other men's labor, which he purchases with the produce, or, what is the same thing, with the price of the produce, of his own. But this purchase cannot be made till such time as the produce of his own labor has not only been completed, but sold. A stock of goods of different kinds, therefore, must be stored up somewhere, sufficient to maintain him, and to supply him with the materials and tools of his work, till such time at least as both these events can be brought about. A weaver cannot apply himself entirely to his peculiar business, unless there is beforehand stored up somewhere, either in his own possession, or in that of some other person, a stock sufficient to maintain him, and to supply him with the materials and tools of his work, till he has not only completed, but sold his web. This accumulation must evidently be previous to his applying his industry for so long a time to such a peculiar business.

As the accumulation of stock must, in the nature of things, be previous to the division of labor, so labor can be more and more subdivided in proportion only as stock is previously more and more accumulated. The quantity of materials which the same number of people can work up, increases in a great proportion as labor comes to be more and more subdivided; and as the operations of each workman are gradually reduced to a greater degree of simplicity, a variety of new machines come to be invented for facilitating and abridging those operations. As the division of labor advances, therefore, in order to give constant employment to an equal number of workmen, an equal stock of provisions, and a greater stock of materials and tools than what would have been necessary in a ruder state of things, must be accumulated beforehand. But the number of workmen in every branch of business generally increases with the division of labor in that branch; or rather it is the increase of their number which enables them to class and subdivide themselves in this manner. . . .

As the accumulation of stock is previously necessary for carrying on this great improvement in the productive powers of labor, so that accumulation naturally leads to this improvement. The person who employs his stock in maintaining labor, necessarily wishes to employ it in such a manner as to produce as great a quantity of work as possible. He endeavors, therefore, both to make among his workmen the most proper distribution of employment, and to furnish them with the best machines which he can either invent or afford to purchase. His abilities, in both these respects, are generally in proportion to the extent of his stock, or to the number of people whom it can employ. The quantity of industry, therefore, not only increases in every country with the increase of the stock which employs it, but, in consequence of that increase, the same quantity of industry produces a much greater quantity of work. . . .

## *Chapter One*

# Of the Division of Stock

W HEN THE STOCK which a man possesses
is no more than sufficient to maintain
him for a few days or a few weeks, he seldom thinks of deriving any revenue from it. He consumes it as sparingly as he can, and endeavors, by his
labor, to acquire something which may supply its place
before it be consumed altogether. His revenue is, in
this case, derived from his labor only. This is the state
of the greater part of the laboring poor in all countries.

But when he possesses stock sufficient to maintain
him for months or years, he naturally endeavors to
derive a revenue from the greater part of it, reserving only so much for his immediate consumption as
may maintain him till this revenue begins to come in.
His whole stock, therefore, is distinguished into two

parts. That part which he expects is to afford him this revenue is called his capital. The other is that which supplies his immediate consumption. . . .

There are two different ways in which a capital may be employed so as to yield a revenue or profit to its employer.

First, it may be employed in raising, manufacturing, or purchasing goods, and selling them again with a profit. The capital employed in this manner yields no revenue or profit to its employer, while it either remains in his possession, or continues in the same shape. The goods of the merchant yield him no revenue or profit till he sells them for money, and the money yields him as little till it is again exchanged for goods. His capital is continually going from him in one shape, and returning to him in another; and it is only by means of such circulation, or successive changes, that it can yield him any profit. Such capitals, therefore, may very properly be called circulating capitals.

Secondly, it may be employed in the improvement of land, in the purchase of useful machines and instruments of trade, or in such like things as yield a revenue or profit without changing masters, or circulating any further. Such capitals, therefore, may very properly be called fixed capitals.

Different occupations require very different proportions between the fixed and circulating capitals employed in them.

The capital of a merchant, for example, is altogether a circulating capital. He has occasion for no machines or instruments of trade, unless his shop or warehouse be considered as such.

Some part of the capital of every master artificer or manufacturer must be fixed in the instruments of his trade. This part, however, is very small in some and very great in others. . . .

. . . The stock that is laid out in a house, if it is to be the dwelling house of the proprietor, ceases from that moment to serve in the function of a capital, or to afford any revenue to its owner. A dwelling house, as such, contributes nothing to the revenue of its inhabitant; and though it is, no doubt, extremely useful to him, it is as his clothes and household furniture are useful to him, which, however, make a part of his expense, and not of his revenue. . . .

In all countries where there is a tolerable security, every man of common understanding will endeavor to employ whatever stock he can command, in procuring either present enjoyment or future profit. If it is employed in procuring present enjoyment, it is a stock reserved for immediate consumption. If it is employed in procuring future profit, it must procure this profit either by staying with him or by going from him. In the one case it is a fixed, in the other it is a circulating capital. A man must be perfectly crazy, who, where there is a tolerable security, does not employ all the stock which he commands, whether it be his own, or borrowed of other people, in some one or other of those three ways.

In those unfortunate countries, indeed, where men are continually afraid of the violence of their superiors, they frequently bury or conceal a great part of their stock, in order to have it always at hand to carry with them to some place of safety, in case of their being threatened with any of those disasters to which they consider themselves at all times exposed. This is said to be a common practice in Turkey, in Indostan, and, I believe, in most other governments of Asia. It seems to have been a common practice among our ancestors during the violence of the feudal government. Treasure-trove was, in these times, considered as no contemptible part of the revenue of the greatest sovereigns in Europe. It consisted in such treasure as was found concealed in the earth, and to which no particular person could prove any right. This was regarded, in those times, as so important an object, that it was always considered as belonging to the sovereign, and neither to the finder nor to the proprietor of the land, unless the right to it had been conveyed to the latter by an express clause in his charter. It was put upon the same footing with gold and silver mines, which, without a special clause in the charter, were never supposed to be comprehended in the general grant of the lands, though mines of lead, copper, tin, and coal were, as things of smaller consequence.

## Chapter Two

# Of Money Considered as a Particular Branch of the General Stock of the Society

I<small>T HAS BEEN</small> shown in the First Book, that the price of the greater part of commodities resolves itself into three parts, of which one pays the wages of the labor, another the profits of the stock, and a third the rent of the land which had been employed in producing and bringing them to market. . . .

Since this is the case, it has been observed, with regard to every particular commodity, taken separately, it must be so with regard to all the commodities which compose the whole annual produce of the land and labor of every country, taken complexly. The whole price or exchangeable value of that annual produce must resolve itself into the same three parts, and be parceled out among the different inhabitants of the country, either as the wages of their labor, the profits of their stock, or the rent of their land. . . .

. . . The amount of the metal pieces which are annually paid to an individual, is often precisely equal to his revenue, and is upon that account the shortest and best expression of its value. But the amount of the metal pieces which circulate in a society can never be equal to the revenue of all its members. As the same guinea which pays the weekly pension of one man today, may pay that of another tomorrow, and that of a third the day thereafter, the amount of the metal pieces which annually circulate in any country, must always be of much less value than the whole money pensions annually paid with them. . . .

There are several different sorts of paper money; but the circulating notes of banks and bankers are the species which is best known, and which seems best adapted for this purpose. When the people of any particular country have such confidence in the fortune, probity and prudence of a particular banker, as to believe that he is always ready to pay upon demand such of his promissory notes as are likely to be at any time presented to him, those notes come to have the same currency as gold and silver money, from the confidence that such money can at any time be had for them.

A particular banker lends among his customers his own promissory notes, to the extent, we shall suppose, of a hundred thousand pounds. As those notes serve all the purposes of money, his debtors pay him the same interest as if he had lent them so much money. This interest is the source of his gain. Though some of those notes are continually coming back upon him for payment, part of them continue to circulate for months and years together. Though he has generally in circulation, therefore, notes to the extent of a hundred thousand pounds, twenty thousand pounds in gold and silver may, frequently, be a sufficient provision for answering occasional demands. By this operation, therefore, twenty thousand pounds in gold and silver perform all the functions which a hundred thousand could otherwise have performed. The same exchanges may be made, the same quantity of consumable goods may be circulated and distributed to their proper consumers, by means of his promissory notes, to the value of a hundred thousand pounds, as by an equal value of gold and silver money. Eighty thousand pounds of gold and silver, therefore, can in this manner be spared from the circulation of the country; and if different operations of the same kind should, at the same time, be carried on by many different banks and bankers, the whole circulation may thus be conducted with a fifth part only of the gold and silver which would otherwise have been requisite.

Let us suppose, for example, that the whole circulating money of some particular country amounted, at a particular time, to one million sterling, that sum being then sufficient for circulating the whole annual produce of their land and labor; let us suppose, too, that some time thereafter, different banks and bankers issued promissory notes payable to the bearer, to the extent of one million, reserving in their different coffers two hundred thousand pounds for answering occasional demands; there would remain, therefore, in circulation, eight hundred thousand pounds in gold and silver, and a million of bank notes, or eighteen hundred thousand pounds of paper and money together. But the annual produce of the land and labor of the country had before required only one million to circulate and distribute it to its proper consumers, and that annual produce cannot be immediately augmented by those operations of banking. One million, therefore, will be sufficient to circulate it after them. The goods to be bought and sold being precisely the same as before, the same quantity of money will be sufficient for buying and selling them. The channel of circulation, if I may be allowed such an expression, will remain precisely the same as before.

One million we have supposed sufficient to fill that channel. Whatever, therefore, is poured into it beyond this sum, cannot run into it, but must overflow. One million eight hundred thousand pounds are poured into it. Eight hundred thousand pounds, therefore, must overflow, that sum being over and above what can be employed in the circulation of the country. But though this sum cannot be employed at home, it is too valuable to be allowed to lie idle. It will, therefore, be sent abroad, in order to seek that profitable employment which it cannot find at home. But the paper cannot go abroad; because at a distance from the banks which issue it, and from the country in which payment of it can be exacted by law, it will not be received in common payments. Gold and silver, therefore, to the amount of eight hundred thousand pounds, will be sent abroad, and the channel of home circulation will remain filled with a million of paper instead of a million of those metals which filled it before.

But though so great a quantity of gold and silver is thus sent abroad, we must not imagine that it is sent abroad for nothing, or that its proprietors make a present of it to foreign nations. They will exchange it for foreign goods of some kind or another, in order to supply the consumption either of some other foreign country, or of their own.

If they employ it in purchasing foreign goods for home consumption, they may either, first, purchase such goods as are likely to be consumed by idle people, who produce nothing, such as foreign wines, foreign silks, etc.; or, secondly, they may purchase an additional stock of materials, tools, and provisions, in order to maintain and employ an additional number of industrious people, who reproduce, with a profit, the value of their annual consumption.

So far as it is employed in the first way, it promotes prodigality, increases expense and consumption, without increasing production, or establishing any permanent fund for supporting that expense, and is in every respect hurtful to the society.

So far as it is employed in the second way, it promotes industry. . . .

That the greater part of the gold and silver which being forced abroad by those operations of banking, is employed in purchasing foreign goods for home consumption, is, and must be, employed in purchasing those of this second kind, seems not only probable, but almost unavoidable. . . . The demand of idle people . . . for foreign goods, being the same, or very nearly the same as before, a very small part of the money which, being forced abroad by those operations of banking, is employed in purchasing foreign goods for home consumption, is likely to be employed in purchasing those for their use. The greater part of it will naturally be destined for the employment of industry, and not for the maintenance of idleness. . . .

When paper is substituted in the room of gold and silver money, the quantity of the materials, tools, and maintenance, which the whole circulating capital can supply, may be increased by the whole value of gold and silver which used to be employed in purchasing them. The whole value of the great wheel of circulation and distribution is added to the goods which are circulated and distributed by means of it. . . .

What is the proportion which the circulating money of any country bears to the whole value of the annual produce circulated by means of it, it is perhaps impossible to determine. It has been computed by different authors at a fifth, at a tenth, at a twentieth, and at a thirtieth, part of that value. But how small soever the proportion which the circulating money may bear to the whole value of the annual produce, as but a part, and frequently but a small part, of that produce, is ever destined for the maintenance of industry, it must always bear a very considerable proportion to that part. When, therefore, by the substitution of paper, the gold and silver necessary for circulation is reduced to, perhaps, a fifth part of the former quantity, if the value of only the greater part of the other four-fifths be added to the funds which are destined for the maintenance of industry, it must make a very considerable addition to the quantity of that industry, and, consequently, to the value of the annual produce of land and labor.

An operation of this kind has, within these five-and-twenty or thirty years, been performed in Scotland, by the erection of new banking companies in almost every considerable town, and even in some country villages. The effects of it have been precisely those above described. The business of the country is almost entirely carried on by means of the paper of those different banking companies, with which purchases and payments of all kinds are commonly made. Silver very seldom appears, except in the change of a twenty-shilling bank note, and gold still seldomer. But though the conduct of all those different companies has not been unexceptionable, and has accordingly required an act of parliament to regulate it, the country, notwithstanding, has evidently derived great benefit from their trade. I have heard it asserted, that the trade of the city of Glasgow doubled in about fifteen years after the first erection of the banks there; and that the trade of Scotland has more than quadrupled since the first erection of the two public banks at Edinburgh; of which the one, called the Bank of Scotland, was established by act of parliament in 1695, and the other, called the Royal Bank, by royal charter in 1727. Whether the trade, either of Scotland in general or of the city of Glasgow in particular, has really increased in so great a proportion, during so short a period, I do not pretend to know. If either of them has increased in this proportion, it seems to be an effect too great to be accounted for by the sole operation of this cause. That the trade and industry of Scotland, however, have increased very considerably during this period, and that the banks have contributed a good deal to this increase, cannot be doubted.

The value of the silver money which circulated in Scotland before the Union in 1707, and which, immediately after it, was brought into the Bank of Scotland, in order to be recoined, amounted to 411,117*l.* 10*s.* 9*d.* sterling. No account has been got of the gold coin; but it appears from the ancient accounts of the mint of Scotland, that the value of the gold annually coined somewhat exceeded that of the silver. . . . The whole value of the gold and silver, therefore, which circulated in Scotland before the Union, cannot be estimated at less than a million sterling. . . . In the present times, the whole circulation of Scotland cannot be estimated at less than two millions, of which that part which consists in gold and silver, most probably, does not amount to half a million. But though the circulating gold and silver of Scotland have suffered so great a diminution during this period, its real riches and prosperity do not appear to have suffered any. Its agriculture, manufactures, and trade, on the contrary, the annual produce of its land and labor, have evidently been augmented. . . .

The commerce of Scotland, which at present is not very great, was still more inconsiderable when the two first banking companies were established; and those companies would have had but little trade, had they confined their business to the discounting of bills of exchange. They invented, therefore, another method of issuing their promissory notes; by granting what they call cash accounts, that is, by giving credit, to the extent of a certain sum (two or three thousand pounds for example), to any individual who could procure two persons of undoubted credit and good landed estate to become surety for him, that whatever money should be advanced to him, within the sum for which the credit had been given, should be repaid upon demand, together with the legal interest. Credits of this kind are, I believe, commonly granted by banks and bankers in all different parts of the world. But the easy terms upon which the Scotch banking companies accept of repayment are, so far as I know, peculiar to them, and have perhaps been the principal cause, both of the great trade of those companies, and of the benefit which the country has received from it.

. . . The banks, when their customers apply to them for money, generally advance it to them in their own promissory notes. These the merchants pay away to the manufacturers for goods, the manufacturers to the farmers for materials and provisions, the farmers to their landlords for rent; the landlords repay them to the merchants for the conveniences and luxuries with which they supply them, and the merchants again return them to the banks, in order to balance their cash accounts, or to replace what they may have borrowed of them; and thus almost the whole money business of the country is transacted by means of them. Hence the great trade of those companies.

By means of those cash accounts, every merchant can, without imprudence, carry on a greater trade than he otherwise could do. If there are two merchants, one in London and the other in Edinburgh, who employ equal stocks in the same branch of trade, the Edinburgh merchant can, without imprudence, carry on a greater trade, and give employment to a greater number of people, than the London merchant. The London merchant must always keep by him a considerable sum of money, either in his own coffers, or in those of his banker, who gives him no interest for it, in order to answer the demands continually coming upon him for payment of the goods which he purchases upon credit. Let the ordinary amount of this sum be supposed five hundred pounds; the value of the goods in his warehouse must always be less, by five hundred pounds, than it would have been, had he not been obliged to keep such a sum unemployed. Let us suppose that he generally disposes of his whole stock upon hand, or of goods to the value of his whole stock upon hand, once in the year. By being obliged to keep so great a sum unemployed, he must sell in a year five hundred pounds worth less goods than he might otherwise have done. His annual profits must be less by all that he could have made by the sale of five hundred pounds worth more goods; and the number of people employed in preparing his goods for the market must be less by all those that five hundred pounds more stock could have employed. The merchant in Edinburgh, on the other hand, keeps no money unemployed for answering such occasional demands. When they actually come upon him, he satisfies them from his cash account with the bank, and gradually replaces the sum borrowed with the money or paper which comes in from the occasional sales of his goods. With the same stock, therefore, he can, without imprudence, have at all times in his warehouse a larger quantity of goods than the London merchant; and can thereby both make a greater profit himself, and give constant employment to a greater number of industrious people who prepare those goods for the market. Hence the great benefit which the country has derived from this trade. . . .*

The whole paper money of every kind which can easily circulate in any country never can exceed the value of the gold and silver, of which it supplies the place, or which (the commerce being supposed the same) would circulate there, if there was no paper money. If twenty-shilling notes, for example, are the lowest paper money current in Scotland, the whole of that currency which can easily circulate there, cannot exceed the sum of gold and silver which would be necessary for transacting the annual exchanges of twenty shillings value and upwards usually transacted within that country. Should the circulating paper at any time exceed that sum, as the excess could neither be sent abroad nor be employed in the circulation of the country, it must immediately return upon the banks, to be exchanged for gold and silver. Many people would immediately perceive that they had more of this paper than was necessary for transacting their business at home; and as they could not send it abroad, they would immediately demand payment for it from the banks. When this superfluous paper was converted into gold and silver, they could easily find a use for it, by sending it abroad; but they could find none while it remained in the shape of paper. There would immediately, therefore, be a run upon the banks to the whole

---

* See Introduction, page 51, for a cautionary note.

extent of this superfluous paper, and if they showed any difficulty or backwardness in payment, to a much greater extent; the alarm which this would occasion necessarily increasing the run....

Let us suppose that all the paper of a particular bank, which the circulation of the country can easily absorb and employ, amounts exactly to forty thousand pounds, and that, for answering occasional demands, this bank is obliged to keep at all times in its coffers ten thousand pounds in gold and silver. Should this bank attempt to circulate forty-four thousand pounds, the four thousand pounds which are over and above what the circulation can easily absorb and employ, will return upon it almost as fast as they are issued. For answering occasional demands, therefore, this bank ought to keep at all times in its coffers, not eleven thousand pounds only, but fourteen thousand pounds. It will thus gain nothing by the interest of the four thousand pounds excessive circulation; and it will lose the whole expense of continually collecting four thousand pounds in gold and silver, which will be continually going out of its coffers as fast as they are brought into them.

Had every particular banking company always understood and attended to its own particular interest, the circulation never could have been overstocked with paper money. But every particular banking company has not always understood or attended to its own particular interest, and the circulation has frequently been overstocked with paper money....

The gold coin which was paid out, either by the Bank of England or by the Scotch banks, in exchange for that part of their paper which was over and above what could be employed in the circulation of the country, being likewise over and above what could be employed in that circulation, was sometimes sent abroad in the shape of coin, sometimes melted down and sent abroad in the shape of bullion, and sometimes melted down and sold to the Bank of England at the high price of four pounds an ounce. It was the newest, the heaviest, and the best pieces only, which were carefully picked out of the whole coin, and either sent abroad or melted down.* At home, and while they remained in the shape of coin, those heavy pieces were of no more value than the light; but they were of more value abroad, or when melted down into bullion at home. The Bank of England, notwithstanding their great annual coinage, found, to their astonishment, that there was every year the same scarcity of coin as there had been the year before; and that, notwithstanding the great quantity of good and new coin which was every year issued from the bank, the state of the coin, instead of growing better and better, became every year worse and worse. Every year they found themselves under the necessity of coining nearly the same quantity of gold as they had coined the year before; and from the continual rise in the price of gold bullion, in consequence of the

---

* I.e., people cherry picked heavier (unclipped or newer) gold coins and took them out of circulation.

continual wearing and clipping of the coin, the expense of this great annual coinage became, every year, greater and greater. The Bank of England, it is to be observed, by supplying its own coffers with coin, is indirectly obliged to supply the whole kingdom, into which coin is continually flowing from those coffers in a great variety of ways. Whatever coin, therefore, was wanted to support this excessive circulation both of Scotch and English paper money, whatever vacuities this excessive circulation occasioned in the necessary coin of the kingdom, the Bank of England was obliged to supply them. The Scotch banks, no doubt, paid all of them very dearly for their own imprudence and inattention: but the Bank of England paid very dearly, not only for its own imprudence, but for the much greater imprudence of almost all the Scotch banks.

The over-trading of some bold projectors in both parts of the United Kingdom was the original cause of this excessive circulation of paper money.*

What a bank can with propriety advance to a merchant or undertaker of any kind, is not either the whole capital with which he trades, or even any considerable part of that capital; but that part of it only which he would otherwise be obliged to keep by him unemployed and in ready money, for answering occasional demands. If the paper money which the bank advances never exceeds this value, it can never exceed the value

---

* See Introduction, page 49, for a contrary view.

of the gold and silver which would necessarily circulate in the country if there was no paper money; it can never exceed the quantity which the circulation of the country can easily absorb and employ. . . .

The banking companies of Scotland, accordingly, were for a long time very careful to require frequent and regular repayments from all their customers, and did not care to deal with any person, whatever might be his fortune or credit, who did not make, what they called, frequent and regular operations with them. . . .

. . . By this attention they secured themselves from the possibility of issuing more paper money than what the circulation of the country could easily absorb and employ. When they observed, that within moderate periods of time, the repayments of a particular customer were, upon most occasions, fully equal to the advances which they had made to him, they might be assured that the paper money which they had advanced to him had not, at any time, exceeded the quantity of gold and silver which he would otherwise have been obliged to keep by him for answering occasional demands; and that, consequently, the paper money, which they had circulated by his means, had not at any time exceeded the quantity of gold and silver which would have circulated in the country, had there been no paper money. . . .*

---

* This argues that banks should not make longer term but only temporary working capital loans.

… A bank cannot, consistently with its own interest, advance to a trader the whole, or even the greater part of the circulating capital with which he trades; because, though that capital is continually returning to him in the shape of money, and going from him in the same shape, yet the whole of the returns is too distant from the whole of the outgoings, and the sum of his repayments could not equal the sum of his advances within such moderate periods of time as suit the conveniency of a bank. Still less could a bank afford to advance him any considerable part of his fixed capital; of the capital which the undertaker of an iron forge, for example, employs in erecting his forge and smelting houses, his workhouses, and warehouses, the dwelling houses of his workmen, etc. . . . The money which is borrowed, and which it is meant should not be repaid till after a period of several years, ought not to be borrowed of a bank, but ought to be borrowed upon bond or mortgage, of such private people as propose to live upon the interest of their money, without taking the trouble themselves to employ the capital. . . .

… The gold and silver money which circulates in any country, and by means of which, the produce of its land and labor is annually circulated and distributed to the proper consumers, is, in the same manner as the ready money of the dealer, all dead stock. It is a very valuable part of the capital of the country, which produces nothing to the country. The judicious operations of banking, by substituting paper in the room of a great part of this gold and silver, enable the country to convert a great part of this dead stock into active and productive stock; into stock which produces something to the country.... The commerce and industry of the country, however, it must be acknowledged, though they may be somewhat augmented, cannot be altogether so secure, when they are thus, as it were, suspended upon the Daedalian wings of paper money, as when they travel about upon the solid ground of gold and silver. Over and above the accidents to which they are exposed from the unskilfullness of the conductors of this paper money, they are liable to several others, from which no prudence or skill of those conductors can guard them.

An unsuccessful war, for example, in which the enemy got possession of the capital, and consequently of that treasure which supported the credit of the paper money, would occasion a much greater confusion in a country where the whole circulation was carried on by paper, than in one where the greater part of it was carried on by gold and silver.... A prince, anxious to maintain his dominions at all times in the state in which he can most easily defend them, ought upon this account to guard not only against that excessive multiplication of paper money which ruins the very banks which issue it, but even against that multiplication of it which enables them to fill the greater part of the circulation of the country with it.

The circulation of every country may be considered as divided into two different branches; the circulation of the dealers with one another, and the circulation between the dealers and the consumers. . . . The circulation between the dealers, as it is carried on by wholesale, requires generally a pretty large sum for every particular transaction. That between the dealers and the consumers, on the contrary, as it is generally carried on by retail, frequently requires but very small ones, a shilling, or even a halfpenny, being often sufficient. But small sums circulate much faster than large ones. A shilling changes masters more frequently than a guinea and a halfpenny more frequently than a shilling. Though the annual purchases of all the consumers, therefore, are at least equal in value to those of all the dealers, they can generally be transacted with a much smaller quantity of money; the same pieces, by a more rapid circulation, serving as the instrument of many more purchases of the one kind than of the other.

Paper money may be so regulated as either to confine itself very much to the circulation between the different dealers, or to extend itself likewise to a great part of that between the dealers and the consumers. Where no bank notes are circulated under ten pounds value, as in London, paper money confines itself very much to the circulation between the dealers. . . . Where bank notes are issued for so small sums as twenty shillings as in Scotland, paper money extends itself to a considerable part of the circulation between dealers and consumers. Before the act of parliament which put a stop to the circulation of ten and five shilling notes, it filled a still greater part of that circulation. . . .

It were better, perhaps, that no bank notes were issued in any part of the kingdom for a smaller sum than five pounds. Paper money would then, probably, confine itself, in every part of the kingdom, to the circulation between the different dealers, as much as it does at present in London, where no bank notes are issued under ten pounds value; five pounds being, in most parts of the kingdom, a sum which, though it will purchase, perhaps, little more than half the quantity of goods, is as much considered, and is as seldom spent all at once, as ten pounds are amidst the profuse expense of London. . . .

To restrain private people, it may be said, from receiving in payment the promissory notes of a banker for any sum, whether great or small, when they themselves are willing to receive them; or, to restrain a banker from issuing such notes, when all his neighbors are willing to accept of them, is a manifest violation of that natural liberty, which it is the proper business of law not to infringe, but to support. Such regulations may, no doubt, be considered as in some respect a violation of natural liberty. But those exertions of the natural liberty of a few individuals, which might endanger the security of the whole society, are, and ought to be, restrained by the laws of all governments; of the most free, as well as or the most despotical. The obligation of building party walls, in order to prevent the communication of fire, is a violation of natural liberty, exactly of the same kind with the regulations of the banking trade which are here proposed. . . .*

The increase of paper money, it has been said, by augmenting the quantity, and consequently diminishing the value, of the whole currency, necessarily augments the money price of commodities. But as the quantity of gold and silver, which is taken from the currency, is always equal to the quantity of paper which is added to it, paper money does not necessarily increase the quantity of the whole currency. From the beginning of the last century to the present time, provisions never were cheaper in Scotland than in 1759, though, from the circulation of ten and five shilling bank notes, there was then more paper money in the country than at present. The proportion between the price of provisions in Scotland and that in England is the same now as before the great multiplication of banking companies in Scotland. Corn is, upon most occasions, fully as cheap in England as in France, though there is a great deal of paper money in England, and scarce any in France. In 1751 and 1752, when Mr. Hume† published his *Political Discourses*, and soon after the great multiplication of paper money in Scotland, there was a very sensible

---

* See Introduction, page 53, for discussion. Smith is acknowledging his own seeming inconsistency about government regulation.

† David Hume (1711–1776), Scottish philosopher, historian, economist, and essayist.

rise in the price of provisions, owing, probably, to the badness of the seasons, and not to the multiplication of paper money.*

It would be otherwise, indeed, with a paper money, consisting in promissory notes, of which the immediate payment depended, in any respect, either upon the good will of those who issued them, or upon a condition which the holder of the notes might not always have it in his power to fulfill, or of which the payment was not eligible till after a certain number of years, and which, in the meantime, bore no interest. Such a paper money would, no doubt, fall more or less below the value of gold and silver, according as the difficulty or uncertainty of obtaining immediate payment was supposed to be greater or less, or according to the greater or less distance of time at which payment was eligible.

Some years ago the different banking companies of Scotland were in the practice of inserting into their bank notes, what they called an optional clause; by which they promised payment to the bearer, either as soon as the note should be presented, or, in the option of the directors, six months after such presentment, together with the legal interest for the said six months. The directors of some of those banks sometimes took advantage of this optional clause, and sometimes threatened those who demanded gold and

---

* Also see Introduction, page 50, for further discussion of whether paper money causes inflation.

silver in exchange for a considerable number of their notes, that they would take advantage of it, unless such demanders would content themselves with a part of what they demanded. The promissory notes of those banking companies constituted, at that time, the far greater part of the currency of Scotland, which this uncertainty of payment necessarily degraded below value of gold and silver money. . . . The same act of parliament which suppressed ten and five shilling bank notes, suppressed likewise this optional clause, and thereby restored the exchange between England and Scotland to its natural rate, or to what the course of trade and remittances might happen to make it. . . .

The paper currencies of North America consisted, not in bank notes payable to the bearer on demand, but in a government paper, of which the payment was not eligible till several years after it was issued; and though the colony governments paid no interest to the holders of this paper, they declared it to be, and in fact rendered it, a legal tender of payment for the full value for which it was issued. But allowing the colony security to be perfectly good, a hundred pounds payable fifteen years hence, for example, in a country where interest is at six percent, is worth little more than forty pounds ready money. To oblige a creditor, therefore, to accept of this as full payment for a debt of hundred pounds actually paid down in ready money, was an act of such violent injustice, as has scarce, perhaps, been attempted by the government of any other country which pretended to be free. It bears the evident marks of having originally been, what the honest and downright Doctor Douglas assures us it was, a scheme of fraudulent debtors to cheat their creditors.

The government of Pennsylvania, indeed, pretended, upon their first emission of paper money, in 1722, to render their paper of equal value with gold and silver, by enacting penalties against all those who made any difference in the price of their goods when they sold them for a colony paper, and when they sold them for gold and silver, a regulation equally tyrannical, but much less, effectual, than that which it was meant to support. A positive law may render a shilling a legal tender for a guinea, because it may direct the courts of justice to discharge the debtor who has made that tender; but no positive law can oblige a person who sells goods, and who is at liberty to sell or not to sell as he pleases, to accept of a shilling as equivalent to a guinea in the price of them. Notwithstanding any regulation of this kind, it appeared, by the course of exchange with Great Britain, that a hundred pounds sterling was occasionally considered as equivalent, in some of the colonies, to a hundred and thirty and in others to so great a sum as eleven hundred currency; this difference in the value arising from the difference in the quantity of paper emitted in the different colonies, and in the distance and probability of the term of its final discharge and redemption.

No law, therefore, could be more equitable than the act of parliament, so unjustly complained of in the colonies, which declared, that no paper currency to be emitted there in time coming, should be a legal tender of payment.

Pennsylvania was always more moderate in its emissions of paper money than any other of our colonies. Its paper currency, accordingly, is said never to have sunk below the value of the gold and silver which was current in the colony before the first emission of its paper money. Before that emission, the colony had raised the denomination of its coin, and had, by act of assembly, ordered five shillings sterling to pass in the colonies for six-and-three pence, and afterwards for six-and-eight pence. A pound, colony currency, therefore, even when that currency was gold and silver, was more than thirty percent below the value of a pound sterling; and when that currency was turned into paper, it was seldom much more than thirty percent below that value. The pretence for raising the denomination of the coin was to prevent the exportation of gold and silver, by making equal quantities of those metals pass for greater sums in the colony than they did in the mother country. It was found, however, that the price of all goods from the mother country rose exactly in proportion as they raised the denomination of their coin, so that their gold and silver were exported as fast as ever. . . .

If bankers are restrained from issuing any circulating bank notes, or notes payable to the bearer, for less than a certain sum; and if they are subjected to the

obligation of an immediate and unconditional payment of such bank notes as soon as presented, their
trade may, with safety to the public, be rendered in all
other respects perfectly free. The late multiplication of
banking companies in both parts of the United Kingdom, an event by which many people have been much
alarmed, instead of diminishing, increases the security of the public. It obliges all of them to be more cir-
cumspect in their conduct, and, by not extending their
currency beyond its due proportion to their cash, to
guard themselves against those malicious runs, which
the rivalship of so many competitors is always ready
to bring upon them. It restrains the circulation of
each particular company within a narrower circle, and
reduces their circulating notes to a smaller number. By
dividing the whole circulation into a greater number
of parts, the failure of any one company, an accident
which, in the course of things, must sometimes happen, becomes of less consequence to the public. This
free competition, too, obliges all bankers to be more
liberal in their dealings with their customers, lest their
rivals should carry them away. In general, if any branch
of trade, or any division of labor, be advantageous to
the public, the freer and more general the competition, it will always be the more so.

## Chapter Three

# Of the Accumulation of Capital, or of Productive and Unproductive Labor

T HERE IS ONE sort of labor which adds to the value of the subject upon which it is bestowed; there is another which has no such effect. The former as it produces a value, may be called productive, the latter, unproductive labor. . . . A man grows rich by employing a multitude of manufacturers; he grows poor by maintaining a multitude or menial servants. The labor of the latter, however, has its value, and deserves its reward as well as that of the former. . . .

The labor of some of the most respectable orders in the society is, like that of menial servants, unproductive of any value, and does not fix or realize itself in any permanent subject, or vendible commodity, which endures after that labor is past, and for which an equal quantity of labor could afterwards be procured. The sovereign, for example, with all the officers both of justice and war who serve under him, the whole army and navy, are unproductive laborers. They are the servants of the public, and are maintained by a part of the annual produce of the industry of other people. Their service, how honorable, how useful, or how necessary soever, produces nothing for which an equal quantity of service can afterwards be procured. The protection, security, and defense, of the commonwealth, the effect of their labor this year, will not purchase its protection, security, and defense, for the year to come. In the same class must be ranked, some both of the gravest and most important, and some of the most frivolous professions; churchmen, lawyers, physicians, men of letters of all kinds; players, buffoons, musicians, opera singers, opera dancers, etc. The labor of the meanest of these has a certain value, regulated by the very same principles which regulate that of every other sort of labor; and that of the noblest and most useful, produces nothing which could afterwards purchase or procure an equal quantity of labor. Like the declamation of the actor, the harangue of the orator, or the tune of the musician, the work of all of them perishes in the very instant of its production.

Both productive and unproductive laborers, and those who do not labor at all, are all equally maintained by the annual produce of the land and labor of the country. This produce, how great soever, can never be infinite, but must have certain limits. According, therefore, as a smaller or greater proportion of it is in any one year employed in maintaining unproductive hands, the more in the one case, and the less in the other, will remain for the productive, and the next year's produce will be greater or smaller accordingly. . . .

Unproductive laborers, and those who do not labor at all, are all maintained by revenue; either, first, by that part of the annual produce which is originally destined for constituting a revenue to some particular persons, either as the rent of land, or as the profits of stock; or, secondly, by that part which, though originally destined for replacing a capital, and for maintaining productive laborers only, yet when it comes into their hands, whatever part of it is over and above their necessary subsistence, may be employed in maintaining indifferently either productive or unproductive hands. Thus, not only the great landlord or the rich merchant, but even the common workman, if his wages are considerable, may maintain a menial servant; or he may sometimes go to a play or a puppet show, and so contribute his share towards maintaining one set of unproductive laborers; or he may pay some taxes, and thus help to maintain another set, more honorable and useful, indeed, but equally unproductive. . . . The workman must have earned his wages by work done, before he can employ any part of them in this manner. That part, too, is generally but a small one. It is his spare revenue only, of which productive laborers have seldom a great deal. They generally have some, however; and in the payment of taxes, the greatness of their number may compensate, in some measure, the smallness of their contribution. The rent of land and the profits of stock are everywhere, therefore, the principal sources from which unproductive hands derive their subsistence. These are the two sorts of revenue of which the owners have generally most to spare. They might both maintain indifferently, either productive or unproductive hands. They seem, however, to have some predilection for the latter. The expense of a great lord feeds generally more idle than industrious people. The rich merchant though with his capital he maintains industrious people only, yet by his expense, that is, by the employment of his revenue, he feeds commonly the very same sort as the great lord. . . .

. . . We are more industrious than our forefathers, because, in the present times, the funds destined for the maintenance of industry are much greater in proportion to those which are likely to be employed in the maintenance of idleness, than they were two or three centuries ago. Our ancestors were idle for want of a sufficient encouragement to industry. It is better, says the proverb, to play for nothing, than to work for nothing. In mercantile and manufacturing towns, where the inferior ranks of people are chiefly maintained by the employment of capital, they are in general industrious, sober, and thriving; as in many English, and in most Dutch towns. In those towns which are principally supported by the constant or occasional residence of a court, and in which the inferior ranks of people are chiefly maintained by the spending of revenue, they are in general idle, dissolute, and poor; as at Rome, Versailles, Compiegne, and Fontainebleau. If you except Rouen and Bordeaux, there is little trade or industry in any of the parliament towns of France; and the inferior ranks of people, being chiefly maintained by the expense of the members of the courts of justice, and of those who come to plead before them, are in general idle and poor. . . .

There was little trade or industry in Edinburgh before the Union. When the Scotch parliament was no longer to be assembled in it, when it ceased to be the necessary residence of the principal nobility and gentry of Scotland, it became a city of some trade and industry. It still continues, however, to be the residence of the principal courts of justice in Scotland, of the boards of customs and excise, etc. A considerable revenue, therefore, still continues to be spent in it. In trade and industry, it is much inferior to Glasgow, of which the inhabitants are chiefly maintained by the employment of capital. The inhabitants of a large village, it has sometimes been observed, after having made considerable progress in manufactures, have become idle and poor, in consequence of a great lord's having taken up his residence in their neighborhood. . . .

[The] capitals [of industry] are increased by parsimony, and diminished by prodigality and misconduct.

Whatever a person saves from his revenue he adds to his capital, and either employs it himself in maintaining an additional number of productive hands, or enables some other person to do so, by lending it to him for an interest, that is, for a share of the profits. As the capital of an individual can be increased only by what he saves from his annual revenue or his annual gains, so the capital of a society, which is the same with that of all the individuals who compose it, can be increased only in the same manner.

Parsimony, and not industry, is the immediate cause of the increase of capital. Industry, indeed, provides the subject which parsimony accumulates; but whatever industry might acquire, if parsimony did not save and store up, the capital would never be the greater. . . .*

What is annually saved is as regularly consumed as what is annually spent and nearly in the same time too: but it is consumed by a different set of people. That portion of his revenue which a rich man annually spends is, in most cases, consumed by idle guests and menial servants, who leave nothing behind them in return for their consumption. That portion, which he annually saves, as, for the sake of the profit, it is immediately employed as a capital, is consumed in the same manner and nearly in the same time too, but by

---

* See page 36 for a discussion of Smith's emphasis on saving.

a different set of people: by laborers, manufacturers, and artificers, who reproduce, with a profit, the value of their annual consumption. . . .

By what a frugal man annually saves, he not only affords maintenance to an additional number of productive hands, for that of the ensuing year, but like the founder of a public workhouse he establishes, as it were, a perpetual fund for the maintenance of an equal number in all times to come. The perpetual allotment and destination of this fund, indeed, is not always guarded by any positive law, by any trust-right or deed of mortmain. It is always guarded, however, by a very powerful principle, the plain and evident interest of every individual to whom any share of it shall ever belong. No part of it can ever afterwards be employed to maintain any but productive hands, without an evident loss to the person who thus perverts it from its proper destination.

The prodigal perverts it in this manner: By not confining his expense within his income, he encroaches upon his capital. Like him who perverts the revenues of some pious foundation to profane purposes, he pays the wages of idleness with those funds which the frugality of his forefathers had, as it were, consecrated to the maintenance of industry. . . . If the prodigality of some were not compensated by the frugality of others, the conduct of every prodigal, by feeding the idle with the bread of the industrious, would tend not only to beggar himself but to impoverish his country. . . .

This [spending], it may be said, indeed, not being in foreign goods, and not occasioning any exportation of gold and silver, the same quantity of money would remain in the country as before. But if the quantity of food and clothing which were thus consumed by unproductive had been distributed among productive hands, they would have reproduced, together with a profit, the full value of their consumption. The same quantity of money would, in this case, equally have remained in the country, and there would, besides, have been a reproduction of an equal value of consumable goods. There would have been two values instead of one.

The same quantity of money, besides, cannot long remain in any country in which the value of the annual produce diminishes. . . . The money which, by this annual diminution of produce, is annually thrown out of domestic circulation will not be allowed to lie idle. The interest of whoever possesses it requires that it should be employed; but having no employment at home, it will, in spite of all laws and prohibitions, be sent abroad, and employed in purchasing consumable goods, which may be of some use at home. Its annual exportation will, in this manner, continue for some time to add something to the annual consumption of the country beyond the value of its own annual produce. . . .

The quantity of money, on the contrary, must in every country naturally increase as the value of the annual produce increases. The value of the consumable goods annually circulated within the society being greater, will require a greater quantity of money to circulate them. A part of the increased produce, therefore, will naturally be employed in purchasing, wherever it is to be had, the additional quantity of gold and silver necessary for circulating the rest. The increase of those metals will, in this case, be the effect, not the cause, of the public prosperity. Gold and silver are purchased everywhere in the same manner. The food, clothing, and lodging, the revenue and maintenance, of all those whose labor or stock is employed in bringing them from the mine to the market, is the price paid for them in Peru as well as in England. . . .*

Whatever, therefore, we may imagine the real wealth and revenue of a country to consist in, whether in the value of the annual produce of its land and labor, as plain reason seems to dictate, or in the quantity of the precious metals which circulate within it, as vulgar prejudices suppose; in either view of the matter, every prodigal appears to be a public enemy, and every frugal man a public benefactor.

The effects of misconduct are often the same as those of prodigality. Every injudicious and unsuccessful project in agriculture, mines, fisheries, trade, or manufactures, tends in the same manner to diminish the funds destined for the maintenance of productive labor. In every such project, though the capital is consumed by

---

* Not true, don't need more money.

productive hands only, yet as, by the injudicious manner in which they are employed, they do not reproduce the full value of their consumption, there must always be some diminution in what would otherwise have been the productive funds of the society.

It can seldom happen, indeed, that the circumstances of a great nation can be much affected either by the prodigality or misconduct of individuals; the profusion or imprudence of some being always more than compensated by the frugality and good conduct of others.

With regard to profusion, the principle which prompts to expense is the passion for present enjoyment; which, though sometimes violent and very difficult to be restrained, is in general only momentary and occasional. But the principle which prompts to save is the desire of bettering our condition; a desire which, though generally calm and dispassionate, comes with us from the womb, and never leaves us till we go into the grave. In the whole interval which separates those two moments, there is scarce, perhaps, a single instance, in which any man is so perfectly and completely satisfied with his situation, as to be without any wish of alteration or improvement of any kind. An augmentation of fortune is the means by which the greater part of men propose and wish to better their condition. It is the means the most vulgar and the most obvious; and the most likely way of augmenting their fortune, is to save and accumulate some part of what they acquire, either regularly and annually, or upon some extraordinary occasion. Though the principle of expense, therefore, prevails in almost all men upon some occasions, and in some men upon almost all occasions; yet in the greater part of men, taking the whole course of their life at an average, the principle of frugality seems not only to predominate, but to predominate very greatly.

With regard to misconduct, the number of prudent and successful undertakings is everywhere much greater than that of injudicious and unsuccessful ones. After all our complaints of the frequency of bankruptcies, the unhappy men who fall into this misfortune, make but a very small part of the whole number engaged in trade, and all other sorts of business; not much more, perhaps, than one in a thousand. Bankruptcy is, perhaps, the greatest and most humiliating calamity which can befall an innocent man. The greater part of men, therefore, are sufficiently careful to avoid it. Some, indeed, do not avoid it; as some do not avoid the gallows.

Great nations are never impoverished by private, though they sometimes are by public prodigality and misconduct. The whole or almost the whole, public revenue is, in most countries, employed in maintaining unproductive hands. Such are the people who compose a numerous and splendid court, a great ecclesiastical establishment, great fleets and armies, who in time of peace produce nothing, and in time of war acquire nothing which can compensate the expense of maintaining them, even while the war lasts. Such people, as they themselves produce nothing, are all maintained by the produce of other men's labor. When multiplied, therefore, to an unnecessary number, they may in a particular year consume so great a share of this produce, as not to leave a sufficiency for maintaining the productive laborers, who should reproduce it next year. The next year's produce, therefore, will be less than that of the foregoing; and if the same disorder should continue, that of the third year will be still less than that of the second. Those unproductive hands who should be maintained by a part only of the spare revenue of the people, may consume so great a share of their whole revenue, and thereby oblige so great a number to encroach upon their capitals, upon the funds destined for the maintenance of productive labor, that all the frugality and good conduct of individuals may not be able to compensate the waste and degradation of produce occasioned by this violent and forced encroachment.

This frugality and good conduct, however, is, upon most occasions, it appears from experience, sufficient to compensate, not only the private prodigality and misconduct of individuals, but the public extravagance of government. The uniform, constant, and uninterrupted effort of every man to better his condition, the principle from which public and national, as well as private opulence is originally derived, is frequently powerful enough to maintain the natural progress of things towards improvement, in spite both of the extravagance of government, and of the greatest errors of administration. Like the unknown principle of animal life, it frequently restores health and vigor to the constitution, in spite not only of the disease, but of the absurd prescriptions of the doctor.

The annual produce of the land and labor of any nation can be increased in its value by no other means, but by increasing either the number of its productive laborers, or the productive powers of those laborers who had before been employed. The number of its productive laborers, it is evident, can never be much increased, but in consequence of an increase of capital, or of the funds destined for maintaining them. The productive powers of the same number of laborers cannot be increased, but in consequence either of some addition and improvement to those machines and instruments which facilitate and abridge labor, or of more proper division and distribution of employment. In either case, an additional capital is almost always required. . . . When we compare, therefore, the state of a nation at two different periods, and find that the annual produce of its land and labor is evidently greater at the latter than at the former, that its lands are better cultivated, its manufactures more numerous and more flourishing, and its trade more extensive; we may be assured that its capital must have increased during the interval between those two periods, and that more must have been added to it by the good conduct of some, than had been taken from it either by the private misconduct of others, or by the public extravagance of government....

The annual produce of the land and labor of England, for example, is certainly much greater than it was a little more than a century ago, at the restoration of Charles II....

... [Yet], in the happiest and most fortunate period of them all, that which has passed since the Restoration, how many disorders and misfortunes have occurred, which, could they have been foreseen, not only the impoverishment, but the total ruin of the country would have been expected from them? The fire and the plague of London, the two Dutch wars, the disorders of the revolution, the war in Ireland, the four expensive French wars of 1688, 1701, 1742, and 1756, together with the two rebellions of 1715 and 1745. In the course of the four French wars, the nation has contracted more than a hundred and forty-five millions of debt, over and above all the other extraordinary annual expense which they occasioned; so that the whole cannot be computed at less than two hundred millions. So great a share of the annual produce of the land and labor of the country, has, since the Revolution, been employed upon different occasions, in maintaining an extraordinary number of unproductive hands. But had not those wars given this particular direction to so large a capital, the greater part of it would naturally have been employed in maintaining productive hands, whose labor would have replaced, with a profit, the whole value of their consumption. The value of the annual produce of the land and labor of the country would have been considerably increased by it every year, and every year's increase would have augmented still more that of the following year. More houses would have been built, more lands would have been improved, and those which had been improved before would have been better cultivated; more manufactures would have been established, and those which had been established before would have been more extended; and to what height the real wealth and revenue of the country might by this time have been raised, it is not perhaps very easy even to imagine.

But though the profusion of government must undoubtedly have retarded the natural progress of England towards wealth and improvement, it has not been able to stop it. The annual produce of its land and labor is undoubtedly much greater at present than it was either at the Restoration or at the Revolution. The capital, therefore, annually employed in cultivating this land, and in maintaining this labor, must likewise be much greater. In the midst of all the exactions of government, this capital has been silently and gradually accumulated by the private frugality and good conduct of individuals, by their universal, continual, and uninterrupted effort to better their own condition. It is this effort, protected by law, and allowed by liberty to exert itself in the manner that is most advantageous, which has maintained the progress of England towards opulence and improvement in almost all former times, and which, it is to be hoped, will do so in all future times. England, however, as it has never been blessed with a very parsimonious government, so parsimony has at no time been the characteristic virtue of its inhabitants. It is the highest impertinence and presumption, therefore, in kings and ministers to pretend to watch over the economy of private people, and to restrain their expense, either by sumptuary laws, or by prohibiting the importation of foreign luxuries. They are themselves always, and without any exception, the greatest spendthrifts in the society. Let them look well after their own expense, and they may safely trust private people with theirs. If their own extravagance does not ruin the state, that of the subject never will.

As frugality increases, and prodigality diminishes, the public capital, so the conduct of those whose expense just equals their revenue, without either accumulating or encroaching, neither increases nor diminishes it. Some modes of expense, however, seem to contribute more to the growth of public opulence than others.

The revenue of an individual may be spent, either in things which are consumed immediately, and in which one day's expense can neither alleviate nor support that of another; or it may be spent in things more durable, which can therefore be accumulated, and in which every day's expense may, as he chooses, either alleviate, or support and heighten, the effect of that of the following day. A man of fortune, for example, may either spend his revenue in a profuse and sumptuous table, and in maintaining a great number of menial servants, and a multitude of dogs and horses; or, contenting himself with a frugal table, and few attendants, he may lay out the greater part of it in adorning his house or his country villa, in useful or ornamental buildings, in useful or ornamental furniture, in collecting books, statues, pictures; or in things more frivolous, jewels, baubles, ingenious trinkets of different kinds; or, what is most trifling of all, in amassing a great wardrobe of fine clothes, like the favorite and minister of a great prince who died a few years ago. Were two men of equal fortune to spend their revenue, the one chiefly in the one way, the other in the other, the magnificence of the person whose expense had been chiefly in durable commodities, would be continually increasing, every day's expense contributing something to support and heighten the effect of that of the following day; that of the other, on the contrary, would be no greater at the end of the period than at the beginning. The former too would, at the end of the period, be the richer man of the two. He would have a stock of goods of some kind or other, which, though it might not be worth all that it cost, would always be worth something. No trace or vestige of the expense of the latter would remain, and the effects of ten or twenty years' profusion would be as completely annihilated as if they had never existed.

As the one mode of expense is more favorable than the other to the opulence of an individual, so is it likewise to that of a nation. The houses, the furniture, the clothing of the rich, in a little time, become useful to the inferior and middling ranks of people. They are able to purchase them when their superiors grow weary of them; and the general accommodation of the whole people is thus gradually improved, when this mode of expense becomes universal among men of fortune. In countries which have long been rich, you will frequently find the inferior ranks of people in possession both of houses and furniture perfectly good and entire, but of which neither the one could have been built, nor the other have been made for their use. What was formerly a seat of the family of Seymour is now an inn upon the Bath road. The marriage bed of James I of Great Britain, which his queen brought with her from Denmark, as a present fit for a sovereign to make to a sovereign, was, a few years ago, the ornament of an alehouse at Dunfermline. In some ancient cities, which either have been long stationary, or have gone somewhat to decay, you will sometimes scarce find a single house which could have been built for its present inhabitants. If you go into those houses, too, you will frequently find many excellent, though antiquated pieces of furniture, which are still very fit for use, and which could as little have been made for them. Noble palaces, magnificent villas, great collections of books, statues, pictures, and other curiosities, are frequently both an ornament and an honor, not only to the neighborhood, but to the whole country to which they belong. Versailles is an ornament and an honor to France, Stowe and Wilton to England. Italy still continues to command some sort of veneration, by the number of monuments of this kind which it possesses, though the wealth which produced them has decayed, and though the genius which planned them seems to be extinguished, perhaps from not having the same employment.

The expense, too, which is laid out in durable commodities, is favorable not only to accumulation, but to frugality. If a person should at any time exceed in it, he can easily reform without exposing himself to the censure of the public. To reduce very much the number of his servants, to reform his table from great profusion to great frugality, to lay down his equipage after he has once set it up, are changes which cannot escape the observation of his neighbors, and which are supposed to imply some acknowledgment of preceding bad conduct. Few, therefore, of those who have once been so unfortunate as to launch out too far into this sort of expense, have afterwards the courage to reform, till ruin and bankruptcy oblige them. But if a person has, at any time, been at too great an expense in building, in furniture, in books, or pictures, no imprudence can be inferred from his changing his conduct. These are things in which further expense is frequently rendered unnecessary by former expense; and when a person stops short, he appears to do so, not because he has exceeded his fortune, but because he has satisfied his fancy. . . .

I would not, however, by all this, be understood to mean, that the one species of expense always betokens a more liberal or generous spirit than the other. When a man of fortune spends his revenue chiefly in hospitality, he shares the greater part of it with his friends and companions; but when he employs it in purchasing such durable commodities he often spends the whole upon his own person, and gives nothing to anybody without an equivalent. The latter species of expense, therefore, especially when directed towards frivolous objects, the little ornaments of dress and furniture, jewels, trinkets, gewgaws, frequently indicates not only a trifling, but a base and selfish disposition. All that I mean is, that the one sort of expense, as it always occasions some accumulation of valuable commodities, as it is more favorable to private frugality, and, consequently, to the increase of the public capital, and as it maintains productive rather than unproductive hands, conduces more than the other to the growth of public opulence.

## Chapter Four

# Of Stock Lent at Interest

THE STOCK WHICH is lent at interest . . . the borrower may use either as a capital, or as a stock reserved for immediate consumption. If he uses it as a capital, he employs it in the maintenance of productive laborers, who reproduce the value, with a profit. He can, in this case, both restore the capital, and pay the interest, without alienating or encroaching upon any other source of revenue. If he uses it as a stock reserved for immediate consumption, he acts the part of a prodigal, and dissipates, in the maintenance of the idle, what was destined for the support of the industrious. . . .

The stock which is lent at interest is, no doubt, occasionally employed in both these ways, but in the former much more frequently than in the latter. The man who borrows in order to spend will soon be ruined, and he who lends to him will generally have occasion to repent of his folly. To borrow or to lend for such a purpose, therefore, is, in all cases, where gross usury is out of the question, contrary to the interest of both parties; and though it no doubt happens sometimes, that people do both the one and the other, yet, from the regard that all men have for their own interest, we may be assured, that it cannot happen so very frequently as we are sometimes apt to imagine. Ask any rich man of common prudence, to which of the two sorts of people he has lent the greater part of his stock, to those who he thinks will employ it profitably, or to those who will spend it idly, and he will laugh at you for proposing the question. Even among borrowers, therefore, not the people in the world most famous for frugality, the number of the frugal and industrious surpasses considerably that of the prodigal and idle.

The only people, to whom stock is commonly lent, without their being expected to make any very profitable use of it, are country gentlemen, who borrow upon mortgage. Even they scarce ever borrow merely to spend. What they borrow, one may say, is commonly spent before they borrow it. They have generally consumed so great a quantity of goods, advanced to them upon credit by shopkeepers and tradesmen, that they find it necessary to borrow at interest, in order to pay the debt. The capital borrowed replaces the capitals of those shopkeepers and tradesmen which the country gentlemen could not have replaced from the rents of their estates. It is not properly borrowed in order to be spent, but in order to replace a capital which had been spent before.

Almost all loans at interest are made in money, either of paper, or of gold and silver; but what the borrower really wants, and what the lender readily supplies him with, is not the money, but the money's worth, or the goods which it can purchase. . . .

As the quantity of stock to be lent at interest increases, the interest, or the price which must be paid for the use of that stock, necessarily diminishes, not only from those general causes which make the market price of things commonly diminish as their quantity increases, but from other causes which are peculiar to this particular case. As capitals increase in any country, the profits which can be made by employing them necessarily diminish. It becomes gradually more and more difficult to find within the country a profitable method of employing any new capital. There arises, in consequence, a competition between different capitals, the owner of one endeavoring to get possession of that employment which is occupied by another; but, upon most occasions, he can hope to jostle that other out of this employment by no other means but by dealing upon more reasonable terms. He must not only sell what he deals in somewhat cheaper, but, in order to get it to sell, he must sometimes, too, buy it dearer. The demand for productive labor, by the increase of the funds which are destined for maintaining it, grows every day greater and greater. Laborers easily find employment; but the owners of capitals find it difficult to get laborers to employ. Their competition raises the wages of labor, and sinks the profits of stock. But when the profits which can be made by the use of a capital are in this manner diminished, as it were, at both ends, the price which can be paid for the use of it, that is, the rate of interest must necessarily be diminished with them.

Mr. Locke,[*] Mr. Lawe,[†] and Mr. Montesquieu,[‡] as well as many other writers, seem to have imagined that the increase of the quantity of gold and silver, in consequence of the discovery of the Spanish West Indies, was the real cause of the lowering of the rate of interest through the greater part of Europe. Those metals, they say, having become of less value themselves, the use of any particular portion of them necessarily became of less value too, and, consequently, the price which could be paid for it. This notion, which at first sight seems so plausible, has been so fully exposed by Mr. Hume, that it is, perhaps, unnecessary to say anything more about it. The following very short and plain argument, however, may serve to explain more distinctly the fallacy which seems to have misled those gentlemen.

---

[*] John Locke (1632–1704), English philosopher and physician.

[†] John Law (1671–1729), Scottish economist. He served King Louis XV of France as controller-general of finance and pursued monetary policies which resulted in the disastrous Mississippi Bubble.

[‡] Baron de Montesquieu, Charles-Louis de Secondat (1689–1755), French social commentator and political thinker.

Before the discovery of the Spanish West Indies, ten percent seems to have been the common rate of interest through the greater part of Europe. It has since that time, in different countries, sunk to six, five, four, and three percent Let us suppose, that in every particular country the value of silver has sunk precisely in the same proportion as the rate of interest; and that in those countries, for example, where interest has been reduced from ten to five percent the same quantity of silver can now purchase just half the quantity of goods which it could have purchased before. This supposition will not, I believe, be found anywhere agreeable to the truth; but it is the most favorable to the opinion which we are going to examine; and, even upon this supposition, it is utterly impossible that the lowering of the value of silver could have the smallest tendency to lower the rate of interest. If a hundred pounds are in those countries now of no more value than fifty pounds were then, ten pounds must now be of no more value than five pounds were then. Whatever were the causes which lowered the value of the capital, the same must necessarily have lowered that of the interest, and exactly in the same proportion. The proportion between the value of the capital and that of the interest must have remained the same, though the rate had never been altered. By altering the rate, on the contrary, the proportion between those two values is necessarily altered. If a hundred pounds now are worth no more than fifty were then, five now can be worth no more than two pounds ten shillings were then. By reducing the rate of interest, therefore, from ten to five percent we give for the use of a capital, which is supposed to be equal to one-half of its former value, an interest which is equal to one-fourth only of the value of the former interest. . . .

In some countries the interest of money has been prohibited by law. But as something can everywhere be made by the use of money, something ought everywhere to be paid for the use of it. This regulation, instead of preventing, has been found from experience to increase the evil of usury. The debtor being obliged to pay, not only for the use of the money, but for the risk which his creditor runs by accepting a compensation for that use, he is obliged, if one may say so, to insure his creditor from the penalties of usury.

In countries where interest is permitted, the law in order to prevent the extortion of usury generally fixes the highest rate which can be taken without incurring a penalty. This rate ought always to be somewhat above the lowest market price, or the price which is commonly paid for the use of money by those who can give the most undoubted security. If this legal rate should be fixed below the lowest market rate, the effects of this fixation must be nearly the same as those of a total prohibition of interest. The creditor will not lend his money for less than the use of it is worth, and the debtor must pay him for the risk which he runs by accepting the full value of that use. If it is fixed precisely at the lowest market price, it ruins, with honest people who respect the laws of their country, the credit of all those who cannot give the very best security, and obliges them to have recourse to exorbitant usurers. In a country such as Great Britain, where money is lent to government at three percent and to private people, upon good security, at four and four-and-a-half, the present legal rate, five percent is perhaps as proper as any.*

The legal rate, it is to be observed, though it ought to be somewhat above, ought not to be much above the lowest market rate. If the legal rate of interest in Great Britain, for example, was fixed so high as eight or ten percent the greater part of the money which was to be lent, would be lent to prodigals and projectors, who alone would be willing to give this high interest. Sober people, who will give for the use of money no more than a part of what they are likely to make by the use of it, would not venture into the competition. A great part of the capital of the country would thus be kept out of the hands which were most likely to make a profitable and advantageous use of it, and thrown into those which were most likely to waste and destroy it. Where the legal rate of interest, on the contrary, is fixed but a very little above the lowest market rate, sober people are universally preferred, as borrowers, to prodigals and projectors. The person who lends money gets nearly as much interest from the former as

---

* He's OK with interest rate control.

he dares to take from the latter, and his money is much safer in the hands of the one set of people than in those of the other. A great part of the capital of the country is thus thrown into the hands in which it is most likely to be employed with advantage.

No law can reduce the common rate of interest below the lowest ordinary market rate at the time when that law is made. Notwithstanding the edict of 1766, by which the French king attempted to reduce the rate of interest from five to four percent, money continued to be lent in France at five percent, the law being evaded in several different ways. . . .

# Chapter Five

# Of the Different
# Employment of Capitals

A CAPITAL MAY BE employed in four different ways; either, first, in procuring the rude produce annually required for the use and consumption of the society; or, secondly, in manufacturing and preparing that rude produce for immediate use and consumption; or, thirdly in transporting either the rude or manufactured produce from the places where they abound to those where they are wanted; or, lastly, in dividing particular portions of either into such small parcels as suit the occasional demands of those who want them. . . .

Unless a capital was employed in breaking and dividing certain portions either of the rude or manufactured produce into such small parcels as suit the occasional demands of those who want them, every man would be obliged to purchase a greater quantity of the goods he wanted than his immediate occasions required. If there was no such trade as a butcher, for example, every man would be obliged to purchase a whole ox or a whole sheep at a time. This would generally be inconvenient to the rich, and much more so to the poor. If a poor workman was obliged to purchase a month's or six months' provisions at a time, a great part of the stock which he employs as a capital in the instruments of his trade, or in the furniture of his shop, and which yields him a revenue, he would be forced to place in that part of his stock which is reserved for immediate consumption, and which yields him no revenue. Nothing can be more convenient for such a person than to be able to purchase his subsistence from day to day, or even from hour to hour, as he wants it. He is thereby enabled to employ almost his whole stock as a capital. He is thus enabled to furnish work to a greater value; and the profit which he makes by it in this way much more than compensates the additional price which the profit of the retailer imposes upon the goods.

The prejudices of some political writers against shopkeepers and tradesmen are altogether without foundation. So far is it from being necessary either to tax them, or to restrict their numbers, that they can never be multiplied so as to hurt the public, though they may so as to hurt one another. The quantity of grocery goods, for example, which can be sold in a particular town, is limited by the demand of that town and its neighborhood. The capital, therefore, which can be employed in the grocery trade, cannot exceed what is sufficient to purchase that quantity. If this capital is divided between two different grocers, their competition will tend to make both of them sell cheaper than if it were in the hands of one only; and if it were divided among twenty, their competition would be just so much the greater, and the chance of their combining together, in order to raise the price, just so much the less. Their competition might, perhaps, ruin some of themselves; but to take care of this, is the business of the parties concerned, and it may safely be trusted to their discretion. It can never hurt either the consumer or the producer; on the contrary, it must tend to make the retailers both sell cheaper and buy dearer, than if the whole trade was monopolized by one or two persons. Some of them, perhaps, may sometimes decoy a weak customer to buy what he has no occasion for. This evil, however, is of too little importance to deserve the public attention, nor would it necessarily be prevented by restricting their numbers. It is not the multitude of alehouses, to give the most suspicious example, that occasions a general disposition to drunkenness among the common people; but that disposition, arising from other causes, necessarily gives employment to a multitude of alehouses....

A particular country, in the same manner as a particular person, may frequently not have capital sufficient both to improve and cultivate all its lands, to manufacture and prepare their whole rude produce for immediate use and consumption, and to transport the surplus part either of the rude or manufactured produce to those distant markets, where it can be exchanged for something for which there is a demand at home. The inhabitants of many different parts of Great Britain have not capital sufficient to improve and cultivate all their lands. The wool of the southern counties of Scotland is, a great part of it, after a long land carriage through very bad roads, manufactured in Yorkshire, for want of a capital to manufacture it at home. There are many little manufacturing towns in Great Britain, of which the inhabitants have not capital sufficient to transport the produce of their own industry to those distant markets where there is demand and consumption for it. . . .

When the capital of any country is not sufficient for all those three purposes, in proportion as a greater share of it is employed in agriculture, the greater will be the quantity of productive labor which it puts into motion within the country; as will likewise be the value which its employment adds to the annual produce of the land and labor of the society. After agriculture, the capital employed in manufactures puts into motion the greatest quantity of productive labor, and adds the greatest value to the annual produce. That which is employed in the trade of exportation has the least effect of any of the three.

The country, indeed, which has not capital sufficient for all those three purposes, has not arrived at that degree of opulence for which it seems naturally destined. To attempt, however, prematurely, and with an insufficient capital, to do all the three, is certainly not the shortest way for a society, no more than it would be for an individual, to acquire a sufficient one. The capital of all the individuals of a nation has its limits, in the same manner as that of a single individual, and is capable of executing only certain purposes. The capital of all the individuals of a nation is increased in the same manner as that of a single individual, by their continually accumulating and adding to it whatever they save out of their revenue. It is likely to increase the fastest, therefore, when it is employed in the way that affords the greatest revenue to all the inhabitants or the country, as they will thus be enabled to make the greatest savings. . . .

It has been the principal cause of the rapid progress of our American colonies towards wealth and greatness, that almost their whole capitals have hitherto been employed in agriculture. They have no manufactures, those household and coarser manufactures excepted, which necessarily accompany the progress of agriculture, and which are the work of the women and children in every private family. The greater part, both of the exportation and coasting trade of America, is carried on by the capitals of merchants who reside in Great Britain. Even the stores and warehouses from which goods are retailed in some provinces, particularly in Virginia and Maryland, belong, many of them, to merchants who reside in the mother country, and afford one of the few instances of the retail trade of a society being carried on by the capitals of those who are not resident members of it. Were the Americans, either by combination, or by any other sort of violence, to stop the importation of European manufactures, and, by thus giving a monopoly to such of their own countrymen as could manufacture the like goods, divert any considerable part of their capital into this employment, they would retard, instead of accelerating, the further increase in the value of their annual produce, and would obstruct, instead of promoting, the progress of their country towards real wealth and greatness. This would be still more the case, were they to attempt, in the same manner, to monopolize to themselves their whole exportation trade. . . .

When the produce of any particular branch of industry exceeds what the demand of the country requires, the surplus must be sent abroad, and exchanged for something for which there is a demand at home. Without such exportation, a part of the productive labor of the country must cease, and the value of its annual produce diminish. The land and labor of Great Britain produce generally more corn, woolens, and hardware, than the demand of the home market requires. The surplus part of them, therefore, must be sent abroad, and exchanged for something for which there is a demand at home. It is only by means of such exportation, that this surplus can acquire value sufficient to compensate the labor and expense of producing it. . . .

When the foreign goods which are thus purchased with the surplus produce of domestic industry exceed the demand of the home market, the surplus part of them must be sent abroad again, and exchanged for something more in demand at home. About ninety-six thousand hogsheads of tobacco are annually purchased in Virginia and Maryland with a part of the surplus produce of British industry. But the demand of Great Britain does not require, perhaps, more than fourteen thousand. If the remaining eighty-two thousand, therefore, could not be sent abroad, and exchanged for something more in demand at home, the importation of them must cease immediately, and with it the productive labor of all those inhabitants of Great Britain who are at present employed in preparing the goods with which these eighty-two thousand hogsheads are annually purchased. Those goods, which are part of the produce of the land and labor of Great Britain, having no market at home, and being deprived of that which they had abroad, must cease to be produced. The most roundabout foreign trade of consumption, therefore, may, upon some occasions, be as necessary for supporting the productive labor of the country, and the value of its annual produce, as the most direct.

When the capital stock of any country is increased to such a degree that it cannot be all employed in supplying the consumption, and supporting the productive labor of that particular country, the surplus part of it naturally disgorges itself into the carrying trade, and is employed in performing the same offices to other countries. The carrying trade is the natural effect and symptom of great national wealth; but it does not seem to be the natural cause of it. Those statesmen, who have been disposed to favor it with particular encouragement, seem to have mistaken the effect and symptom for the cause. Holland, in proportion to the extent of the land and the number of its inhabitants, by far the richest country in Europe, has accordingly the greatest share of the carrying trade of Europe. England, perhaps the second richest country of Europe, is likewise supposed to have a considerable share in it; though what commonly passes for the carrying trade of England will frequently, perhaps, be found to be no more than a roundabout foreign trade of consumption. . . .

*Book Three*

# Of the Different Progress of Opulence in Different Nations

## Chapter One

# Of the Natural Progress of Opulence

COMMERCE AND MANUFACTURES gradually introduced order and good government, and with them, the liberty and security of individuals, among the inhabitants of the country, who had before lived almost in a continual state of war with their neighbors, and of servile dependency upon their superiors.*

The great commerce of every civilized society is that carried on between the inhabitants of the town and those of the country. It consists in the exchange of rude for manufactured produce, either immediately, or by

---

* This passage moved from Book Three, Chapter Four.

the intervention of money, or of some sort of paper which represents money. The country supplies the town with the means of subsistence and the materials of manufacture. The town repays this supply, by sending back a part of the manufactured produce to the inhabitants of the country. The town in which there neither is nor can be any reproduction of substances, may very properly be said to gain its whole wealth and subsistence from the country. We must not, however, upon this account, imagine that the gain of the town is the loss of the country. The gains of both are mutual and reciprocal, and the division of labor is in this, as in all other cases, advantageous to all the different persons employed in the various occupations into which it is subdivided. The inhabitants of the country purchase of the town a greater quantity of manufactured goods with the produce of a much smaller quantity of their own labor, than they must have employed had they attempted to prepare them themselves.... Among all the absurd speculations that have been propagated concerning the balance of trade, it has never been pretended that either the country loses by its commerce with the town, or the town by that with the country which maintains it....

. . . Upon equal or nearly equal profits, most men will choose to employ their capitals, rather in the improvement and cultivation of land, than either in manufactures or in foreign trade. The man who employs his capital in land, has it more under his view and command; and his fortune is much less liable to accidents than that of the trader, who is obliged frequently to commit it, not only to the winds and the waves, but to the more uncertain elements of human folly and injustice, by giving great credits, in distant countries, to men with whose character and situation he can seldom be thoroughly acquainted. The capital of the landlord, on the contrary, which is fixed in the improvement of his land, seems to be as well secured as the nature of human affairs can admit of. The beauty of the country, besides, the pleasure of a country life, the tranquility of mind which it promises, and, wherever the injustice of human laws does not disturb it, the independency which it really affords, have charms that, more or less, attract everybody; and as to cultivate the ground was the original destination of man, so, in every stage of his existence, he seems to retain a predilection for this primitive employment.

Without the assistance of some artificers, indeed, the cultivation of land cannot be carried on, but with great inconveniency and continual interruption. Smiths, carpenters, wheelwrights and plough wrights, masons and bricklayers, tanners, shoemakers, and tailors, are people whose service the farmer has frequent occasion for. Such artificers, too, stand occasionally in need of the assistance of one another; and as their residence is not, like that of the farmer, necessarily tied down to a precise spot, they naturally settle in the neighborhood of one another, and thus form a small town or village.

The butcher, the brewer, and the baker, soon join them, together with many other artificers and retailers, necessary or useful for supplying their occasional wants, and who contribute still further to augment the town. The inhabitants of the town, and those of the country, are mutually the servants of one another. . . .

In our North American colonies, where uncultivated land is still to be had upon easy terms, no manufactures for distant sale have ever yet been established in any of their towns. When an artificer has acquired a little more stock than is necessary for carrying on his own business in supplying the neighboring country, he does not, in North America, attempt to establish with it a manufacture for more distant sale, but employs it in the purchase and improvement of uncultivated land. From artificer he becomes planter; and neither the large wages nor the easy subsistence which that country affords to artificers, can bribe him rather to work for other people than for himself. He feels that an artificer is the servant of his customers, from whom he derives his subsistence; but that a planter who cultivates his own land, and derives his necessary subsistence from the labor of his own family, is really a master, and independent of all the world. . . .

In seeking for employment to a capital, manufactures are, upon equal or nearly equal profits, naturally preferred to foreign commerce, for the same reason that agriculture is naturally preferred to manufactures. As the capital of the landlord or farmer is more secure than that of the manufacturer, so the capital of the manufacturer, being at all times more within his view and command, is more secure than that of the foreign merchant. In every period, indeed, of every society, the surplus part both of the rude and manufactured produce, or that for which there is no demand at home, must be sent abroad, in order to be exchanged for something for which there is some demand at home. But whether the capital which carries this surplus produce abroad be a foreign or a domestic one is of very little importance. . . . The wealth of ancient Egypt, that of China and Indostan, sufficiently demonstrate that a nation may attain a very high degree of opulence, though the greater part of its exportation trade be carried on by foreigners. The progress of our North American and West Indian colonies, would have been much less rapid, had no capital but what belonged to themselves been employed in exporting their surplus produce.

According to the natural course of things, therefore, the greater part of the capital of every growing society is, first, directed to agriculture, afterwards to manufactures, and, last of all, to foreign commerce. This order of things is so very natural, that in every society that had any territory, it has always, I believe, been in some degree observed. . . .

## Book Four

# Of Systems of
# Political Economy

# Introduction

P OLITICAL ECONOMY, CONSIDERED as a
branch of the science of a statesman or legislator, proposes two distinct objects; first, to provide a plentiful revenue or subsistence for the people,
or, more properly, to enable them to provide such a
revenue or subsistence for themselves; and, secondly,
to supply the state or commonwealth with a revenue
sufficient for the public services. It proposes to enrich
both the people and the sovereign. . . .

## Chapter One

# Of the Principle of the Commercial or Mercantile System

THAT WEALTH CONSISTS in money, or in gold and silver, is a popular notion which naturally arises from the double function of money, as the instrument of commerce, and as the measure of value. In consequence of its being the instrument of commerce, when we have money we can more readily obtain whatever else we have occasion for, than by means of any other commodity. The great affair, we always find, is to get money. When that is obtained, there is no difficulty in making any subsequent purchase. In consequence of its being the measure of value, we estimate that of all other commodities by the quantity of money which they will exchange for. We say of a rich man, that he is worth a great deal, and of a poor man, that he is worth very little money. A frugal man, or a man eager to be rich, is said to love money; and a careless, a generous, or a profuse man, is said to be indifferent about it. To grow rich is to get money; and wealth and money, in short, are, in common language, considered as in every respect synonymous.

A rich country, in the same manner as a rich man, is supposed to be a country abounding in money; and to heap up gold and silver in any country is supposed to be the readiest way to enrich it. For some time after the discovery of America, the first inquiry of the Spaniards, when they arrived upon any unknown coast, used to be, if there was any gold or silver to be found in the neighborhood? By the information which they received, they judged whether it was worthwhile to make a settlement there, or if the country was worth the conquering. Plano Carpine, a monk sent ambassador from the King of France to one of the sons of the famous Genghis Khan, says, that the Tartars used frequently to ask him, if there were plenty of sheep and oxen in the kingdom of France? Their inquiry had the same object with that of the Spaniards. They wanted to know if the country was rich enough to be worth the conquering. Among the Tartars, as among all other nations of shepherds, who are generally ignorant of the use of money, cattle are the instruments of commerce and the measures of value. Wealth, therefore, according to them, consisted in cattle, as, according to the

Spaniards, it consisted in gold and silver. Of the two, the Tartar notion, perhaps, was the nearest to the truth.

Mr. Locke remarks a distinction between money and other moveable goods. All other moveable goods, he says, are of so consumable a nature, that the wealth which consists in them cannot be much depended on; and a nation which abounds in them one year may, without any exportation, but merely by their own waste and extravagance, be in great want of them the next. Money, on the contrary, is a steady friend, which, though it may travel about from hand-to-hand, yet if it can be kept from going out of the country, is not very liable to be wasted and consumed. Gold and silver, therefore, are, according to him, the most solid and substantial part of the moveable wealth of a nation; and to multiply those metals ought, he thinks, upon that account, to be the great object of its political economy.

Others admit that if a nation could be separated from all the world it would be of no consequence how much or how little money circulated in it. The consumable goods, which were circulated by means of this money, would only be exchanged for a greater or a smaller number of pieces; but the real wealth or poverty of the country, they allow, would depend altogether upon the abundance or scarcity of those consumable goods. But it is otherwise, they think, with countries which have connections with foreign nations, and which are obliged to carry on foreign wars, and to maintain fleets and armies in distant countries. This, they say, cannot be done, but by sending abroad money to pay them with; and a nation cannot send much money abroad, unless it has a good deal at home. Every such nation, therefore, must endeavor, in time of peace, to accumulate gold and silver, that when occasion requires, it may have wherewithal to carry on foreign wars.

In consequence of those popular notions, all the different nations of Europe have studied, though to little purpose, every possible means of accumulating gold and silver in their respective countries. Spain and Portugal, the proprietors of the principal mines which supply Europe with those metals, have either prohibited their exportation under the severest penalties, or subjected it to a considerable duty. The like prohibition seems anciently to have made a part of the policy of most other European nations. It is even to be found, where we should least of all expect to find it, in some old Scotch acts of Parliament, which forbid, under heavy penalties, the carrying gold or silver *forth of the kingdom*. The like policy anciently took place both in France and England.

When those countries became commercial, the merchants found this prohibition, upon many occasions, extremely inconvenient. They could frequently buy more advantageously with gold and silver, than with any other commodity, the foreign goods which they wanted, either to import into their own, or to carry to some other foreign country. They remonstrated, therefore, against this prohibition as hurtful to trade.

They represented, first, that the exportation of gold and silver, in order to purchase foreign goods, did not always diminish the quantity of those metals in the kingdom; that, on the contrary, it might frequently increase the quantity; because, if the consumption of foreign goods was not thereby increased in the country, those goods might be re-exported to foreign countries, and being there sold for a large profit, might bring back much more treasure than was originally sent out to purchase them. Mr. Mun* compares this operation of foreign trade to the seedtime and harvest of agriculture.…

They represented, secondly, that this prohibition could not hinder the exportation of gold and silver, which, on account of the smallness of their bulk in proportion to their value, could easily be smuggled abroad. That this exportation could only be prevented by a proper attention to what they called the balance of trade. That when the country exported to a greater value than it imported, a balance became due to it from foreign nations, which was necessarily paid to it in gold and silver, and thereby increased the quantity of those metals in the kingdom. But that when it imported to a greater value than it exported, a contrary balance became due to foreign nations, which was necessarily paid to them in the same manner, and thereby diminished that quantity. That in this case, to

---

* Thomas Mun (1571–1641), one of the directors of the British East India Company.

prohibit the exportation of those metals, could not prevent it, but only, by making it more dangerous, render it more expensive. . . .

Those arguments were partly solid and partly sophistical. They were solid, so far as they asserted that the exportation of gold and silver in trade might frequently be advantageous to the country. They were solid, too, in asserting that no prohibition could prevent their exportation, when private people found any advantage in exporting them. But they were sophistical, in supposing, that either to preserve or to augment the quantity of those metals required more the attention of government, than to preserve or to augment the quantity of any other useful commodities, which the freedom of trade, without any such attention, never fails to supply in the proper quantity. . . .

Such as they were, however, those arguments convinced the people to whom they were addressed. They were addressed by merchants to parliaments and to the councils of princes, to nobles, and to country gentlemen; by those who were supposed to understand trade, to those who were conscious to themselves that they knew nothing about the matter. That foreign trade enriched the country, experience demonstrated to the nobles and country gentlemen, as well as to the merchants; but how, or in what manner, none of them well knew. The merchants knew perfectly in what manner it enriched themselves, it was their business to know it. But to know in what manner it enriched the country was no part of their business. The subject never came into their consideration, but when they had occasion to apply to their country for some change in the laws relating to foreign trade. It then became necessary to say something about the beneficial effects of foreign trade, and the manner in which those effects were obstructed by the laws as they then stood. To the judges who were to decide the business, it appeared a most satisfactory account of the matter, when they were told that foreign trade brought money into the country, but that the laws in question hindered it from bringing so much as it otherwise would do.

Those arguments . . . produced the wished-for effect. The prohibition of exporting gold and silver was, in France and England, confined to the coin of those respective countries. The exportation of foreign coin and of bullion was made free. In Holland, and in some other places, this liberty was extended even to the coin of the country. The attention of government was turned away from guarding against the exportation of gold and silver, to watch over the balance of trade, as the only cause which could occasion any augmentation or diminution of those metals. From one fruitless care, it was turned away to another care much more intricate, much more embarrassing, and just equally fruitless. The title of Mun's book, *England's Treasure in Foreign Trade*, became a fundamental maxim in the political economy, not of England only, but of all other commercial countries. The inland or home trade, the most important of all, the trade in which an equal capital affords the greatest revenue, and creates the greatest employment to the people of the country, was considered as subsidiary only to foreign trade. It neither brought money into the country, it was said, nor carried any out of it. The country, therefore, could never become either richer or poorer by means of it, except so far as its prosperity or decay might indirectly influence the state of foreign trade.

A country that has no mines of its own must undoubtedly draw its gold and silver from foreign countries, in the same manner as one that has no vineyards of its own must draw its wines. It does not seem necessary, however, that the attention of government should be more turned towards the one than towards the other object. A country that has wherewithal to buy wine, will always get the wine which it has occasion for; and a country that has wherewithal to buy gold and silver, will never be in want of those metals. They are to be bought for a certain price, like all other commodities; and as they are the price of all other commodities, so all other commodities are the price of those metals. We trust, with perfect security, that the freedom of trade, without any attention of government, will always supply us with the wine which we have occasion for; and we may trust, with equal security, that it will always supply us with all the gold and silver which we can afford to purchase or to employ, either in circulating our commodities or in other uses. . . .

... The attention of government never was so unnecessarily employed, as when directed to watch over the preservation or increase of the quantity of money in any country.

No complaint, however, is more common than that of a scarcity of money. Money, like wine, must always be scarce with those who have neither wherewithal to buy it, nor credit to borrow it. Those who have either will seldom be in want either of the money, or of the wine which they have occasion for. This complaint, however, of the scarcity of money, is not always confined to improvident spendthrifts. It is sometimes general through a whole mercantile town and the country in its neighborhood. Over-trading is the common cause of it. Sober men, whose projects have been disproportioned to their capitals, are as likely to have neither wherewithal to buy money, nor credit to borrow it, as prodigals, whose expense has been disproportioned to their revenue. Before their projects can be brought to bear, their stock is gone, and their credit with it. They run about everywhere to borrow money, and everybody tells them that they have none to lend. Even such general complaints of the scarcity of money do not always prove that the usual number of gold and silver pieces are not circulating in the country, but that many people want those pieces who have nothing to give for them.

When the profits of trade happen to be greater than ordinary, over-trading becomes a general error, both among great and small dealers. They do not always send more money abroad than usual, but they buy upon credit, both at home and abroad, an unusual quantity of goods, which they send to some distant market, in hopes that the returns will come in before the demand for payment. The demand comes before the returns, and they have nothing at hand with which they can either purchase money or give solid security for borrowing. It is not any scarcity of gold and silver, but the difficulty which such people find in borrowing, and which their creditors find in getting payment, that occasions the general complaint of the scarcity of money....*

The gold and silver which can properly be considered as accumulated, or stored up in any country, may be distinguished into three parts; first, the circulating money; secondly, the plate of private families; and, last of all, the money which may have been collected by many years parsimony, and laid up in the treasury of the prince....

... The last French war cost Great Britain upwards of ninety millions, including not only the seventy-five millions of new debt that was contracted, but the additional two shillings in the pound land tax, and what was annually borrowed of the sinking fund. More than two-thirds of this expense were laid out in distant countries; in Germany, Portugal, America, in the ports

---

* See Introduction, page 53, for discussion. Smith misses the role of too easy money leading to tight money.

of the Mediterranean, in the East and West Indies. The kings of England had no accumulated treasure. We never heard of any extraordinary quantity of plate being melted down. The circulating gold and silver of the country had not been supposed to exceed eighteen millions. Since the late recoinage of the gold, however, it is believed to have been a good deal underrated. Let us suppose, therefore, according to the most exaggerated computation which I remember to have either seen or heard of, that, gold and silver together, it amounted to thirty millions. Had the war been carried on by means of our money, the whole of it must, even according to this computation, have been sent out and returned again, at least twice in a period of between six and seven years. . . .

Besides the three sorts of gold and silver above mentioned, there is in all great commercial countries a good deal of bullion alternately imported and exported, for the purposes of foreign trade. This bullion, as it circulates among different commercial countries, in the same manner as the national coin circulates in every country, may be considered as the money of the great mercantile republic. The national coin receives its movement and direction from the commodities circulated within the precincts of each particular country; the money in the mercantile republic, from those circulated between different countries. Both are employed in facilitating exchanges, the one between different individuals of the same, the other between those of different nations. Part of this money of the great mercantile republic may have been, and probably was, employed in carrying on the late war. In time of a general war, it is natural to suppose that a movement and direction should be impressed upon it, different from what it usually follows in profound peace, that it should circulate more about the seat of the war, and be more employed in purchasing there, and in the neighboring countries, the pay and provisions of the different armies. But whatever part of this money of the mercantile republic Great Britain may have annually employed in this manner, it must have been annually purchased, either with British commodities, or with something else that had been purchased with them; which still brings us back to commodities, to the annual produce of the land and labor of the country, as the ultimate resources which enabled us to carry on the war. . . .

The importation of gold and silver is not the principal, much less the sole benefit, which a nation derives from its foreign trade. Between whatever places foreign trade is carried on, they all of them derive two distinct benefits from it. It carries out that surplus part of the produce of their land and labor for which there is no demand among them, and brings back in return for it something else for which there is a demand. It gives a value to their superfluities, by exchanging them for something else, which may satisfy a part of their wants and increase their enjoyments. By means of it, the narrowness of the home market does not hinder the division of labor in any particular branch of art or manufacture from being carried to the highest perfection. By opening a more extensive market for whatever part of the produce of their labor may exceed the home consumption, it encourages them to improve its productive power, and to augment its annual produce to the utmost, and thereby to increase the real revenue and wealth of the society. These great and important services foreign trade is continually occupied in performing to all the different countries between which it is carried on. They all derive great benefit from it, though that in which the merchant resides generally derives the greatest, as he is generally more employed in supplying the wants, and carrying out the superfluities of his own, than of any other particular country. To import the gold and silver which may be wanted into the countries which have no mines, is, no doubt, a part of the business of foreign commerce. It is, however, a most insignificant part of it. A country which carried on foreign trade merely upon this account could scarce have occasion to freight a ship in a century.

It is not by the importation of gold and silver that the discovery of America has enriched Europe. By the abundance of the American mines, those metals have become cheaper. A service of plate can now be purchased for about a third part of the corn, or a third part of the labor, which it would have cost in the fifteenth century. . . . The cheapness of gold and silver renders those metals rather less fit for the purposes of money than they were before. In order to make the same purchases, we must load ourselves with a greater quantity of them, and carry about a shilling in our pocket, where a groat would have done before. . . . The discovery of America, however, certainly made a most essential . . . [change in the State of Europe]. By opening a new and inexhaustible market to all the commodities of Europe, it gave occasion to new divisions of labor and improvements of art, which in the narrow circle of the ancient commerce could never have taken place, for want of a market to take off the greater part of their produce. The productive powers of labor were improved, and its produce increased in all the different countries of Europe, and together with it the real revenue and wealth of the inhabitants. The commodities of Europe were almost all new to America, and many of those of America were new to Europe. A new set of exchanges, therefore, began to take place, which had never been thought of before, and which should naturally have proved as advantageous to the new, as it certainly did to the old continent. The savage injustice of the Europeans rendered an event, which ought to have been beneficial to all, ruinous and destructive to several of those unfortunate countries.

The discovery of a passage to the East Indies by the Cape of Good Hope, which happened much about the same time, opened perhaps a still more extensive range to foreign commerce, than even that of America, notwithstanding the greater distance. There were but two nations in America, in any respect, superior to the savages, and these were destroyed almost as soon as discovered. The rest were mere savages. But the empires of China, Indostan, Japan, as well as several others in the East Indies, without having richer mines of gold or silver, were, in every other respect, much richer, better cultivated, and more advanced in all arts and manufactures, than either Mexico or Peru, even though we should credit, what plainly deserves no credit, the exaggerated accounts of the Spanish writers concerning the ancient state of those empires. But rich and civilized nations can always exchange to a much greater value with one another, than with savages and barbarians. Europe, however, has hitherto derived much less advantage from its commerce with the East Indies, than from that with America.

The Portuguese monopolized the East India trade to themselves for about a century; and it was only indirectly, and through them, that the other nations of Europe could either send out or receive any goods from that country. When the Dutch, in the beginning of the last century, began to encroach upon them, they vested their whole East India commerce in an exclusive company. The English, French, Swedes, and Danes, have all followed their example; so that no great nation of Europe has ever yet had the benefit of a free commerce to the East Indies. No other reason need be assigned why it has never been so advantageous as the trade to America, which, between almost every nation of Europe and its own colonies, is free to all its subjects. The exclusive privileges of those East India companies, their great riches, the great favor and protection which these have procured them from their respective governments, have excited much envy against them. This envy has frequently represented their trade as altogether pernicious, on account of the great quantities of silver which it every year exports from the countries from which it is carried on. The parties concerned have replied, that their trade by this continual exportation of silver, might indeed tend to impoverish Europe in general, but not the particular country from which it was carried on; because, by the exportation of a part of the returns to other European countries, it annually brought home a much greater quantity of that metal than it carried out. Both the objection and the reply are founded in the popular notion which I have been just now examining. It is therefore unnecessary to say anything further about either.

By the annual exportation of silver to the East Indies, plate is probably somewhat dearer in Europe than it otherwise might have been; and coined silver probably purchases a larger quantity both of labor and commodities. The former of these two effects is a very small loss, the latter a very small advantage; both too insignificant to deserve any part of the public attention. The trade to the East Indies, by opening a market to the commodities of Europe, or, what comes nearly to the same thing, to the gold and silver which is purchased with those commodities, must necessarily tend to increase the annual production of European commodities, and consequently the real wealth and revenue of Europe. That it has hitherto increased them so little, is probably owing to the restraints which it everywhere labors under.

I thought it necessary, though at the hazard of being tedious, to examine at full length this popular notion, that wealth consists in money or in gold and silver. Money, in common language, as I have already observed, frequently signifies wealth; and this ambiguity of expression has rendered this popular notion so familiar to us, that even they who are convinced of its absurdity, are very apt to forget their own principles, and, in the course of their reasonings, to take it for granted as a certain and undeniable truth. Some of the best English writers upon commerce set out with observing, that the wealth of a country consists, not in its gold and silver only, but in its lands, houses, and consumable goods of all different kinds. In the course of their reasonings, however, the lands, houses, and consumable goods, seem to slip out of their memory; and the strain of their argument frequently supposes that all wealth consists in gold and silver, and that to multiply those metals is the great object of national industry and commerce.

The two principles being established, however, that wealth consisted in gold and silver, and that those metals could be brought into a country which had no mines, only by the balance of trade, or by exporting to a greater value than it imported; it necessarily became the great object of political economy to diminish as much as possible the importation of foreign goods for home consumption, and to increase as much as possible the exportation of the produce of domestic industry. Its two great engines for enriching the country, therefore, were restraints upon importation, and encouragement to exportation.

The restraints upon importation were of two kinds.

- First, restraints upon the importation of such foreign goods for home consumption as could be produced at home, from whatever country they were imported.
- Secondly, restraints upon the importation of goods of almost all kinds, from those particular countries with which the balance of trade was supposed to be disadvantageous.

Those different restraints consisted sometimes in high duties, and sometimes in absolute prohibitions.

Exportation was encouraged sometimes by drawbacks, sometimes by bounties, sometimes by advantageous treaties of commerce with foreign states, and sometimes by the establishment of colonies in distant countries.

Drawbacks were given upon two different occasions. When the home manufactures were subject to any duty or excise, either the whole or a part of it was frequently drawn back upon their exportation; and when foreign goods liable to a duty were imported, in order to be exported again, either the whole or a part of this duty was sometimes given back upon such exportation.

Bounties were given for the encouragement, either of some beginning manufactures, or of such sorts of industry of other kinds as were supposed to deserve particular favor.

By advantageous treaties of commerce, particular privileges were procured in some foreign state for the goods and merchants of the country, beyond what were granted to those of other countries.

By the establishment of colonies in distant countries, not only particular privileges, but a monopoly was frequently procured for the goods and merchants of the country which established them.

The two sorts of restraints upon importation above mentioned, together with these four encouragements to exportation, constitute the six principal means by which the commercial system proposes to increase the quantity of gold and silver in any country, by turning the balance of trade in its favor. I shall consider each of them in a particular chapter, and, without taking much farther notice of their supposed tendency to bring money into the country, I shall examine chiefly what are likely to be the effects of each of them upon the annual produce of its industry. . . .

## Chapter Two

# Of Restraints upon Importation from Foreign Countries of Such Goods as Can Be Produced at Home

B Y RESTRAINING, EITHER by high duties, or by absolute prohibitions, the importation of such goods from foreign countries as can be produced at home, the monopoly of the home market is more or less secured to the domestic industry employed in producing them. Thus the prohibition of importing either live cattle or salt provisions* from foreign countries,

---

* "Salt provisions" refers to salted meat.

secures to the graziers of Great Britain the monopoly of the home market for butcher's meat. The high duties upon the importation of corn, which, in times of moderate plenty, amount to a prohibition, give a like advantage to the growers of that commodity. The prohibition of the importation of foreign woolen is equally favorable to the woolen manufacturers. The silk manufacture, though altogether employed upon foreign materials, has lately obtained the same advantage. The linen manufacture has not yet obtained it, but is making great strides towards it. Many other sorts of manufactures have, in the same manner obtained in Great Britain, either altogether, or very nearly, a monopoly against their countrymen. The variety of goods, of which the importation into Great Britain is prohibited, either absolutely, or under certain circumstances, greatly exceeds what can easily be suspected by those who are not well acquainted with the laws of the customs.

That this monopoly of the home market frequently gives great encouragement to that particular species of industry which enjoys it, and frequently turns towards that employment a greater share of both the labor and stock of the society than would otherwise have gone to it, cannot be doubted. But whether it tends either to increase the general industry of the society, or to give it the most advantageous direction, is not, perhaps, altogether so evident.

The general industry of the society can never exceed what the capital of the society can employ. As the number of workmen that can be kept in employment by any particular person must bear a certain proportion to his capital, so the number of those that can be continually employed by all the members of a great society must bear a certain proportion to the whole capital of the society, and never can exceed that proportion. No regulation of commerce can increase the quantity of industry in any society beyond what its capital can maintain. It can only divert a part of it into a direction into which it might not otherwise have gone; and it is by no means certain that this artificial direction is likely to be more advantageous to the society, than that into which it would have gone of its own accord.

Every individual is continually exerting himself to find out the most advantageous employment for whatever capital he can command. It is his own advantage, indeed, and not that of the society, which he has in view. But the study of his own advantage naturally, or rather necessarily, leads him to prefer that employment which is most advantageous to the society.

First, every individual endeavors to employ his capital as near home as he can, and consequently as much as he can in the support of domestic industry, provided always that he can thereby obtain the ordinary, or not a great deal less than the ordinary profits of stock. . . .

. . . Upon equal or only nearly equal profits, therefore, every individual naturally inclines to employ his capital in the manner in which it is likely to afford the

greatest support to domestic industry, and to give revenue and employment to the greatest number of people
of his own country.

Secondly, every individual who employs his capital in the support of domestic industry necessarily
endeavors so to direct that industry, that its produce
may be of the greatest possible value.

The produce of industry is what it adds to the subject or materials upon which it is employed. In proportion as the value of this produce is great or small,
so will likewise be the profits of the employer. But it
is only for the sake of profit that any man employs a
capital in the support of industry; and he will always,
therefore, endeavor to employ it in the support of that
industry of which the produce is likely to be of the
greatest value, or to exchange for the greatest quantity
either of money or of other goods.

But the annual revenue of every society is always
precisely equal to the exchangeable value of the whole
annual produce of its industry, or rather is precisely the
same thing with that exchangeable value. As every individual, therefore, endeavors as much as he can, both to
employ his capital in the support of domestic industry,
and so to direct that industry that its produce may be
of the greatest value; every individual necessarily labors
to render the annual revenue of the society as great as
he can. He generally, indeed, neither intends to promote the public interest, nor knows how much he is
promoting it. By preferring the support of domestic to

that of foreign industry, he intends only his own security; and by directing that industry in such a manner as its produce may be of the greatest value, he intends only his own gain; and he is in this, as in many other cases, led by an invisible hand to promote an end which was no part of his intention. Nor is it always the worse for the society that it was no part of it. By pursuing his own interest, he frequently promotes that of the society more effectually than when he really intends to promote it. I have never known much good done by those who affected to trade for the public good. It is an affectation, indeed, not very common among merchants, and very few words need be employed in dissuading them from it.

What is the species of domestic industry which his capital can employ, and of which the produce is likely to be of the greatest value, every individual, it is evident, can in his local situation judge much better than any statesman or lawgiver can do for him. The statesman, who should attempt to direct private people in what manner they ought to employ their capitals, would not only load himself with a most unnecessary attention, but assume an authority which could safely be trusted, not only to no single person, but to no council or senate whatever, and which would nowhere be so dangerous as in the hands of a man who had folly and presumption enough to fancy himself fit to exercise it.

To give the monopoly of the home market to the produce of domestic industry, in any particular art or manufacture, is in some measure to direct private people in what manner they ought to employ their capitals, and must in almost all cases be either a useless or a hurtful regulation. If the produce of domestic can be brought there as cheap as that of foreign industry, the regulation is evidently useless. If it cannot, it must generally be hurtful. It is the maxim of every prudent master of a family, never to attempt to make at home what it will cost him more to make than to buy. The tailor does not attempt to make his own shoes, but buys them of the shoemaker. The shoemaker does not attempt to make his own clothes, but employs a tailor. The farmer attempts to make neither the one nor the other, but employs those different artificers. All of them find it for their interest to employ their whole industry in a way in which they have some advantage over their neighbors, and to purchase with a part of its produce, or, what is the same thing, with the price of a part of it, whatever else they have occasion for.

What is prudence in the conduct of every private family can scarce be folly in that of a great kingdom. If a foreign country can supply us with a commodity cheaper than we ourselves can make it, better buy it of them with some part of the produce of our own industry, employed in a way in which we have some advantage. The general industry of the country being always in proportion to the capital which employs it, will not thereby be diminished, no more than that of the above-mentioned artificers; but only left to find out the way in which it can be employed with the greatest advantage. It is certainly not employed to the greatest advantage, when it is thus directed towards an object which it can buy cheaper than it can make. The value of its annual produce is certainly more or less diminished, when it is thus turned away from producing commodities evidently of more value than the commodity which it is directed to produce. According to the supposition, that commodity could be purchased from foreign countries cheaper than it can be made at home; it could therefore have been purchased with a part only of the commodities, or, what is the same thing, with a part only of the price of the commodities, which the industry employed by an equal capital would have produced at home, had it been left to follow its natural course. The industry of the country, therefore, is thus turned away from a more to a less advantageous employment; and the exchangeable value of its annual produce, instead of being increased, according to the intention of the lawgiver, must necessarily be diminished by every such regulation.

By means of such regulations, indeed, a particular manufacture may sometimes be acquired sooner than it could have been otherwise, and after a certain time may be made at home as cheap, or cheaper, than in the foreign country. But though the industry of the society may be thus carried with advantage into a particular channel sooner than it could have been otherwise, it will by no means follow that the sum-total, either of its industry, or of its revenue, can ever be augmented by any such regulation. The industry of the society can augment only in proportion as its capital augments, and its capital can augment only in proportion to what can be gradually saved out of its revenue. But the immediate effect of every such regulation is to diminish its revenue; and what diminishes its revenue is certainly not very likely to augment its capital faster than it would have augmented of its own accord, had both capital and industry been left to find out their natural employments.

Though, for want of such regulations, the society should never acquire the proposed manufacture, it would not upon that account necessarily be the poorer in any one period of its duration. In every period of its duration its whole capital and industry might still have been employed, though upon different objects, in the manner that was most advantageous at the time. In every period its revenue might have been the greatest which its capital could afford, and both capital and revenue might have been augmented with the greatest possible rapidity.

The natural advantages which one country has over another, in producing particular commodities, are sometimes so great, that it is acknowledged by all the world to be in vain to struggle with them. By means of glasses, hot-beds, and hot-walls, very good grapes can be raised in Scotland, and very good wine, too, can be made of them, at about thirty times the expense for which at least equally good can be brought from foreign countries. Would it be a reasonable law to prohibit the importation of all foreign wines, merely to encourage the making of claret and Burgundy in Scotland? But if there would be a manifest absurdity in turning towards any employment thirty times more of the capital and industry of the country than would be necessary to purchase from foreign countries an equal quantity of the commodities wanted, there must be an absurdity, though not altogether so glaring, yet exactly of the same kind, in turning towards any such employment a thirtieth, or even a three hundredth part more of either. Whether the advantages which one country has over another be natural or acquired is in this respect of no consequence. As long as the one country has those advantages, and the other wants them, it will always be more advantageous for the latter rather to buy of the former than to make. It is an acquired advantage only, which one artificer has over his neighbor, who exercises another trade; and yet they both find it more advantageous to buy of one another, than to make what does not belong to their particular trades.

Merchants and manufacturers are the people who derive the greatest advantage from this monopoly of the home market The prohibition of the importation of foreign cattle and of salt provisions, together with the high duties upon foreign corn, which in times of moderate plenty amount to a prohibition, are not near so advantageous to the graziers and farmers of Great

Britain, as other regulations of the same kind are to its merchants and manufacturers. Manufactures, those of the finer kind especially, are more easily transported from one country to another than corn or cattle. It is in the fetching and carrying manufactures, accordingly, that foreign trade is chiefly employed. In manufactures, a very small advantage will enable foreigners to undersell our own workmen, even in the home market. It will require a very great one to enable them to do so in the rude produce of the soil. If the free importation of foreign manufactures were permitted, several of the home manufactures would probably suffer, and some of them perhaps go to ruin altogether, and a considerable part of the stock and industry at present employed in them, would be forced to find out some other employment. But the freest importation of the rude produce of the soil could have no such effect upon the agriculture of the country. . . .

Even the free importation of foreign corn could very little affect the interest of the farmers of Great Britain. Corn is a much more bulky commodity than butcher's meat. A pound of wheat at a penny is as dear as a pound of butcher's meat at four pence. The small quantity of foreign corn imported even in times of the greatest scarcity, may satisfy our farmers that they can have nothing to fear from the freest importation. The average quantity imported, one year with another, amounts only, according to the very well informed author of the Tracts upon the corn trade, to twenty-three thousand seven hundred and twenty-weight quarters of all sorts of grain, and does not exceed the five hundredth and seventy-one part of the annual consumption. But as the bounty upon corn occasions a greater exportation in years of plenty, so it must, of consequence, occasion a greater importation in years of scarcity, than in the actual state of tillage would otherwise take place. By means of it, the plenty of one year does not compensate the scarcity of another; and as the average quantity exported is necessarily augmented by it, so must likewise, in the actual state of tillage, the average quantity imported. If there were no bounty, as less corn would be exported, suit is probable that, one year with another, less would be imported than at present. The corn merchants, the fetchers and carriers of corn between Great Britain and foreign countries, would have much less employment, and might suffer considerably; but the country gentlemen and farmers could suffer very little. It is in the corn merchants, accordingly, rather than the country gentlemen and farmers, that I have observed the greatest anxiety for the renewal and continuation of the bounty.

Country gentlemen and farmers are, to their great honor, of all people, the least subject to the wretched spirit of monopoly. The undertaker of a great manufactory is sometimes alarmed if another work of the same kind is established within twenty miles of him; the Dutch undertaker of the woolen manufacture at Abbeville, stipulated that no work of the same kind should be established within thirty leagues of that city. Farmers and country gentlemen, on the contrary, are generally disposed rather to promote, than to obstruct, the cultivation and improvement of their neighbors farms and estates. They have no secrets, such as those of the greater part of manufacturers, but are generally rather fond of communicating to their neighbors, and of extending as far as possible any new practice which they may have found to be advantageous. "*Pius quaestus,*" says old Cato, "*stabilissimusque, minimeque invidiosus; minimeque male cogitantes sunt, qui in eo studio occupati sunt.*"* Country gentlemen and farmers, dispersed in different parts of the country, cannot so easily combine as merchants and manufacturers, who being collected into towns, and accustomed to that exclusive corporation spirit which prevails in them, naturally endeavor to obtain, against all their countrymen, the same exclusive privilege which they generally possess against the inhabitants of their respective towns. They accordingly seem to have been the original inventors of those restraints upon the importation of foreign goods, which secure to them the monopoly of the home market. It was probably in imitation of them, and to put themselves upon a level with those who, they found, were disposed to oppress them, that the country gentlemen

---

* "[Farming is] the most stable income and the least subject to envy; and those occupied in this pursuit are the least duplicitous."

and farmers of Great Britain so far forgot the generosity which is natural to their station, as to demand the exclusive privilege of supplying their countrymen with corn and butcher's meat. They did not, perhaps, take time to consider how much less their interest could be affected by the freedom of trade, than that of the people whose example they followed.

To prohibit, by a perpetual law, the importation of foreign corn and cattle, is in reality to enact, that the population and industry of the country shall, at no time, exceed what the rude produce of its own soil can maintain.

There seem, however, to be two cases, in which it will generally be advantageous to lay some burden upon foreign, for the encouragement of domestic industry.

The first is, when some particular sort of industry is necessary for the defense of the country. The defense of Great Britain, for example, depends very much upon the number of its sailors and shipping. The act of navigation, therefore, very properly endeavors to give the sailors and shipping of Great Britain the monopoly of the trade of their own country, in some cases, by absolute prohibitions, and in others, by heavy burdens upon the shipping of foreign countries. . . .

When the act of navigation was made, though England and Holland were not actually at war, the most violent animosity subsisted between the two nations. It had begun during the government of the long parliament, which first framed this act, and it broke out soon after in the Dutch wars, during that of the Protector and of Charles II. It is not impossible, therefore, that some of the regulations of this famous act may have proceeded from national animosity. They are as wise, however, as if they had all been dictated by the most deliberate wisdom. National animosity, at that particular time, aimed at the very same object which the most deliberate wisdom would have recommended, the diminution of the naval power of Holland, the only naval power which could endanger the security of England. . . .

The second case, in which it will generally be advantageous to lay some burden upon foreign for the encouragement of domestic industry, is when some tax is imposed at home upon the produce of the latter. In this case, it seems reasonable that an equal tax should be imposed upon the like produce of the former. This would not give the monopoly of the borne market to domestic industry, nor turn towards a particular employment a greater share of the stock and labor of the country, than what would naturally go to it. It would only hinder any part of what would naturally go to it from being turned away by the tax into a less natural direction, and would leave the competition between foreign and domestic industry, after the tax, as nearly as possible upon the same footing as before it. In Great Britain, when any such tax is laid upon the produce of domestic industry, it is usual, at the same time, in order to stop the clamorous complaints of our merchants and manufacturers, that they will be undersold at home, to lay a much heavier duty upon the importation of all foreign goods of the same kind. . . .

. . . Every commodity, therefore, which is the produce of domestic industry, though not immediately taxed itself, becomes dearer in consequence of such taxes, because the labor which produces it becomes so. Such taxes, therefore, are really equivalent, they say, to a tax upon every particular commodity produced at home. In order to put domestic upon the same footing with foreign industry, therefore, it becomes necessary, they think, to lay some duty upon every foreign commodity, equal to this enhancement of the price of the home commodities with which it can come into competition.

Whether taxes upon the necessaries of life, such as those in Great Britain upon soap, salt, leather, candles, etc. necessarily raise the price of labor, and consequently that of all other commodities, I shall consider hereafter, when I come to treat of taxes. Supposing, however, in the meantime, that they have this effect, and they have it undoubtedly, . . . would be impossible . . . to proportion, with any tolerable exactness, the tax of every foreign, to the enhancement of the price of every home commodity.

. . . Taxes upon the necessaries of life have nearly the same effect upon the circumstances of the people as a poor soil and a bad climate. Provisions are thereby rendered dearer, in the same manner as if it required extraordinary labor and expense to raise them. As, in the natural scarcity arising from soil and climate, it would be absurd to direct the people in what manner they ought to employ their capitals and industry, so is it likewise in the artificial scarcity arising from such taxes. To be left to accommodate, as well as they could, their industry to their situation, and to find out those employments in which, notwithstanding their unfavorable circumstances, they might have some advantage either in the home or in the foreign market, is what, in both cases, would evidently be most for their advantage. To lay a new tax upon them, because they are already overburdened with taxes, and because they already pay too dear for the necessaries of life, to make them likewise pay too dear for the greater part of other commodities, is certainly a most absurd way of making amends.

Such taxes, when they have grown up to a certain height, are a curse equal to the barrenness of the earth, and the inclemency of the heavens, and yet it is in the richest and most industrious countries that they have been most generally imposed. No other countries could support so great a disorder. As the strongest bodies only can live and enjoy health under an unwholesome regimen, so the nations only, that in every sort of industry have the greatest natural and acquired advantages, can subsist and prosper under such taxes. Holland is the country in Europe in which they abound most, and which, from peculiar circumstances, continues to prosper, not by means of them, as has been most absurdly supposed, but in spite of them.

As there are two cases in which it will generally be advantageous to lay some burden upon foreign for the encouragement of domestic industry, so there are two others in which it may sometimes be a matter of deliberation, in the one, how far it is proper to continue the free importation of certain foreign goods; and, in the other, how far, or in what manner, it may be proper to restore that free importation, after it has been for some time interrupted.

The case in which it may sometimes be a matter of deliberation how far it is proper to continue the free importation of certain foreign goods, is when some foreign nation restrains, by high duties or prohibitions, the importation of some of our manufactures into their country. Revenge, in this case, naturally dictates retaliation, and that we should impose the like duties and prohibitions upon the importation of some or all of their manufactures into ours. Nations, accordingly, seldom fail to retaliate in this manner.

The French have been particularly forward to favor their own manufactures, by restraining the importation of such foreign goods as could come into competition with them. In this consisted a great part of the policy of Mr. Colbert,* who, notwithstanding his great abilities, seems in this case to have been imposed upon by the sophistry of merchants and manufacturers, who are

---

* Jean-Baptiste Colbert, controller-general of finances of France from 1665 to 1683. His policies were mercantilist and thus represented what Smith was attacking.

always demanding a monopoly against their country-men. It is at present the opinion of the most intelligent men in France, that his operations of this kind have not been beneficial to his country. That minister, by the tariff of 1667, imposed very high duties upon a great number of foreign manufactures. Upon his refusing to moderate them in favor of the Dutch, they, in 1671, prohibited the importation of the wines, brandies, and manufactures of France. The war of 1672 seems to have been in part occasioned by this commercial dispute. The peace of Nimeguen put an end to it in 1678, by moderating some of those duties in favor of the Dutch, who in consequence took off their prohibition.

It was about the same time that the French and English began mutually to oppress each other's industry, by the like duties and prohibitions, of which the French, however, seem to have set the first example, The spirit of hostility which has subsisted between the two nations ever since, has hitherto hindered them from being moderated on either side. In 1697, the English prohibited the importation of bone lace, the manufacture of Flanders. The government of that country, at that time under the dominion of Spain, prohibited, in return, the importation of English woolens. In 1700, the prohibition of importing bone lace into England was taken off; upon condition that the importation of English woolens into Flanders should be put on the same footing as before.

There may be good policy in retaliations of this kind, when there is a probability that they will procure the repeal of the high duties or prohibitions complained of. The recovery of a great foreign market will generally more than compensate the transitory inconveniency of paying dearer during a short time for some sorts of goods. To judge whether such retaliations are likely to produce such an effect, does not, perhaps, belong so much to the science of a legislator, whose deliberations ought to be governed by general principles, which are always the same, as to the skill of that insidious and crafty animal vulgarly called a statesman or politician, whose councils are directed by the momentary fluctuations of affairs. When there is no probability that any such repeal can be procured, it seems a bad method of compensating the injury done to certain classes of our people, to do another injury ourselves, not only to those classes, but to almost all the other classes of them. When our neighbors prohibit some manufacture of ours, we generally prohibit, not only the same, for that alone would seldom affect them considerably, but some other manufacture of theirs. This may, no doubt, give encouragement to some particular class of workmen among ourselves, and, by excluding some of their rivals, may enable them to raise their price in the home market. Those workmen however, who suffered by our neighbors prohibition, will not be benefited by ours. On the contrary, they, and almost all the other classes of our citizens, will thereby be obliged to pay dearer than before for certain goods. Every such law, therefore, imposes a real tax upon the whole country, not in favor of that particular class of workmen who were injured by our neighbors' prohibitions, but of some other class.

The case in which it may sometimes be a matter of deliberation, how far, or in what manner, it is proper to restore the free importation of foreign goods, after it has been for some time interrupted, is when particular manufactures, by means of high duties or prohibitions upon all foreign goods which can come into competition with them, have been so far extended as to employ a great multitude of hands. Humanity may in this case require that the freedom of trade should be restored only by slow gradations, and with a good deal of reserve and circumspection. Were those high duties and prohibitions taken away all at once, cheaper foreign goods of the same kind might be poured so fast into the home market, as to deprive all at once many thousands of our people of their ordinary employment and means of subsistence. The disorder which this would occasion might no doubt be very considerable. It would in all probability, however, be much less than is commonly imagined, for the two following reasons.

First, all those manufactures of which any part is commonly exported to other European countries without a bounty, could be very little affected by the freest importation of foreign goods. Such manufactures must be sold as cheap abroad as any other foreign goods of the same quality and kind, and consequently must be sold cheaper at home. They would still, therefore, keep possession of the home market; and though a capricious man of fashion might sometimes prefer foreign wares, merely because they were foreign, to cheaper and better goods of the same kind that were made at home, this folly could, from the nature of things, extend to so few, that it could make no sensible impression upon the general employment of the people. . . .

Secondly, though a great number of people should, by thus restoring the freedom of trade, be thrown all at once out of their ordinary employment and common method of subsistence, it would by no means follow that they would thereby be deprived either of employment or subsistence. By the reduction of the army and navy at the end of the late war, more than a hundred thousand soldiers and seamen, a number equal to what is employed in the greatest manufactures, were all at once thrown out of their ordinary employment; but though they no doubt suffered some inconveniency, they were not thereby deprived of all employment and subsistence. The greater part of the seamen, it is probable, gradually betook themselves to the merchant service as they could find occasion, and in the meantime both they and the soldiers were absorbed in the great mass of the people, and employed in a great variety of occupations. Not only no great convulsion, but no sensible disorder, arose from so great a change in the situation of more than a hundred thousand men, all accustomed to the use of arms, and many of them to rapine and plunder. The number of vagrants was scarce anywhere sensibly increased by it; even the wages of labor were not reduced by it in any occupation, so far as I have been able to learn, except in that of seamen in the merchant service. But if we compare together the habits of a soldier and of any sort of manufacturer, we shall find that those of the latter do not tend so much to disqualify him from being employed in a new trade, as those of the former from being employed in any. The manufacturer has always been accustomed to look for his subsistence from his labor only; the soldier to expect it from his pay. Application and industry have been familiar to the one; idleness and dissipation to the other. But it is surely much easier to change the direction of industry from one sort of labor to another, than to turn idleness and dissipation to any. . . .

Soldiers and seamen, indeed, when discharged from the king's service, are at liberty to exercise any trade within any town or place of Great Britain or Ireland. Let the same natural liberty of exercising what species of industry they please, be restored to all his Majesty's subjects, in the same manner as to soldiers and seamen; that is, break down the exclusive privileges of corporations, and repeal the statute of apprenticeship, both which are really encroachments upon natural Liberty, and add to those the repeal of the law of settlements, so that a poor workman, when thrown out of employment, either in one trade or in one place, may seek for it in another trade or in another place, without the fear either of a prosecution or of a removal; and neither the public nor the individuals will suffer much more from the occasional disbanding of some particular classes of manufacturers, than from that of the soldiers. Our manufacturers have no doubt great merit with their country, but they cannot have more than those who defend it with their blood, nor deserve to be treated with more delicacy.

To expect, indeed, that the freedom of trade should ever be entirely restored in Great Britain, is as absurd as to expect that an Oceana or Utopia should ever be established in it. Not only the prejudices of the public, but what is much more unconquerable, the private interests of many individuals, irresistibly oppose it. Were the officers of the army to oppose, with the same zeal and unanimity, any reduction in the number of forces, with which master manufacturers set themselves against every law that is likely to increase the number of their rivals in the home market; were the former to animate their soldiers, in the same manner as the latter inflame their workmen, to attack with violence and outrage the proposers of any such regulation; to attempt to reduce the army would be as dangerous as it has now become to attempt to diminish, in any respect, the monopoly which our manufacturers have obtained against us. This monopoly has so much increased the number of some particular tribes of them, that, like an overgrown standing army, they have become formidable to the government, and, upon many occasions, intimidate the legislature. The member of parliament who supports every proposal for strengthening this monopoly, is sure to acquire not only the reputation of understanding trade, but great popularity and influence with an order of men whose numbers and wealth render them of great importance. If he opposes them, on the contrary, and still more, if he has authority enough to be able to thwart them, neither the most acknowledged probity, nor the highest rank, nor the greatest public services, can protect him from the most infamous abuse and detraction, from personal insults, nor sometimes from real danger, arising from the insolent outrage of furious and disappointed monopolists.

The undertaker of a great manufacture, who, by the home markets being suddenly laid open to the competition of foreigners, should be obliged to abandon his trade, would no doubt suffer very considerably. That part of his capital which had usually been employed in purchasing materials, and in paying his workmen, might, without much difficulty, perhaps, find another employment; but that part of it which was fixed in workhouses, and in the instruments of trade, could scarce be disposed of without considerable loss. The equitable regard, therefore, to his interest, requires that changes of this kind should never be introduced suddenly, but slowly, gradually, and after a very long warning. The legislature, were it possible that its deliberations could be always directed, not by the clamorous importunity of partial interests, but by an extensive view of the general good, ought, upon this very account, perhaps, to be particularly careful, neither to establish any new monopolies of this kind, nor to extend further those which are already established. Every such regulation introduces some degree of real disorder into the constitution of the state, which it will be difficult afterwards to cure without occasioning another disorder.

How far it may be proper to impose taxes upon the importation of foreign goods, in order not to prevent their importation, but to raise a revenue for government, I shall consider hereafter when I come to treat of taxes. Taxes imposed with a view to prevent, or even to diminish importation, are evidently as destructive of the revenue of the customs as of the freedom of trade.

# Of the Extraordinary Restraints upon the Importation of Goods of Almost All Kinds, from Those Countries with Which the Balance Is Supposed to Be Disadvantageous

## Of the Unreasonableness of Those Restraints, Even upon the Principles of the Commercial System

To LAY EXTRAORDINARY restraints upon the importation of goods of almost all kinds, from those particular countries with which the balance of trade is supposed to be disadvantageous, is the second expedient by which the commercial system proposes to increase the quantity of gold and silver. Thus, in Great Britain, Silesia lawns may be imported for home consumption, upon paying certain duties; but French cambrics and lawns are prohibited to be imported, except into the port of London, there to be warehoused for exportation. Higher duties are imposed upon the wines of France than upon those of Portugal, or indeed of any other country. By what is called the impost 1692, a duty of five-and-twenty percent of the rate or value, was laid upon all French goods; while the goods of other nations were, the greater part of them, subjected to much lighter duties, seldom exceeding five percent. . . . Before the commencement of the present war, seventy-five percent may be considered as the lowest duty to which the greater part of the goods of the growth, produce, or manufacture of France, were liable. But upon the greater part of goods, those duties are equivalent to a prohibition. The French, in their turn, have, I believe, treated our goods and manufactures just as hardly; though I am not so well acquainted with the particular hardships which they have imposed upon them. Those mutual restraints have put an end to almost all fair commerce between the two nations; and smugglers are now the principal importers, either of British goods into France, or of French goods into Great Britain. The principles which I have been examining, in the foregoing chapter, took their origin from private interest and the spirit of monopoly; those which I am going to examine in this, from national prejudice and animosity. They are, accordingly, as might well be expected, still more unreasonable. They are so, even upon the principles of the commercial system.

First, though it were certain that in the case of a free trade between France and England, for example, the balance would be in favor of France, it would by no means follow that such a trade would be disadvantageous to England, or that the general balance of its whole trade would thereby be turned more against it. If the wines of France are better and cheaper than those of Portugal, or its linens than those of Germany, it would be more advantageous for Great Britain to purchase both the wine and the foreign linen which it had occasion for of France, than of Portugal and Germany. Though the value of the annual importations from France would thereby be greatly augmented, the value of the whole annual importations would be diminished, in proportion as the French goods of the same quality were cheaper than those of the other two countries. This would be the case, even upon the supposition that the whole French goods imported were to be consumed in Great Britain.

But, secondly, a great part of them might be re-exported to other countries, where, being sold with profit, they might bring back a return, equal in value, perhaps, to the prime cost of the whole French goods imported. . . .

Thirdly, and lastly, there is no certain criterion by which we can determine on which side what is called the balance between any two countries lies, or which of them exports to the greatest value. National prejudice and animosity, prompted always by the private interest of particular traders, are the principles which generally direct our judgment upon all questions concerning it. There are two criterions, however, which have frequently been appealed to upon such occasions, the customhouse books, and the course of exchange. The customhouse books, I think, it is now generally acknowledged, are a very uncertain criterion, on account of the inaccuracy of the valuation at which the greater part of goods are rated in them. The course of exchange is, perhaps, almost equally so.

. . . Though the ordinary course of exchange shall be allowed to be a sufficient indication of the ordinary state of debt and credit between any two places, it would not from thence follow, that the balance of trade was in favor of that place which had the ordinary state of debt and credit in its favor. The ordinary state of debt and credit between any two places is not always entirely regulated by the ordinary course of their dealings with one another, but is often influenced by that of the dealings of either with many other places. . . .

In the way, besides, in which the par of exchange has hitherto been computed, the ordinary course of exchange can afford no sufficient indication that the ordinary state of debt and credit is in favor of that country which seems to have, or which is supposed to have, the ordinary course of exchange in its favor; or, in other words, the real exchange may be, and in fact often is, so very different from the computed one, that, from the course of the latter, no certain conclusion can, upon many occasions, be drawn concerning that of the former.

When for a sum of money paid in England, containing, according to the standard of the English mint, a certain number of ounces of pure silver, you receive a bill for a sum of money to be paid in France, containing, according to the standard of the French mint, an equal number of ounces of pure silver, exchange is said to be at par between England and France. When you pay more, you are supposed to give a premium, and exchange is said to be against England, and in favor of France. When you pay less, you are supposed to get a premium, and exchange is said to be against France, and in favor of England.

But, first, we cannot always judge of the value of the current money of different countries by the standard of their respective mints. In some it is more, in others it is less worn, clipped, and otherwise degenerated from that standard. But the value of the current coin of every country, compared with that of any other country, is in proportion, not to the quantity of pure silver which it ought to contain, but to that which it actually does contain. Before the reformation of the silver coin in King William's time, exchange between England and Holland, computed in the usual manner, according to the standard of their respective mints, was five-and-twenty percent against England. But the value of the current coin of England, as we learn from Mr. Lowndes,* was at that time rather more than five-and-twenty percent below its standard value. The real exchange, therefore, may even at that time have been in favor of England, notwithstanding the computed exchange was so much against it; a smaller number of ounces of pure silver, actually paid in England, may have purchased a bill for a greater number of ounces of pure silver to be paid in Holland, and the man who was supposed to give, may in reality have got the premium. . . .

Secondly, in some countries the expense of coinage is defrayed by the government; in others, it is defrayed by the private people, who carry their bullion to the mint, and the government even derives some revenue from the coinage. In England it is defrayed by the government; and if you carry a pound weight of standard silver to the mint, you get back sixty-two shillings, containing a pound weight of the like standard silver. In France a duty of eight percent is deducted for the coinage, which not only defrays the expense of it, but affords a small revenue to the government. In England, as the coinage costs nothing, the current coin

---

* William Lowndes (1652–1724), Secretary to the Treasury of Great Britain under King William III and Queen Anne, and a Member of Parliament under William III, Anne and George I.

can never be much more valuable than the quantity of bullion which it actually contains. In France, the workmanship, as you pay for it, adds to the value, in the same manner as to that of wrought plate. A sum of French money, therefore, containing an equal weight of pure silver, is more valuable than a sum of English money containing an equal weight of pure silver, and must require more bullion, or other commodities, to purchase it. . . .

Thirdly, and lastly, in some places, as at Amsterdam, Hamburg, Venice, etc. foreign bills of exchange are paid in what they call bank money; while in others, as at London, Lisbon, Antwerp, Leghorn, etc. they are paid in the common currency of the country. . . . Supposing the current money of the two countries equally near to the standard of their respective mints, and that the one pays foreign bills in this common currency, while the other pays them in bank money, it is evident that the computed exchange may be in favor of that which pays in bank money, though the real exchange should be in favor of that which pays in current money; for the same reason that the computed exchange may be in favor of that which pays in better money, or in money nearer to its own standard, though the real exchange should be in favor of that which pays in worse. . . .

## *Part Two*

# Of the Unreasonableness of Those Extraordinary Restraints, upon Other Principles

In the foregoing part of this chapter, I have endeavored to show, even upon the principles of the commercial system, how unnecessary it is to lay extraordinary restraints upon the importation of goods from those countries with which the balance of trade is supposed to be disadvantageous.

Nothing, however, can be more absurd than this whole doctrine of the balance of trade, upon which, not only these restraints, but almost all the other regulations of commerce, are founded. When two places trade with one another, this doctrine supposes that, if the balance be even, neither of them either loses or gains; but if it leans in any degree to one side, that one of them loses, and the other gains, in proportion to its declension from the exact equilibrium. Both suppositions are false. A trade, which is forced by means of bounties and monopolies, may be, and commonly is, disadvantageous to the country in whose favor it is meant to be established, as I shall endeavor to show hereafter. But that trade which, without force or constraint, is naturally and regularly carried on between any two places, is always advantageous, though not always equally so, to both.

By advantage or gain, I understand, not the increase of the quantity of gold and silver, but that of the exchangeable value of the annual produce of the land and labor of the country, or the increase of the annual revenue of its inhabitants. . . .

There is not, probably, between any two countries, a trade which consists altogether in the exchange, either of native commodities on both sides, or of native commodities on one side, and of foreign goods on the other. Almost all countries exchange with one another, partly native and partly foreign goods. That country, however, in whose cargoes there is the greatest proportion of native, and the least of foreign goods, will always be the principal gainer. . . .

It is a losing trade, it is said, which a workman carries on with the alehouse; and the trade which a manufacturing nation would naturally carry on with a wine country, may be considered as a trade of the same nature. I answer, that the trade with the alehouse is not necessarily a losing trade. In its own nature it is just as advantageous as any other, though, perhaps, somewhat more liable to be abused. The employment of a brewer, and even that of a retailer of fermented liquors, are as necessary divisions of labor as any other. It will generally be more advantageous for a workman to buy of the brewer the quantity he has occasion for, than to brew it himself; and if he is a poor workman, it will generally be more advantageous for him to buy it by little and little of the retailer, than a large quantity of the brewer. He may no doubt buy too much of either, as he may of any other dealers in his neighborhood; of the butcher, if he is a glutton; or of the draper, if he affects to be a beau among his companions. It is advantageous to the great body of workmen, notwithstanding, that all these trades should be free, though this freedom may be abused in all of them, and is more likely to be so, perhaps, in some than in others.

Though individuals, besides, may sometimes ruin their fortunes by an excessive consumption of fermented liquors, there seems to be no risk that a nation should do so. Though in every country there are many people who spend upon such liquors more than they can afford, there are always many more who spend less. It deserves to be remarked, too, that if we consult experience, the cheapness of wine seems to be a cause, not of drunkenness, but of sobriety. The inhabitants of the wine countries are in general the soberest people of Europe; witness the Spaniards, the Italians, and the inhabitants of the southern provinces of France. People are seldom guilty of excess in what is their daily fare. Nobody affects the character of liberality and good fellowship, by being profuse of a liquor which is as cheap as small beer. On the contrary, in the countries which, either from excessive heat or cold, produce no grapes, and where wine consequently is dear and a rarity, drunkenness is a common vice, as among the northern nations, and all those who live between the tropics, the negroes, for example on the coast of

Guinea. When a French regiment comes from some of the northern provinces of France, where wine is somewhat dear, to be quartered in the southern, where it is very cheap, the soldiers, I have frequently heard it observed, are at first debauched by the cheapness and novelty of good wine; but after a few months residence, the greater part of them become as sober as the rest of the inhabitants.

Were the duties upon foreign wines, and the excises upon malt, beer, and ale, to be taken away all at once, it might, in the same manner, occasion in Great Britain a pretty general and temporary drunkenness among the middling and inferior ranks of people, which would probably be soon followed by a permanent and almost universal sobriety. At present, drunkenness is by no means the vice of people of fashion, or of those who can easily afford the most expensive liquors. A gentleman drunk with ale has scarce ever been seen among us. The restraints upon the wine trade in Great Britain, besides, do not so much seem calculated to hinder the people from going, if I may say so, to the alehouse, as from going where they can buy the best and cheapest liquor. They favor the wine trade of Portugal, and discourage that of France. The Portuguese, it is said, indeed, are better customers for our manufactures than the French, and should therefore be encouraged in preference to them. As they give us their custom, it is pretended we should give them ours. The sneaking arts of underling tradesmen are thus erected into political maxims for the conduct of a great empire; for it is the most underling tradesmen only who make it a rule to employ chiefly their own customers. A great trader purchases his goods always where they are cheapest and best, without regard to any little interest of this kind.

By such maxims as these, however, nations have been taught that their interest consisted in beggaring all their neighbors. Each nation has been made to look with an invidious eye upon the prosperity of all the nations with which it trades, and to consider their gain as its own loss. Commerce, which ought naturally to be, among nations as among individuals, a bond of union and friendship, has become the most fertile source of discord and animosity. The capricious ambition of kings and ministers has not, during the present and the preceding century, been more fatal to the repose of Europe, than the impertinent jealousy of merchants and manufacturers. The violence and injustice of the rulers of mankind is an ancient evil, for which, I am afraid, the nature of human affairs can scarce admit of a remedy. But the mean rapacity, the monopolizing spirit, of merchants and manufacturers, who neither are, nor ought to be, the rulers of mankind, though it cannot, perhaps, be corrected, may very easily be prevented from disturbing the tranquility of anybody but themselves.

That it was the spirit of monopoly which originally both invented and propagated this doctrine, cannot be doubted and they, who first taught it, were by no means such fools as they who believed it. In every country it always is, and must be, the interest of the great body of the people, to buy whatever they want of those who sell it cheapest. The proposition is so very manifest, that it seems ridiculous to take any pains to prove it; nor could it ever have been called in question, had not the interested sophistry of merchants and manufacturers confounded the common sense of mankind. Their interest is, in this respect, directly opposite to that of the great body of the people. As it is the interest of the freemen of a corporation to hinder the rest of the inhabitants from employing any workmen but themselves; so it is the interest of the merchants and manufacturers of every country to secure to themselves the monopoly of the home market. Hence, in Great Britain, and in most other European countries, the extraordinary duties upon almost all goods imported by alien merchants. Hence the high duties and prohibitions upon all those foreign manufactures which can come into competition with our own. Hence, too, the extraordinary restraints upon the importation of almost all sorts of goods from those countries with which the balance of trade is supposed to be disadvantageous; that is, from those against whom national animosity happens to be most violently inflamed.

The wealth of neighboring nations, however, though dangerous in war and politics, is certainly advantageous in trade. In a state of hostility, it may enable our enemies to maintain fleets and armies superior to our own; but in a state of peace and commerce it must likewise enable them to exchange with us to a greater value, and to afford a better market, either for the immediate produce of our own industry, or for whatever is purchased with that produce. As a rich man is likely to be a better customer to the industrious people in his neighborhood, than a poor, so is likewise a rich nation. A rich man, indeed, who is himself a manufacturer, is a very dangerous neighbor to all those who deal in the same way. All the rest of the neighborhood, however, by far the greatest number, profit by the good market which his expense affords them. They even profit by his underselling the poorer workmen who deal in the same way with him. The manufacturers of a rich nation, in the same manner, may no doubt be very dangerous rivals to those of their neighbors. This very competition, however, is advantageous to the great body of the people, who profit greatly, besides, by the good market which the great expense of such a nation affords them in every other way. Private people, who want to make a fortune, never think of retiring to the remote and poor provinces of the country, but resort either to the capital, or to some of the great commercial towns. They know that where little wealth circulates, there is little to be got; but that where a great deal is in motion, some share of it may fall to them. The same maxims which would in this manner direct the common sense of one, or ten, or twenty individuals, should regulate the judgment of one, or ten, or twenty millions, and should make a whole nation regard the riches of its neighbors, as a probable cause and occasion for itself to acquire riches. A nation that would enrich itself by foreign trade is certainly most likely to do so, when its neighbors are all rich, industrious, and commercial nations. A great nation, surrounded on all sides by wandering savages and poor barbarians, might, no doubt, acquire riches by the cultivation of its own lands, and by its own interior commerce, but not by foreign trade. It seems to have been in this manner that the ancient Egyptians and the modern Chinese acquired their great wealth. The ancient Egyptians, it is said, neglected foreign commerce, and the modern Chinese, it is known, hold it in the utmost contempt, and scarce deign to afford it the decent protection of the laws. The modern maxims of foreign commerce, by aiming at the impoverishment of all our neighbors, so far as they are capable of producing their intended effect, tend to render that very commerce insignificant and contemptible.

It is in consequence of these maxims, that the commerce between France and England has, in both countries, been subjected to so many discouragements and restraints. If those two countries, however, were to consider their real interest, without either mercantile jealousy or national animosity, the commerce of France might be more advantageous to Great Britain than that of any other country, and, for the same reason, that of Great Britain to France. France is the nearest neighbor to Great Britain. . . . Between the parts of France and Great Britain most remote from one another, the returns might be expected, at least, once in the year; and even this trade would so far be at least equally advantageous, as the greater part of the other branches of our foreign European trade. It would be, at least, three times more advantageous than the boasted trade with our North American colonies, in which the returns were seldom made in less than three years, frequently not in less than four or five years. France, besides, is supposed to contain twenty-four millions of inhabitants. Our North American colonies were never supposed to contain more than three millions; and France is a much richer country than North America; though, on account of the more unequal distribution of riches, there is much more poverty and beggary in the one country than in the other. France, therefore, could afford a market at least eight times more extensive, and, on account of the superior frequency of the returns, four-and-twenty times more advantageous than that which our North American colonies ever afforded. The trade of Great Britain would be just as advantageous to France, and, in proportion to the wealth, population, and proximity of the respective countries, would have the same superiority over that which France carries on with her own colonies. Such is the very great difference between that trade which the wisdom of both nations has thought proper to discourage, and that which it has favored the most.

But the very same circumstances which would have rendered an open and free commerce between the two countries so advantageous to both have occasioned the principal obstructions to that commerce. . . . They are both rich and industrious nations; and the merchants and manufacturers of each dread the competition of the skill and activity of those of the other. Mercantile jealousy is excited, and both inflames, and is itself inflamed, by the violence of national animosity, and the traders of both countries have announced, with all the passionate confidence of interested falsehood, the certain ruin of each, in consequence of that unfavorable balance of trade, which, they pretend, would be the infallible effect of an unrestrained commerce with the other.

There is no commercial country in Europe, of which the approaching ruin has not frequently been foretold by the pretended doctors of this system, from all unfavorable balance of trade. After all the anxiety, however, which they have excited about this, after all the vain attempts of almost all trading nations to turn that balance in their own favor, and against their neighbors, it does not appear that any one nation in Europe has been, in any respect, impoverished by this cause. Every town and country, on the contrary, in proportion as they have opened their ports to all nations, instead of being ruined by this free trade, as the principles of the commercial system would lead us to expect, have been enriched by it. . . .

There is another balance, indeed, which has already been explained, very different from the balance of trade, and which, according as it happens to be either favorable or unfavorable, necessarily occasions the prosperity or decay of every nation. This is the balance of the annual produce and consumption. If the exchangeable value of the annual produce, it has already been observed, exceeds that of the annual consumption, the capital of the society must annually increase in proportion to this excess. The society in this case lives within its revenue; and what is annually saved out of its revenue, is naturally added to its capital, and employed so as to increase still further the annual produce. If the exchangeable value of the annual produce, on the contrary, falls short of the annual consumption, the capital of the society must annually decay in proportion to this deficiency. The expense of the society, in this case, exceeds its revenue, and necessarily encroaches upon its capital. Its capital, therefore, must necessarily decay, and, together with it, the exchangeable value of the annual produce of its industry.

This balance of produce and consumption is entirely different from what is called the balance of trade. It might take place in a nation which had no foreign trade, but which was entirely separated from all the world. It may take place in the whole globe of the earth, of which the wealth, population, and improvement, may be either gradually increasing or gradually decaying.

The balance of produce and consumption may be constantly in favor of a nation, though what is called the balance of trade be generally against it. A nation may import to a greater value than it exports for half a century, perhaps, together; the gold and silver which comes into it during all this time, may be all immediately sent out of it; its circulating coin may gradually decay, different sorts of paper money being substituted in its place, and even the debts, too, which it contracts in the principal nations with whom it deals, may be gradually increasing; and yet its real wealth, the exchangeable value of the annual produce of its lands and labor, may, during the same period, have been increasing in a much greater proportion. The state of our North American colonies, and of the trade which they carried on with Great Britain, before the commencement of the present disturbances, may serve as a proof that this is by no means an impossible supposition.

## Chapter Four

# Of Drawbacks

MERCHANTS AND MANUFACTURERS are not contented with the monopoly of the home market, but desire likewise the most extensive foreign sale for their goods. Their country has no jurisdiction in foreign nations, and therefore can seldom procure them any monopoly there. They are generally obliged, therefore, to content themselves with petitioning for certain encouragements to exportation.

Of these encouragements, what are called drawbacks seem to be the most reasonable. To allow the merchant to draw back upon exportation, either the whole, or a part of whatever excise or inland duty is imposed upon domestic industry, can never occasion the exportation of a greater quantity of goods than what would have been exported had no duty been imposed. Such encouragements do not tend to turn towards any particular employment a greater share of the capital of the country, than what would go to that employment of its own accord, but only to hinder the duty from driving away any part of that share to other employments. They tend not to overturn that balance which naturally establishes itself among all the various employments of the society, but to hinder it from being overturned by the duty. They tend not to destroy, but to preserve, what it is in most cases advantageous to preserve, the natural division and distribution of labor in the society. . . .

Drawbacks, however, it must always be understood, are useful only in those cases in which the goods, for the exportation of which they are given, are really exported to some foreign country, and not clandestinely re-imported into our own. That some drawbacks, particularly those upon tobacco, have frequently been abused in this manner, and have given occasion to many frauds, equally hurtful both to the revenue and to the fair trader, is well known.

## Chapter Five

# Of Bounties

**B**OUNTIES UPON EXPORTATION are, in Great Britain, frequently petitioned for, and sometimes granted, to the produce of particular branches of domestic industry. By means of them, our merchants and manufacturers, it is pretended, will be enabled to sell their goods as cheap as or cheaper than their rivals in the foreign market. A greater quantity, it is said, will thus be exported, and the balance of trade consequently turned more in favor of our own country. We cannot give our workmen a monopoly in the foreign, as we have done in the home market. We cannot force foreigners to buy their goods, as we have done our own countrymen. The next best expedient, it has been thought, therefore, is to pay them for buying. It is in this manner that the mercantile system proposes to enrich the whole country, and to put money into all our pockets, by means of the balance of trade.

Bounties, it is allowed, ought to be given to those branches of trade only which cannot be carried on without them. But . . . those trades only require bounties, in which the merchant is obliged to sell his goods for a price which does not replace to him his capital, together with the ordinary profit, or in which he is obliged to sell them for less than it really cost him to send them to market. The bounty is given in order to make up this loss, and to encourage him to continue, or, perhaps, to begin a trade, of which the expense is supposed to be greater than the returns, of which every operation eats up a part of the capital employed in it, and which is of such a nature, that if all other trades resembled it, there would soon be no capital left in the country. . . .

The effect of bounties, like that of all the other expedients of the mercantile system, can only be to force the trade of a country into a channel much less advantageous than that in which it would naturally run of its own accord. . . .

The corn bounty, it is to be observed, as well as every other bounty upon exportation, imposes two different taxes upon the people; first, the tax which they are obliged to contribute, in order to pay the bounty; and, secondly, the tax which arises from the advanced price of the commodity in the home market, and which, as the whole body of the people are purchasers of corn, must, in this particular commodity, be paid by the whole body of the people. In this particular commodity, therefore, this second tax is by much the heavier of the two. . . .

According to the very well informed author of the tracts upon the corn trade,* the average proportion of the corn exported to that consumed at home, is not more than that of one to thirty-one. For every five shillings therefore, which they contribute to the payment of the first tax, they must contribute six pounds four shillings to the payment of the second. So very heavy a tax upon the first necessary of life must either reduce the subsistence of the laboring poor or it must occasion some augmentation in their pecuniary wages, proportional to that in the pecuniary price of their subsistence. So far as it operates in the one way, it must reduce the ability of the laboring poor to educate and bring up their children, and must, so far, tend to restrain the population of the country. So far as it operates in the other, it must reduce the ability of the employers of the poor, to employ so great a number as they otherwise might do, and must so far tend to restrain the industry of the country. The extraordinary exportation of corn, therefore occasioned by the bounty, not only in every particular year diminishes the home, just as much as it extends the foreign market and consumption, but, by restraining the population and industry of the country, its final tendency is

---

* The author is referring to Charles Smith's *Three Tracts on the Corn Trade and Corn Laws* (1766).

to stint and restrain the gradual extension of the home market; and thereby, in the long run, rather to diminish than to augment the whole market and consumption of corn.

This enhancement of the money price of corn, however, it has been thought, by rendering that commodity more profitable to the farmer, must necessarily encourage its production.

I answer, that this might be the case, if the effect of the bounty was to raise the real price of corn, or to enable the farmer, with an equal quantity of it, to maintain a greater number of laborers in the same manner, whether liberal, moderate, or scanty, than other laborers are commonly maintained in his neighborhood. But neither the bounty, it is evident, nor any other human institution, can have any such effect. It is not the real, but the nominal price of corn, which can in any considerable degree be affected by the bounty. And though the tax, which that institution imposes upon the whole body of the people, may be very burdensome to those who pay it, it is of very little advantage to those who receive it. . . .

Though in consequence of the bounty . . . the farmer should be enabled to sell his corn for four shilling the bushel, instead of three and six pence and to pay his landlord a money rent proportional to this rise in the money price of his produce; yet if, in consequence of this rise in the price of corn, four shillings will purchase no more home made goods of any other kind than three and six pence would have done before, neither the circumstances of the farmer, nor those of the landlord, will be much mended by this change. The farmer will not be able to cultivate much better; the landlord will not be able to live much better. In the purchase of foreign commodities, this enhancement in the price of corn may give them some little advantage. In that of homemade commodities, it can give them none at all. And almost the whole expense of the farmer, and the far greater part even of that of the landlord, is in home-made commodities. . . .

It is the peculiar situation of Spain and Portugal, as proprietors of the mines, to be the distributors of gold and silver to all the other countries of Europe. Those metals ought naturally, therefore, to be somewhat cheaper in Spain and Portugal than in any other part of Europe. The difference, however, should be no more than the amount of the freight and insurance; and, on account of the great value and small bulk of those metals, their freight is no great matter, and their insurance is the same as that of any other goods of equal value. Spain and Portugal, therefore, could suffer very little from their peculiar situation, if they did not aggravate its disadvantages by their political institutions.

Spain by taxing, and Portugal by prohibiting, the exportation of gold and silver, load that exportation with the expense of smuggling, and raise the value of those metals in other countries so much more above what it is in their own, by the whole amount of this expense. . . .

The cheapness of gold and silver, or, what is the same thing, the dearness of all commodities, which is the necessary effect of this redundancy of the precious metals, discourages both the agriculture and manufactures of Spain and Portugal, and enables foreign nations to supply them with many sorts of rude, and with almost all sorts of manufactured produce, for a smaller quantity of gold and silver than what they themselves can either raise or make them for at home. The tax and prohibition operate in two different ways. They not only lower very much the value of the precious metals in Spain and Portugal, but by detaining there a certain quantity of those metals which would otherwise flow over other countries, they keep up their value in those other countries somewhat above what it otherwise would be, and thereby give those countries a double advantage in their commerce with Spain and Portugal....

Remove the tax and the prohibition, and as the quantity of gold and silver will diminish considerably in Spain and Portugal, so it will increase somewhat in other countries; and the value of those metals, their proportion to the annual produce of land and labor, will soon come to a level, or very near to a level, in all.... The gold and silver which would go abroad would not go abroad for nothing, but would bring back an equal value of goods of some kind or other. Those goods, too, would not be all matters of mere luxury and expense, to be consumed by idle people, who produce nothing in return for their consumption.

As the real wealth and revenue of idle people would not be augmented by this extraordinary exportation of gold and silver, so neither would their consumption be much augmented by it. Those goods would probably, the greater part of them, and certainly some part of them, consist in materials, tools, and provisions, for the employment and maintenance of industrious people, who would reproduce, with a profit, the full value of their consumption. A part of the dead stock of the society would thus be turned into active stock, and would put into motion a greater quantity of industry than had been employed before. The annual produce of their land and labor would immediately be augmented a little, and in a few years would probably be augmented a great deal; their industry being thus relieved from one of the most oppressive burdens which it at present labors under.

The bounty upon the exportation of corn necessarily operates exactly in the same way as this absurd policy of Spain and Portugal. Whatever be the actual state of tillage, it renders our corn somewhat dearer in the home market than it otherwise would be in that state, and somewhat cheaper in the foreign; and as the average money price of corn regulates, more or less, that of all other commodities, it lowers the value of silver considerably in the one, and tends to raise it a little in the other. It enables foreigners, the Dutch in particular, not only to eat our corn cheaper than they otherwise could do, but sometimes to eat it cheaper than even our own people can do upon the same occasions; as we are assured by an excellent authority, that of Sir Matthew Decker. It hinders our own workmen from furnishing their goods for so small a quantity of silver as they otherwise might do, and enables the Dutch to furnish theirs for a smaller. It tends to render our manufactures somewhat dearer in every market and theirs somewhat cheaper than they otherwise would be, and consequently to give their industry a double advantage over our own.

The bounty, as it raises in the home market, not so much the real, as the nominal price of our corn; as it augments, not the quantity of labor which a certain quantity of corn can maintain and employ, but only the quantity of silver which it will exchange for; it discourages our manufactures, without rendering any considerable service, either to our farmers or country gentlemen. It puts, indeed, a little more money into the pockets of both, and it will perhaps be somewhat difficult to persuade the greater part of them that this is not rendering them a very considerable service. But if this money sinks in its value, in the quantity of labor, provisions, and homemade commodities of all different kinds which it is capable of purchasing, as much as it rises in its quantity, the service will be little more than nominal and imaginary.

There is, perhaps, but one set of men in the whole commonwealth to whom the bounty either was or could be essentially serviceable. These were the corn merchants, the exporters and importers of corn. In years of plenty, the bounty necessarily occasioned a greater exportation than would otherwise have taken place; and by hindering the plenty of the one year from relieving the scarcity of another, it occasioned in years of scarcity a greater importation than would otherwise have been necessary. It increased the business of the corn merchant in both; and in the years of scarcity, it not only enabled him to import a greater quantity, but to sell it for a better price, and consequently with a greater profit, than he could otherwise have made, if the plenty of one year had not been more or less hindered from relieving the scarcity of another. It is in this set of men, accordingly, that I have observed the greatest zeal for the continuance or renewal of the bounty. . . .

Bounties upon the exportation of any homemade commodity are liable, first, to that general objection which may be made to all the different expedients of the mercantile system; the objection of forcing some part of the industry of the country into a channel less advantageous than that in which it would run of its own accord; and, secondly, to the particular objection of forcing it not only into a channel that is less advantageous, but into one that is actually disadvantageous; the trade which cannot be carried on but by means of a bounty being necessarily a losing trade. The bounty upon the exportation of corn is liable to this further objection, that it can in no respect promote the raising of that particular commodity of which it was meant to encourage the production. When our country gentlemen, therefore, demanded the establishment of the bounty, though they acted in imitation of our merchants and manufacturers, they did not act with that complete comprehension of their own interest, which commonly directs the conduct of those two other orders of people. They loaded the public revenue with a very considerable expense: they imposed a very heavy tax upon the whole body of the people; but they did not, in any sensible degree, increase the real value of their own commodity; and by lowering somewhat the real value of silver, they discouraged, in some degree, the general industry of the country, and, instead of advancing, retarded more or less the improvement of their own lands, which necessarily depend upon the general industry of the country.

To encourage the production of any commodity, a bounty upon production, one should imagine, would have a more direct operation than one upon exportation. It would, besides, impose only one tax upon the people, that which they must contribute in order to pay the bounty. Instead of raising, it would tend to lower the price of the commodity in the home market; and thereby, instead of imposing a second tax upon the people, it might, at least in part, repay them for what they had contributed to the first. Bounties upon production, however, have been very rarely granted. The prejudices established by the commercial system have taught us to believe, that national wealth arises more immediately from exportation than from production. It has been more favored, accordingly, as the more immediate means of bringing money into the country. Bounties upon production, it has been said too, have been found by experience more liable to frauds than those upon exportation. How far this is true, I know not. That bounties upon exportation have been abused, to many fraudulent purposes, is very well known. But it is not the interest of merchants and manufacturers, the great inventors of all these expedients, that the home market should be overstocked with their goods; an event which a bounty upon production might sometimes occasion. A bounty upon exportation, by enabling them to send abroad their surplus part, and to keep up the price of what remains in the home market, effectually prevents this. Of all the expedients of the mercantile system, accordingly, it is the one of which they are the fondest. . . .

If any particular manufacture was necessary, indeed, for the defense of the society, it might not always be prudent to depend upon our neighbors for the supply; and if such manufacture could not otherwise be supported at home, it might not be unreasonable that all the other branches of industry should be taxed in order to support it. The bounties upon the exportation of British made sailcloth, and British made gunpowder, may, perhaps, both be vindicated upon this principle.

. . . It can very seldom be reasonable to tax the industry of the great body of the people, in order to support that of some particular class of manufacturers; yet, in the wantonness of great prosperity, when the public enjoys a greater revenue than it knows well what to do with, to give such bounties to favorite manufactures, may, perhaps, be as natural as to incur any other idle expense. In public, as well as in private expenses, great wealth may, perhaps, frequently be admitted as an apology for great folly. But there must surely be something more than ordinary absurdity in continuing such profusion in times of general difficulty and distress.

That system of laws, therefore, which is connected with the establishment of the bounty, seems to deserve no part of the praise which has been bestowed upon it. The improvement and prosperity of Great Britain, which has been so often ascribed to those laws, may very easily be accounted for by other causes. . . . The natural effort of every individual to better his own condition, when suffered to exert itself with freedom and security, is so powerful a principle that it is alone, and without any assistance, not only capable of carrying on the society to wealth and prosperity, but of surmounting a hundred impertinent obstructions with which the folly of human laws too often encumbers its operations; though the effect of these obstructions is always more or less either to encroach upon its freedom, or to diminish its security. In Great Britain industry is perfectly secure; and though it is far from being perfectly free, it is as free as or freer than in any other part of Europe. . . .

Premiums given by the public to artists and manu-facturers, who excel in their particular occupations, are not liable to the same objections as bounties. By encouraging extraordinary dexterity and ingenuity, they serve to keep up the emulation of the workmen actually employed in those respective occupations, and are not considerable enough to turn towards any one of them a greater share of the capital of the coun-try than what would go to it of its own accord. Their tendency is not to overturn the natural balance of employments, but to render the work which is done in each as perfect and complete as possible. The expense of premiums, besides, is very trifling, that of bounties very great. The bounty upon corn alone has sometimes cost the public, in one year, more than three hundred thousand pounds.

Bounties are sometimes called premiums, as draw-backs are sometimes called bounties. But we must, in all cases, attend to the nature of the thing, without paying any regard to the word.

## *Chapter Six*

# Of Treaties of Commerce

W HEN A NATION binds itself by treaty, either to permit the entry of certain goods from one foreign country which it prohibits from all others, or to exempt the goods of one country from duties to which it subjects those of all others, the country, or at least the merchants and manufacturers of the country, whose commerce is so favored, must necessarily derive great advantage from the treaty. Those merchants and manufacturers enjoy a sort of monopoly in the country which is so indulgent to them. That country becomes a market, both more extensive and more advantageous for their goods: more extensive, because the goods of other nations being either excluded or subjected to heavier duties, it takes off a greater quantity of theirs; more advantageous, because the merchants of the favored country, enjoying a sort of monopoly there, will often sell their goods for a better price than if exposed to the free competition of all other nations.

Such treaties, however, though they may be advantageous to the merchants and manufacturers of the favored, are necessarily disadvantageous to those of the favoring country. A monopoly is thus granted against them to a foreign nation; and they must frequently buy the foreign goods they have occasion for, dearer than if the free competition of other nations was admitted. That part of its own produce with which such a nation purchases foreign goods, must consequently be sold cheaper; because, when two things are exchanged for one another, the cheapness of the one is a necessary consequence, or rather is the same thing, with the dearness of the other. The exchangeable value of its annual produce, therefore, is likely to be diminished by every such treaty. This diminution, however, can scarce amount to any positive loss, but only to a lessening of the gain which it might otherwise make. Though it sells its goods cheaper than it otherwise might do, it will not probably sell them for less than they cost; nor, as in the case of bounties, for a price which will not replace the capital employed in bringing them to market, together with the ordinary profits of stock. The trade could not go on long if it did. Even the favoring country, therefore, may still gain by the trade, though less than if there was a free competition.

Some treaties of commerce, however, have been supposed advantageous, upon principles very different from these; and a commercial country has sometimes granted a monopoly of this kind, against itself, to certain goods of a foreign nation, because it expected, that in the whole commerce between them, it would annually sell more than it would buy, and that a balance in gold and silver would be annually returned to it. It is upon this principle that the treaty of commerce between England and Portugal, concluded in 1703 by Mr. Methuen,* has been so much commended. . . .

By this treaty, the crown of Portugal becomes bound to admit the English woolens upon the same footing as before the prohibition; that is, not to raise the duties which had been paid before that time. But it does not become bound to admit them upon any better terms than those of any other nation, of France or Holland, for example. The crown of Great Britain, on the contrary, becomes bound to admit the wines of Portugal, upon paying only two-thirds of the duty which is paid for those of France, the wines most likely to come into competition with them. So far this treaty, therefore, is evidently advantageous to Portugal, and disadvantageous to Great Britain.

---

* John Methuen (c.1650–1706) who served as a member of Parliament, Lord Chancellor of Ireland, Privy Councilor, envoy and then ambassador extraordinary to Portugal where he negotiated the Methuen Treaty of 1703; the Treaty cemented allegiances in the War of Spanish Succession.

It has been celebrated, however, as a masterpiece of the commercial policy of England. Portugal receives annually from the Brazils a greater quantity of gold than can be employed in its domestic commerce, whether in the shape of coin or of plate. The surplus is too valuable to be allowed to lie idle and locked up in coffers; and as it can find no advantageous market at home, it must, notwithstanding any prohibition, be sent abroad, and exchanged for something for which there is a more advantageous market at home. A large share of it comes annually to England, in return either for English goods, or for those of other European nations that receive their returns through England. . . .

[But] though Britain were entirely excluded from the Portugal trade, it could find very little difficulty in procuring all the annual supplies of gold which it wants, either for the purposes of plate, or of coin, or of foreign trade. Gold, like every other commodity, is always somewhere or another to be got for its value by those who have that value to give for it. . . .

It was upon this silly notion, however, that England could not subsist without the Portugal trade, that, towards the end of the late war, France and Spain, without pretending either offence or provocation, required the King of Portugal to exclude all British ships from his ports, and, for the security of this exclusion, to receive into them French or Spanish garrisons. Had the King of Portugal submitted to those ignominious terms which his brother-in-law the King of Spain proposed to him, Britain would have been freed from a much greater inconveniency than the loss of the Portugal trade, the burden of supporting a very weak ally, so unprovided of everything for his own defense, that the whole power of England, had it been directed to that single purpose, could scarce, perhaps, have defended him for another campaign.

The loss of the Portugal trade would, no doubt, have occasioned a considerable embarrassment to the merchants at that time engaged in it, who might not, perhaps, have found out, for a year or two, any other equally advantageous method of employing their capitals; and in this would probably have consisted all the inconveniency which England could have suffered from this notable piece of commercial policy. . . .

## Chapter Seven

# Conclusion of the Mercantile System

THOUGH THE ENCOURAGEMENT of exportation, and the discouragement of importation, are the two great engines by which the mercantile system proposes to enrich every country, yet, with regard to some particular commodities, it seems to follow an opposite plan: to discourage exportation, and to encourage importation. Its ultimate object, however, it pretends, is always the same, to enrich the country by an advantageous balance of trade. It discourages the exportation of the materials of manufacture, and of the instruments of trade, in order to give our own workmen an advantage, and to enable them to undersell those of other nations in all foreign markets;

and by restraining, in this manner, the exportation of a few commodities, of no great price, it proposes to occasion a much greater and more valuable exportation of others. It encourages the importation of the materials of manufacture, in order that our own people may be enabled to work them up more cheaply, and thereby prevent a greater and more valuable importation of the manufactured commodities. . . .

The importation of the materials of manufacture has sometimes been encouraged by an exemption from the duties to which other goods are subject, and sometimes by bounties.

The importation of sheep's wool from several different countries, of cotton wool from all countries, of undressed flax, of the greater part of dyeing drugs, of the greater part of undressed hides from Ireland, or the British colonies, of seal skins from the British Greenland fishery, of pig and bar iron from the British colonies, as well as of several other materials of manufacture, has been encouraged by an exemption from all duties, if properly entered at the customhouse. The private interest of our merchants and manufacturers may, perhaps, have extorted from the legislature these exemptions, as well as the greater part of our other commercial regulations. They are, however, perfectly just and reasonable; and if, consistently with the necessities of the state, they could be extended to all the other materials of manufacture, the public would certainly be a gainer. . . .

Our spinners are poor people; women commonly scattered about in all different parts of the country, without support or protection. It is not by the sale of their work, but by that of the complete work of the weavers, that our great master manufacturers make their profits. As it is their interest to sell the complete manufacture as dear, so it is to buy the materials as cheap as possible. By extorting from the legislature bounties upon the exportation of their own linen, high duties upon the importation of all foreign linen, and a total prohibition of the home consumption of some sorts of French linen, they endeavor to sell their own goods as dear as possible. By encouraging the importation of foreign linen yarn, and thereby bringing it into competition with that which is made by our own people, they endeavor to buy the work of the poor spinners as cheap as possible. They are as intent to keep down the wages of their own weavers, as the earnings of the poor spinners; and it is by no means for the benefit of the workmen that they endeavor either to raise the price of the complete work, or to lower that of the rude materials. It is the industry which is carried on for the benefit of the rich and the powerful, that is principally encouraged by our mercantile system. That which is carried on for the benefit of the poor and the indigent is too often either neglected or oppressed.

The exportation of the materials of manufacture is sometimes discouraged by absolute prohibitions, and sometimes by high duties.

Our woolen manufacturers have been more successful than any other class of workmen, in persuading the legislature that the prosperity of the nation depended upon the success and extension of their particular business.* They have not only obtained a monopoly against the consumers, by an absolute prohibition of importing woolen cloths from any foreign country; but they have likewise obtained another monopoly against the sheep farmers and growers of wool, by a similar prohibition of the exportation of live sheep and wool. The severity of many of the laws which have been enacted for the security of the revenue is very justly complained of, as imposing heavy penalties upon actions which, antecedent to the statutes that declared them to be crimes, had always been understood to be innocent. But the cruelest of our revenue laws, I will venture to affirm, are mild and gentle, in comparison to some of those which the clamor of our merchants and manufacturers has extorted from the legislature, for the support of their own absurd and oppressive monopolies. Like the laws of Draco, these laws may be said to be all written in blood.

By the 8th of Elizabeth, chap. 3, the exporter of sheep, lambs, or rams, was for the first offence, to forfeit all his goods forever, to suffer a year's imprisonment, and then to have his left hand cut off in a market town, upon a market day, to be there nailed up;

---

* See footnote on page 145 re: the revolution in cheap cotton.

and for the second offence, to be adjudged a felon, and to suffer death accordingly. To prevent the breed of our sheep from being propagated in foreign countries seems to have been the object of this law. By the 13th and 14th of Charles II, chap. 18, the exportation of wool was made a felony, and the exporter subjected to the same penalties and forfeitures as a felon.

For the honor of the national humanity, it is to be hoped that neither of these statutes was ever executed. The first of them, however, so far as I know, has never been directly repealed, and Sergeant Hawkins seems to consider it as still in force. It may, however, perhaps be considered as virtually repealed by the 12th of Charles II, chap. 32, sect. 3, which, without expressly taking away the penalties imposed by former statutes, imposes a new penalty, viz. that of 20*s* for every sheep exported, or attempted to be exported, together with the forfeiture of the sheep, and of the owner's share of the sheep. The second of them was expressly repealed by the 7th and 8th of William III, chap. 28, sect. 4, by which it is declared that "Whereas the statute of the 13th and 14th of King Charles II made against the exportation of wool, among other things in the said act mentioned, doth enact the same to be deemed felony, by the severity of which penalty the prosecution of offenders hath not been so effectually put in execution; be it therefore enacted, by the authority aforesaid, that so much of the said act, which relates to the making the said offence felony, be repealed and made void."

The penalties, however, which are either imposed by this milder statute, or which, though imposed by former statutes, are not repealed by this one, are still sufficiently severe. Besides the forfeiture of the goods, the exporter incurs the penalty of three shillings for every pound weight of wool, either exported or attempted to be exported, that is, about four or five times the value. Any merchant, or other person convicted of this offence, is disabled from requiring any debt or account belonging to him from any factor or other person. Let his fortune be what it will, whether he is or is not able to pay those heavy penalties, the law means to ruin him completely. But, as the morals of the great body of the people are not yet so corrupt as those of the contrivers of this statute, I have not heard that any advantage has ever been taken of this clause. If the person convicted of this offence is not able to pay the penalties within three months after judgment, he is to be transported for seven years; and if he returns before the expiration of that term, he is liable to the pains of felony, without benefit of clergy. The owner of the ship, knowing this offence, forfeits all his interest in the ship and furniture. The master and mariners, knowing this offence, forfeit all their goods and chattels, and suffer three months imprisonment. By a subsequent statute, the master suffers six months imprisonment.

In order to prevent exportation, the whole inland commerce of wool is laid under very burdensome and oppressive restrictions. It cannot be packed in any box, barrel, cask, case, chest, or any other package, but only in packs of leather or pack-cloth, on which must be marked on the outside the words *wool* or *yarn*, in large letters, not less than three inches long, on pain of forfeiting the same and the package, and three shillings for every pound weight, to be paid by the owner or packer. It cannot be loaden on any horse or cart, or carried by land within five miles of the coast, but between sun rising, and sun setting, on pain of forfeiting the same, the horses and carriages. The hundred next adjoining to the seacoast, out of, or through which the wool is carried or exported, forfeits twenty pounds, if the wool is under the value of ten pounds; and if of greater value, then treble that value, together with treble costs, to be sued for within the year. The execution to be against any two of the inhabitants, whom the sessions must reimburse, by an assessment on the other inhabitants, as in the cases of robbery. And if any person compounds with the hundred for less than this penalty, he is to be imprisoned for five years; and any other person may prosecute. These regulations take place through the whole kingdom.

But in the particular counties of Kent and Sussex, the restrictions are still more troublesome. Every owner of wool within ten miles of the seacoast must give an account in writing, three days after shearing, to the next officer of the customs, of the number of his fleeces, and of the places where they are lodged. And before he removes any part of them, he must give the like notice of the number and weight of the fleeces, and of the name and abode of the person to whom they are sold, and of the place to which it is intended they should be carried. No person within fifteen miles of the sea, in the said counties, can buy any wool, before he enters into bond to the king, that no part of the wool which he shall so buy shall be sold by him to any other person within fifteen miles of the sea. If any wool is found carrying towards the sea side in the said counties, unless it has been entered and security given as aforesaid, it is forfeited, and the offender also forfeits three shillings for every pound weight, if any person lay any wool, not entered as aforesaid, within fifteen miles of the sea, it must be seized and forfeited; and if, after such seizure, any person shall claim the same, he must give security to the exchequer, that if he is cast upon trial he shall pay treble costs, besides all other penalties.

When such restrictions are imposed upon the inland trade, the coasting trade, we may believe, cannot be left very free. Every owner of wool, who carrieth, or causeth to be carried, any wool to any port or place on the seacoast, in order to be from thence transported by sea to any other place or port on the coast, must first cause an entry thereof to be made at the port from whence it is intended to be conveyed, containing the weight, marks, and number, of the packages, before he brings the same within five miles of that port, on pain of forfeiting the same, and also the horses, carts, and other carriages; and also of suffering and forfeiting, as by the other laws in force against the exportation of wool. This law, however (1st of William III, chap. 32), is so very indulgent as to declare, that this shall not hinder any person from carrying his wool home from the place of shearing, though it be within five miles of the sea, provided that in ten days after shearing, and before he remove the wool, he do under his hand certify to the next officer of the customs the true number of fleeces, and where it is housed; and do not remove the same, without certifying to such officer, under his hand, his intention so to do, three days before. Bond must be given that the wool to be carried coast-ways is to be landed at the particular port for which it is entered outwards; and if my part of it is landed without the presence of an officer, not only the forfeiture of the wool is incurred, as in other goods, but the usual additional penalty of three shillings for every pound weight is likewise incurred.

Our woolen manufacturers, in order to justify their demand of such extraordinary restrictions and regulations, confidently asserted, that English wool was of a peculiar quality, superior to that of any other country; that the wool of other countries could not, without some mixture of it, be wrought up into any tolerable manufacture; that fine cloth could not be made without it; that England, therefore, if the exportation of it could be totally prevented, could monopolize to herself almost the whole woolen trade of the world;

and thus, having no rivals, could sell at what price she pleased, and in a short time acquire the most incredible degree of wealth by the most advantageous balance of trade. This doctrine, like most other doctrines which are confidently asserted by any considerable number of people, was, and still continues to be, most implicitly believed by a much greater number: by almost all those who are either unacquainted with the woolen trade, or who have not made particular inquiries. It is, however, so perfectly false, that English wool is in any respect necessary for the making of fine cloth, that it is altogether unfit for it. Fine cloth is made altogether of Spanish wool. English wool cannot be even so mixed with Spanish wool, as to enter into the composition without spoiling and degrading, in some degree, the fabric of the cloth.

It has been shown in the foregoing part of this work, that the effect of these regulations has been to depress the price of English wool, not only below what it naturally would be in the present times, but very much below what it actually was in the time of Edward III. The price of Scotch wool, when, in consequence of the Union, it became subject to the same regulations, is said to have fallen about one-half. It is observed by the very accurate and intelligent author of the *Memoirs of Wool*, the Reverend Mr. John Smith, that the price of the best English wool in England, is generally below what wool of a very inferior quality commonly sells for in the market of Amsterdam. To depress the price of this commodity below what may be called its natural and proper price was the avowed purpose of those regulations; and there seems to be no doubt of their having produced the effect that was expected from them.

This reduction of price, it may perhaps be thought, by discouraging the growing of wool, must have reduced very much the annual produce of that commodity, though not below what it formerly was, yet below what, in the present state of things, it would probably have been, had it, in consequence of an open and free market, been allowed to rise to the natural and proper price. I am, however, disposed to believe, that the quantity of the annual produce cannot have been much, though it may, perhaps, have been a little affected by these regulations. The growing of wool is not the chief purpose for which the sheep farmer employs his industry and stock. He expects his profit, not so much from the price of the fleece, as from that of the carcass; and the average or ordinary price of the latter must even, in many cases, make up to him whatever deficiency there may be in the average or ordinary price of the former. It has been observed, in the foregoing part of this work, that

> whatever regulations tend to sink the price, either of wool or of raw hides, below what it naturally would be, must, in an improved and cultivated country, have some tendency to raise the price of butcher's meat. The price,

both of the great and small cattle which are fed on improved and cultivated land, must be sufficient to pay the rent which the landlord, and the profit which the farmer, has reason to expect from improved and cultivated land. If it is not, they will soon cease to feed them. Whatever part of this price, therefore, is not paid by the wool and the hide must be paid by the carcass. The less there is paid for the one, the more must be paid for the other. In what manner this price is to be divided upon the different parts of the beast, is indifferent to the landlords and farmers, provided it is all paid to them. In an improved and cultivated country, therefore, their interest as landlords and farmers cannot be much affected by such regulations, though their interest as consumers may, by the rise in the price of provisions.

According to this reasoning, therefore, this degradation in the price of wool is not likely, in an improved and cultivated country, to occasion any diminution in the annual produce of that commodity; except so far as, by raising the price of mutton, it may somewhat diminish the demand for, and consequently the production of, that particular species of butcher's meat. Its effect, however, even in this way, it is probable, is not very considerable.

But though its effect upon the quantity of the annual produce may not have been very considerable, its effect upon the quality, it may perhaps be thought, must necessarily have been very great. The degradation in the quality of English wool, if not below what it was in former times, yet below what it naturally would have been in the present state of improvement and cultivation, must have been, it may perhaps be supposed, very nearly in proportion to the degradation of price. As the quality depends upon the breed, upon the pasture, and upon the management and cleanliness of the sheep, during the whole progress of the growth of the fleece, the attention to these circumstances, it may naturally enough be imagined, can never be greater than in proportion to the recompense which the price of the fleece is likely to make for the labor and expense which that attention requires. It happens, however, that the goodness of the fleece depends, in a great measure, upon the health, growth, and bulk of the animal: the same attention which is necessary for the improvement of the carcass is, in some respect, sufficient for that of the fleece. Notwithstanding the degradation of price, English wool is said to have been improved considerably during the course even of the present century. The improvement, might, perhaps, have been greater if the price had been better; but the lowness of price, though it may have obstructed, yet certainly it has not altogether prevented that improvement. . . .

To hurt, in any degree, the interest of any one order of citizens, for no other purpose but to promote that of some other, is evidently contrary to that justice and equality of treatment which the sovereign owes to all the different orders of his subjects. But the prohibition certainly hurts, in some degree, the interest of the growers of wool, for no other purpose but to promote that of the manufacturers. . . .

The prohibition, notwithstanding all the penalties which guard it, does not prevent the exportation of wool. It is exported, it is well known, in great quantities. The great difference between the price in the home and that in the foreign market, presents such a temptation to smuggling, that all the rigor of the law cannot prevent it. This illegal exportation is advantageous to nobody but the smuggler. A legal exportation, subject to a tax, by affording a revenue to the sovereign, and thereby saving the imposition of some other, perhaps more burdensome and inconvenient taxes, might prove advantageous to all the different subjects of the state.

The exportation of fuller's earth, or fuller's clay, supposed to be necessary for preparing and cleansing the woolen manufactures, has been subjected to nearly the same penalties as the exportation of wool. Even tobacco pipe clay, though acknowledged to be different from fuller's clay, yet, on account of their resemblance, and because fuller's clay might sometimes be exported as tobacco pipe clay, has been laid under the same prohibitions and penalties.

By the 13th and 14th of Charles II, chap. 7, the exportation, not only of raw hides, but of tanned leather, except in the shape of boots, shoes, or slippers, was prohibited; and the law gave a monopoly to our boot makers and shoemakers, not only against our graziers, but against our tanners. By subsequent statutes, our tanners have got themselves exempted from this monopoly, upon paying a small tax of only one shilling on the hundredweight of tanned leather, weighing one hundred and twelve pounds. They have obtained likewise the drawback of two-thirds of the excise duties imposed upon their commodity, even when exported without further manufacture. All manufactures of leather may be exported duty-free; and the exporter is besides entitled to the drawback of the whole duties of excise. Our graziers still continue subject to the old monopoly. Graziers, separated from one another, and dispersed through all the different corners of the country, cannot, without great difficulty, combine together for the purpose either of imposing monopolies upon their fellow citizens or of exempting themselves from such as may have been imposed upon them by other people. Manufacturers of all kinds, collected together in numerous bodies in all great cities, easily can. Even the horns of cattle are prohibited to be exported; and the two insignificant trades of the horner and comb maker enjoy, in this respect, a monopoly against the graziers. . . .

The exportation . . . of the instruments of trade, properly so called, is commonly restrained, not by high duties, but by absolute prohibitions. Thus, by the 7th and 8th of William III, chap. 20, sect. 8, the exportation of frames or engines for knitting [wool] gloves or stockings, is prohibited, under the penalty, not only of the forfeiture of such frames or engines, so exported, or attempted to be exported, but of forty pounds, one-half to the king, the other to the person who shall inform or sue for the same. In the same manner, by the 14th George III, chap. 71, the exportation to foreign parts, of any utensils made use of in the cotton, linen, woolen, and silk manufactures, is prohibited under the penalty, not only of the forfeiture of such utensils, but of two hundred pounds, to be paid by the person who shall offend in this manner; and likewise of two hundred pounds, to be paid by the master of the ship, who shall knowingly suffer such utensils to be loaded on board his ship.

When such heavy penalties were imposed upon the exportation of the dead instruments of trade, it could not well be expected that the living instrument, the artificer, should be allowed to go free. Accordingly, by the 5th George I, chap. 27, the person who shall be convicted of enticing any artificer, of or in any of the manufactures of Great Britain, to go into any foreign parts, in order to practice or teach his trade, is liable, for the first offence, to be fined in any sum not exceeding one hundred pounds, and to three months imprisonment, and until the fine shall be paid; and for the second offence, to be fined in any sum, at the discretion of the court, and to imprisonment for twelve months, and until the fine shall be paid.

By the 23rd George II, chap. 13, this penalty is increased, for the first offence, to five hundred pounds for every artificer so enticed, and to twelve months imprisonment, and until the fine shall be paid; and for the second offence, to one thousand pounds, and to two years imprisonment, and until the fine shall be paid.

By the former of these two statutes, upon proof that any person has been enticing any artificer, or that any artificer has promised or contracted to go into foreign parts, for the purposes aforesaid, such artificer may be obliged to give security, at the discretion of the court, that he shall not go beyond the seas, and may be committed to prison until he give such security.

If any artificer has gone beyond the seas, and is exercising or teaching his trade in any foreign country, upon warning being given to him by any of his majesty's ministers or consuls abroad, or by one of his majesty's secretaries of state, for the time being, if he does not, within six months after such warning, return into this realm, and from henceforth abide and inhabit continually within the same, he is from thenceforth declared incapable of taking any legacy devised to him within this kingdom, or of being executor or administrator to any person, or of taking any lands within this kingdom, by descent, devise, or purchase. He likewise forfeits to the king all his lands, goods, and chattels; is declared an alien in every respect; and is put out of the king's protection.

It is unnecessary, I imagine, to observe how contrary such regulations are to the boasted liberty of the subject, of which we affect to be so very jealous; but which, in this case, is so plainly sacrificed to the futile interests of our merchants and manufacturers.

The laudable motive of all these regulations is to extend our own manufactures, not by their own improvement, but by the depression of those of all our neighbors, and by putting an end, as much as possible, to the troublesome competition of such odious and disagreeable rivals. Our master manufacturers think it reasonable that they themselves should have the monopoly of the ingenuity of all their countrymen. Though by restraining, in some trades, the number of apprentices which can be employed at one time, and by imposing the necessity of a long apprenticeship in all trades, they endeavor, all of them, to confine the knowledge of their respective employments to as small a number as possible; they are unwilling, however, that any part of this small number should go abroad to instruct foreigners.

Consumption is the sole end and purpose of all production; and the interest of the producer ought to be attended to, only so far as it may be necessary for promoting that of the consumer.* The maxim is so perfectly self-evident, that it would be absurd to attempt

---

* John Maynard Keynes quoted this in arguing against Say's Law and for the proposition that, spending being as useful as investment, saving was usually a problem rather than a solution. Smith would likely have strongly disagreed with this. For more on Keynes, see Hunter Lewis's *Where Keynes Went Wrong*.

to prove it. But in the mercantile system, the interest of the consumer is almost constantly sacrificed to that of the producer; and it seems to consider production, and not consumption, as the ultimate end and object of all industry and commerce.

In the restraints upon the importation of all foreign commodities which can come into competition with those of our own growth or manufacture, the interest of the home consumer is evidently sacrificed to that of the producer. It is altogether for the benefit of the latter, that the former is obliged to pay that enhancement of price which this monopoly almost always occasions. . . .

. . . In the system of laws which has been established for the management of our American and West Indian colonies, the interest of the home consumer has been sacrificed to that of the producer, with a more extravagant profusion than in all our other commercial regulations. A great empire has been established for the sole purpose of raising up a nation of customers, who should be obliged to buy, from the shops of our different producers, all the goods with which these could supply them. For the sake of that little enhancement of price which this monopoly might afford our producers, the home consumers have been burdened with the whole expense of maintaining and defending that empire. For this purpose, and for this purpose only, in the two last wars, more than two hundred millions have been spent, and a new debt of more than a hundred and seventy millions has been contracted, over and above all that had been expended for the same purpose in former wars. The interest of this debt alone is not only greater than the whole extraordinary profit which, it never could be pretended, was made by the monopoly of the colony trade, but than the whole value of that trade, or than the whole value of the goods which, at an average, have been annually exported to the colonies.

It cannot be very difficult to determine who have been the contrivers of this whole mercantile system; not the consumers, we may believe, whose interest has been entirely neglected; but the producers, whose interest has been so carefully attended to; and among this latter class, our merchants and manufacturers have been by far the principal architects. In the mercantile regulations which have been taken notice of in this chapter, the interest of our manufacturers has been most peculiarly attended to; and the interest, not so much of the consumers, as that of some other sets of producers, has been sacrificed to it.

## Chapter Eight

## Of the Agricultural Systems ... of Political Economy Which Represent the Produce of Land as Either the Sole or the Principal Source of the Revenue and Wealth of Every Country

M R. COLBERT, THE famous minister of Lewis XIV was a man of probity, of great industry, and knowledge of detail; of great experience and acuteness in the examination of public accounts; and of abilities, in short, every way fitted for introducing method and good order into the collection and expenditure of the public revenue. That minister had unfortunately embraced all the prejudices of the mercantile system, in its nature and essence a system of restraint and regulation. . . . The industry and commerce of a great country, he endeavored to regulate upon the same model as the departments of a public office; and instead of allowing every man to pursue his own interest his own way, upon the liberal plan of equality, liberty, and justice, he bestowed upon certain branches of industry extraordinary privileges, while he laid others under as extraordinary restraints. He was not only disposed, like other European ministers, to encourage more the industry of the towns than that of the country; but, in order to support the industry of the towns, he was willing even to depress and keep down that of the country.

In order to render provisions cheap to the inhabitants of the towns, and thereby to encourage manufactures and foreign commerce, he prohibited altogether the exportation of corn, and thus excluded the inhabitants of the country from every foreign market, for by far the most important part of the produce of their industry. This prohibition, joined to the restraints imposed by the ancient provincial laws of France upon the transportation of corn from one province to another, and to the arbitrary and degrading taxes which are levied upon the cultivators in almost all the provinces, discouraged and kept down the agriculture of that country very much below the state to which it would naturally have risen in so very fertile a soil, and so very happy a climate. This state of discouragement and depression was felt more or less in every different part of the country, and many different inquiries were set on foot concerning the causes of it. One of those causes appeared to be the preference given, by the institutions of Mr. Colbert, to the industry of the towns above that of the country.

If the rod be bent too much one way says the proverb, in order to make it straight, you must bend it as much the other. The French philosophers, who have proposed the system which represents agriculture as the sole source of the revenue and wealth of every country, seem to have adopted this proverbial maxim; and, as in the plan of Mr. Colbert, the industry of the towns was certainly overvalued in comparison with that of the country, so in their system it seems to be as certainly undervalued.

The different orders of people, who have ever been supposed to contribute in any respect towards the annual produce of the land and labor of the country, they divide into three classes. The first is the class of the proprietors of land. The second is the class of the cultivators, of farmers and country laborers, whom they honor with the peculiar appellation of the productive class. The third is the class of artificers, manufacturers, and merchants, whom they endeavor to degrade by the humiliating appellation of the barren or unproductive class. . . .

The . . . expenses of the landlord . . . together with the . . . expenses of the farmer, are the only three sorts of expenses which in this system are considered as productive. All other expenses, and all other orders of people, even those who, in the common apprehensions of men, are regarded as the most productive, are, in this account of things, represented as altogether barren and unproductive. . . .

Artificers, manufacturers, and merchants, can augment the revenue and wealth of their society by parsimony only; or, as it is expressed in this system, by privation, that is, by depriving themselves of a part of the funds destined for their own subsistence. They annually reproduce nothing but those funds. Unless, therefore, they annually save some part of them, unless they annually deprive themselves of the enjoyment of some part of them, the revenue and wealth of their society can never be, in the smallest degree, augmented by means of their industry. Farmers and country laborers, on the contrary, may enjoy completely the whole funds destined for their own subsistence, and yet augment, at the same time, the revenue and wealth of their society. . . .

Nations . . . which, like France or England, consist in a great measure, of proprietors and cultivators, can be enriched by industry and enjoyment. Nations, on the contrary, which, like Holland and Hamburg, are composed chiefly of merchants, artificers, and manufacturers, can grow rich only through parsimony and privation. As the interest of nations so differently circumstanced is very different, so is likewise the common character of the people. In those of the former kind, liberality, frankness, and good fellowship, naturally make a part of their common character; in the latter, narrowness, meanness, and a selfish disposition, averse to all social pleasure and enjoyment.

The unproductive class, that of merchants, artificers, and manufacturers, is maintained and employed altogether at the expense of the two other classes, of that of proprietors, and of that of cultivators. They furnish it both with the materials of its work, and with the fund of its subsistence, with the corn and cattle which it consumes while it is employed about that work. The proprietors and cultivators finally pay both the wages of all the workmen of the unproductive class, and the profits of all their employers. Those workmen and their employers are properly the servants of the proprietors and cultivators. They are only servants who work without doors, as menial servants work within. Both the one and the other, however, are equally maintained at the expense of the same masters. The labor of both is equally unproductive. It adds nothing to the value of the sum total of the rude produce of the land. Instead of increasing the value of that sum total, it is a charge and expense which must be paid out of it.

The unproductive class, however, is not only useful, but greatly useful, to the other two classes. By means of the industry of merchants, artificers, and manufacturers, the proprietors and cultivators can purchase both the foreign goods and the manufactured produce of their own country, which they have occasion for, with the produce of a much smaller quantity of their own labor, than what they would be obliged to employ, if they were to attempt, in an awkward and unskillful manner, either to import the one, or to make the other, for their own use. By means of the unproductive class, the cultivators are delivered from many cares, which would otherwise distract their attention from the cultivation of land. The superiority of produce, which in consequence of this undivided attention, they are enabled to raise, is fully sufficient to pay the whole expense which the maintenance and employment of the unproductive class costs either the proprietors or themselves. The industry of merchants, artificers, and manufacturers, though in its own nature altogether unproductive, yet contributes in this manner indirectly to increase the produce of the land. It increases the productive powers of productive labor, by leaving it at liberty to confine itself to its proper employment, the cultivation of land; and the plough goes frequently the easier and the better, by means of the labor of the man whose business is most remote from the plough.

It can never be the interest of the proprietors and cultivators, to restrain or to discourage, in any respect, the industry of merchants, artificers, and manufacturers. The greater the liberty which this unproductive class enjoys, the greater will be the competition in all the different trades which compose it, and the cheaper will the other two classes be supplied, both with foreign goods and with the manufactured produce of their own country.

It can never be the interest of the unproductive class to oppress the other two classes. It is the surplus produce of the land, or what remains after deducting the maintenance, first of the cultivators, and afterwards of the proprietors, that maintains and employs the unproductive class. The greater this surplus, the greater must likewise be the maintenance and employment of that class. The establishment of perfect justice, of perfect liberty, and of perfect equality, is the very simple secret which most effectually secures the highest degree of prosperity to all the three classes.

The merchants, artificers, and manufacturers of those mercantile states, which, like Holland and Hamburg, consist chiefly of this unproductive class, are in the same manner maintained and employed altogether at the expense of the proprietors and cultivators of land. The only difference is, that those proprietors and cultivators are, the greater part of them, placed at a most inconvenient distance from the merchants, artificers, and manufacturers, whom they supply with the materials of their work and the fund of their subsistence; they are the inhabitants of other countries, and the subjects of other governments.

Such mercantile states, however, are not only useful, but greatly useful, to the inhabitants of those other countries. They fill up, in some measure, a very important void; and supply the place of the merchants, artificers, and manufacturers, whom the inhabitants of those countries ought to find at home, but whom, from some defect in their policy, they do not find at home.

It can never be the interest of those landed nations, if I may call them so, to discourage or distress the industry of such mercantile states, by imposing high duties upon their trade, or upon the commodities which they furnish. Such duties, by rendering those commodities dearer, could serve only to sink the real value of the surplus produce of their own land, with which, or, what comes to the same thing, with the price of which those commodities are purchased.

Such duties could only serve to discourage the increase of that surplus produce, and consequently the improvement and cultivation of their own land. The most effectual expedient, on the contrary, for raising the value of that surplus produce, for encouraging its increase, and consequently the improvement and cultivation of their own land, would be to allow the most perfect freedom to the trade of all such mercantile nations.

This perfect freedom of trade would even be the most effectual expedient for supplying them, in due time, with all the artificers, manufacturers, and merchants, whom they wanted at home; and for filling up, in the properest and most advantageous manner, that very important void which they felt there. . . .

According to this liberal and generous system, therefore, the most advantageous method in which a landed nation can raise up artificers, manufacturers, and merchants of its own, is to grant the most perfect freedom of trade to the artificers, manufacturers, and merchants of all other nations. It thereby raises the value of the surplus produce of its own land, of which the continual increase gradually establishes a fund, which, in due time, necessarily raises up all the artificers, manufacturers, and merchants, whom it has occasion for.

When a landed nation on the contrary, oppresses, either by high duties or by prohibitions, the trade of foreign nations, it necessarily hurts its own interest in two different ways. First, by raising the price of all foreign goods, and of all sorts of manufactures, it necessarily sinks the real value of the surplus produce of its own land, with which, or, what comes to the same thing, with the price of which, it purchases those foreign goods and manufactures. Secondly, by giving a sort of monopoly of the home market to its own merchants, artificers, and manufacturers, it raises the rate of mercantile and manufacturing profit, in proportion to that of agricultural profit; and, consequently, either draws from agriculture a part of the capital which had before been employed in it, or hinders from going to it a part of what would otherwise have gone to it. This policy, therefore, discourages agriculture in two different ways; first, by sinking the real value of its produce, and thereby lowering the rate of its profits; and, secondly, by raising the rate of profit in all other employments. Agriculture is rendered less advantageous, and trade and manufactures more advantageous, than they otherwise would be; and every man is tempted by his own interest to turn, as much as he can, both his capital and his industry from the former to the latter employments.

Though, by this oppressive policy, a landed nation should be able to raise up artificers, manufacturers, and merchants of its own, somewhat sooner than it could do by the freedom of trade; a matter, however, which is not a little doubtful; yet it would raise them up, if one may say so, prematurely, and before it was perfectly ripe for them. By raising up too hastily one species of industry, it would depress another more valuable species of industry. . . .

In what manner, according to this system, the sum total of the annual produce of the land is distributed among the three classes above mentioned, and in what manner the labor of the unproductive class does no more than replace the value of its own consumption, without increasing in any respect the value of that sum total, is represented by Mr. Quesnay,* the very ingenious and profound author of this system, in some arithmetical formularies. The first of these formularies, which, by way of eminence, he peculiarly distinguishes by the name of the Economical Table, represents the manner in which he supposes this distribution takes place, in a state of the most perfect liberty, and, therefore, of the

---

* François Quesnay, the leader of the French physiocrats. Smith had lived in France and originally proposed to dedicate *Wealth of Nations* to Quensay.

highest prosperity; in a state where the annual produce is such as to afford the greatest possible neat produce, and where each class enjoys its proper share of the whole annual produce. Some subsequent formularies represent the manner in which he supposes this distribution is made in different states of restraint and regulation; in which, either the class of proprietors, or the barren and unproductive class, is more favored than the class of cultivators; and in which either the one or the other encroaches, more or less, upon the share which ought properly to belong to this productive class. . . . Those subsequent formularies represent the different degrees of declension which, according to this system, correspond to the different degrees in which this natural distribution of things is violated.

Some speculative physicians seem to have imagined that the health of the human body could be preserved only by a certain precise regimen of diet and exercise, of which every, the smallest violation, necessarily occasioned some degree of disease or disorder proportionate to the degree of the violation. Experience, however, would seem to show, that the human body frequently preserves, to all appearance at least, the most perfect state of health under a vast variety of different regimens; even under some which are generally believed to be very far from being perfectly wholesome. But the healthful state of the human body, it would seem, contains in itself some unknown principle of preservation, capable either of preventing or of correcting, in many respects, the bad effects even of a very faulty regimen. Mr. Quesnay, who was himself a physician, and a very speculative physician, seems to have entertained a notion of the same kind concerning the political body, and to have imagined that it would thrive and prosper only under a certain precise regimen, the exact regimen of perfect liberty and perfect justice. He seems not to have considered, that in the political body, the natural effort which every man is continually making to better his own condition, is a principle of preservation capable of preventing and correcting, in many respects, the bad effects of a political economy, in some degree both partial and oppressive. Such a political economy, though it no doubt retards more or less, is not always capable of stopping altogether, the natural progress of a nation towards wealth and prosperity, and still less of making it go backwards. If a nation could not prosper without the enjoyment of perfect liberty and perfect justice, there is not in the world a nation which could ever have prospered. In the political body, however, the wisdom of nature has fortunately made ample provision for remedying many of the bad effects of the folly and injustice of man; in the same manner as it has done in the natural body, for remedying those of his sloth and intemperance.

The capital error of this system, however, seems to lie in its representing the class of artificers, manufacturers, and merchants, as altogether barren and unproductive.

The following observations may serve to show the impropriety of this representation.

First, this class, it is acknowledged, reproduces annually the value of its own annual consumption, and continues, at least, the existence of the stock or capital which maintains and employs it. But, upon this account alone, the denomination of barren or unproductive should seem to be very improperly applied to it. . . .

. . . It seems, on this account, altogether improper to consider artificers, manufacturers, and merchants, in the same light as menial servants. The labor of menial servants does not continue the existence of the fund which maintains and employs them. Their maintenance and employment is altogether at the expense of their masters, and the work which they perform is not of a nature to repay that expense. That work consists in services which perish generally in the very instant of their performance, and does not fix or realize itself in any vendible commodity, which can replace the value of their wages and maintenance.* The labor, on the contrary, of artificers, manufacturers, and merchants, naturally does fix and realize itself in some such vendible commodity. It is upon this account that, in the chapter in which I treat of productive and unproductive labor, I have classed artificers, manufacturers, and merchants among the productive laborers, and menial servants among the barren or unproductive.

---

* More on potential productivity of services.

... It [also] seems, upon every supposition, improper to say, that the labor of artificers, manufacturers, and merchants, does not increase the real revenue of the society. Though we should suppose, for example, as it seems to be supposed in this system, that the value of the daily, monthly, and yearly consumption of this class was exactly equal to that of its daily, monthly, and yearly production; yet it would not from thence follow, that its labor added nothing to the real revenue, to the real value of the annual produce of the land and labor of the society. An artificer, for example, who, in the first six months after harvest, executes ten pounds worth of work, though he should, in the same time, consume ten pounds worth of corn and other necessaries, yet really adds the value of ten pounds to the annual produce of the land and labor of the society. While he has been consuming a half-yearly revenue of ten pounds worth of corn and other necessaries, he has produced an equal value of work, capable of purchasing, either to himself, or to some other person, an equal half-yearly revenue. The value, therefore, of what has been consumed and produced during these six months, is equal, not to ten, but to twenty pounds. . . .

. . . Farmers and country laborers can no more augment, without parsimony, the real revenue, the annual produce of the land and labor of their society, than artificers, manufacturers, and merchants. The annual produce of the land and labor of any society can be augmented only in two ways; either, first, by some improvement in the productive powers of the useful labor actually maintained within it; or, secondly, by some increase in the quantity of that labor.

The improvement in the productive powers of useful labor depends, first, upon the improvement in the ability of the workman; and, secondly, upon that of the machinery with which he works. But the labor of artificers and manufacturers, as it is capable of being more subdivided, and the labor of each workman reduced to a greater simplicity of operation, than that of farmers and country laborers; so it is likewise capable of both these sorts of improvement in a much higher degree. In this respect, therefore, the class of cultivators can have no sort of advantage over that of artificers and manufacturers.

The increase in the quantity of useful labor actually employed within any society must depend altogether upon the increase of the capital which employs it; and the increase of that capital, again, must be exactly equal to the amount of the savings from the revenue, either of the particular persons who manage and direct the employment of that capital, or of some other persons, who lend it to them. If merchants, artificers, and manufacturers are, as this system seems to suppose, naturally more inclined to parsimony and saving than proprietors and cultivators, they are, so far, more likely to augment the quantity of useful labor employed within their society, and consequently to increase its real revenue, the annual produce of its land and labor.

... Lastly, though the revenue of the inhabitants of every country was supposed to consist altogether, as this system seems to suppose, in the quantity of subsistence which their industry could procure to them; yet, even upon this supposition, the revenue of a trading and manufacturing country must, other things being equal, always be much greater than that of one without trade or manufactures. By means of trade and manufactures, a greater quantity of subsistence can be annually imported into a particular country, than what its own lands, in the actual state of their cultivation, could afford....

This system, [of Quesnay,] with all its imperfections, is perhaps the nearest approximation to the truth that has yet been published upon the subject of political economy; and is upon that account, well worth the consideration of every man who wishes to examine with attention the principles of that very important science. Though in representing the labor which is employed upon land as the only productive labor, the notions which it inculcates are, perhaps, too narrow and confined; yet in representing the wealth of nations as consisting, not in the unconsumable riches of money, but in the consumable goods annually reproduced by the labor of the society, and in representing perfect liberty as the only effectual expedient for rendering this annual reproduction the greatest possible, its doctrine seems to be in every respect as just as it is generous and liberal. Its followers are very numerous; and as men are fond of paradoxes, and of appearing to understand what surpasses the comprehensions of ordinary people, the paradox which it maintains, concerning the unproductive nature of manufacturing labor, has not, perhaps, contributed a little to increase the number of its admirers.* They have for some years past made a pretty considerable sect, distinguished in the French republic of letters by the name of the Economists. Their works have certainly been of some service to their country; not only by bringing into general discussion, many subjects which had never been well examined before, but by influencing, in some measure, the public administration in favor of agriculture. . . . The ancient provincial restraints upon the transportation of corn from one province of the kingdom to another have been entirely taken away; and the liberty of exporting it to all foreign countries, has been established as the common law of the kingdom in all ordinary cases.

This sect, in their works, which are very numerous, and which treat not only of what is properly called Political Economy, or of the nature and causes of the wealth of nations, but of every other branch of the system of civil government, all follow implicitly, and without any sensible variation, the doctrine of Mr. Quesnay. There is, upon this account, little variety in the greater part of their works. . . . The admiration of this whole sect for their master, who was himself a

---

* In the 20th century, the art of economic paradox was carried to an extreme by John Maynard Keynes. See Lewis, *Where Keynes Went Wrong*.

man of the greatest modesty and simplicity, is not inferior to that of any of the ancient philosophers for the founders of their respective systems.

"There have been since the world began," says a very diligent and respectable author, the Marquis de Mirabeau, "three great inventions which have principally given stability to political societies, independent of many other inventions which have enriched and adorned them. The first is the invention of writing, which alone gives human nature the power of transmitting, without alteration, its laws, its contracts, its annals, and its discoveries. The second is the invention of money, which binds together all the relations between civilized societies. The third is the economical table, the result of the other two, which completes them both by perfecting their object; the great discovery of our age, but of which our posterity will reap the benefit."

The greatest and most important branch of the commerce of every nation, it has already been observed, is that which is carried on between the inhabitants of the town and those of the country. The inhabitants of the town draw from the country the rude produce, which constitutes both the materials of their work and the fund of their subsistence; and they pay for this rude produce by sending back to the country a certain portion of it manufactured and prepared for immediate use. The trade which is carried on between these two different sets of people consists ultimately in a certain quantity of rude produce exchanged for a certain quantity of manufactured produce. The dearer the latter, therefore, the cheaper the former; and whatever tends in any country to raise the price of manufactured produce, tends to lower that of the rude produce of the land, and thereby to discourage agriculture. The smaller the quantity of manufactured produce, which any given quantity of rude produce, or, what comes to the same thing, which the price of any given quantity of rude produce is capable of purchasing, the smaller the exchangeable value of that given quantity of rude produce; the smaller the encouragement which either the landlord has to increase its quantity by improving, or the farmer by cultivating the land. Whatever, besides, tends to diminish in any country the number of artificers and manufacturers, tends to diminish the home market, the most important of all markets, for the rude produce of the land, and thereby still further to discourage agriculture.

Those systems, therefore, which preferring agriculture to all other employments, in order to promote it, impose restraints upon manufactures and foreign trade, act contrary to the very end which they propose, and indirectly discourage that very species of industry which they mean to promote. They are so far, perhaps, more inconsistent than even the mercantile system. That system, by encouraging manufactures and foreign trade more than agriculture, turns a certain portion of the capital of the society, from supporting a more advantageous, to support a less advantageous species of industry. But still it really, and in the end, encourages that species of industry which it means to promote. Those agricultural systems, on the contrary, really, and in the end, discourage their own favorite species of industry.

It is thus that every system which endeavors, either, by extraordinary encouragements to draw towards a particular species of industry a greater share of the capital of the society than what would naturally go to it, or, by extraordinary restraints, to force from a particular species of industry some share of the capital which would otherwise be employed in it, is, in reality, subversive of the great purpose which it means to promote. It retards, instead of accelerating the progress of the society towards real wealth and greatness; and diminishes, instead of increasing, the real value of the annual produce of its land and labor.

All systems, either of preference or of restraint, therefore, being thus completely taken away, the obvious and simple system of natural liberty establishes itself of its own accord. Every man, as long as he does not violate the laws of justice, is left perfectly free to pursue his own interest his own way, and to bring both his industry and capital into competition with those of any other man, or order of men. The sovereign is completely discharged from a duty, in the attempting to perform which he must always be exposed to innumerable delusions, and for the proper performance of which, no human wisdom or knowledge could ever be sufficient; the duty of superintending the industry of private people, and of directing it towards the employments most suitable to the interests of the society. According to the system of natural liberty, the sovereign has only three duties to attend to; three duties of great importance, indeed, but plain and intelligible to common understandings: first, the duty of protecting the society from the violence and invasion of other independent societies; secondly, the duty of protecting, as far as possible, every member of the society from the injustice or oppression of every other member of it, or the duty of establishing an exact administration of justice; and, thirdly, the duty of erecting and maintaining certain public works, and certain public institutions, which it can never be for the interest of any individual, or small number of individuals to erect and maintain; because the profit could never repay the expense to any individual, or small number of individuals, though it may frequently do much more than repay it to a great society.

The proper performance of those several duties of the sovereign necessarily supposes a certain expense; and this expense again necessarily requires a certain revenue to support it. In the following book, therefore, I shall endeavor to explain, first, what are the necessary expenses of the sovereign or commonwealth; and which of those expenses ought to be defrayed by the general contribution of the whole society; and which of them, by that of some particular part only, or of some particular members of the society; secondly, what are the different methods in which the whole society may be made to contribute towards defraying the expenses incumbent on the whole society; and what are the principal advantages and inconveniencies of each of those methods; and thirdly, what are the reasons and causes which have induced almost all modern governments to mortgage some part of this revenue, or to contract debts; and what have been the effects of those debts upon the real wealth, the annual produce of the land and labor of the society. The following book, therefore, will naturally be divided into three chapters.

*Book Five*

# Of the Revenue of the Sovereign or Commonwealth

### Chapter One

# Of the Expenses of the Sovereign or Commonwealth

### Part One

## Of the Expense of Defense

THE FIRST DUTY of the sovereign, that of protecting the society from the violence and invasion of other independent societies, can be performed only by means of a military force. . . .

. . . A well-regulated standing army is superior to every militia. Such an army, as it can best be maintained by an opulent and civilized nation, so it can alone defend such a nation against the invasion of a poor and barbarous neighbor. It is only by means of a standing army, therefore, that the civilization of any country can be perpetuated, or even preserved, for any considerable time. . . .

Men of republican principles have been jealous of a standing army, as dangerous to liberty. It certainly is so, wherever the interest of the general, and that of the principal officers, are not necessarily connected with the support of the constitution of the state. The standing army of Caesar destroyed the Roman republic. The standing army of Cromwell turned the long parliament out of doors. But . . . it may, in some cases, be favorable to liberty. The security which it gives to the sovereign renders unnecessary that troublesome jealousy, which, in some modern republics, seems to watch over the minutest actions, and to be at all times ready to disturb the peace of every citizen. Where the security of the magistrate, though supported by the principal people of the country, is endangered by every popular discontent; where a small tumult is capable of bringing about in a few hours a great revolution, the whole authority of government must be employed to suppress and punish every murmur and complaint against it. To a sovereign, on the contrary, who feels himself supported, not only by the natural aristocracy of the country, but by a well-regulated standing army, the rudest, the most groundless, and the most licentious remonstrances, can give little disturbance. He can safely pardon or neglect them, and his consciousness of his own superiority naturally disposes him to do so. . . .

The great change introduced into the art of war by the invention of firearms, has enhanced still further both the expense of exercising and disciplining any particular number of soldiers in time of peace, and that of employing them in time of war. Both their arms and their ammunition are become more expensive. . . .

In modern war, the great expense of firearms gives an evident advantage to the nation which can best afford that expense; and, consequently, to an opulent and civilized, over a poor and barbarous nation. In ancient times, the opulent and civilized found it difficult to defend themselves against the poor and barbarous nations. In modern times, the poor and barbarous find it difficult to defend themselves against the opulent and civilized. The invention of firearms, an invention which at first sight appears to be so pernicious, is certainly favorable, both to the permanency and to the extension of civilization.

## *Part Two*
# Of the Expense of Justice

The second duty of the sovereign, that of protecting, as far as possible, every member of the society from the injustice or oppression of every other member of it, or the duty of establishing an exact administration of justice, requires two very different degrees of expense in the different periods of society.

Justice, however, never was in reality administered gratis in any country. Lawyers and attorneys, at least, must always be paid by the parties; and if they were not, they would perform their duty still worse than they actually perform it. The fees annually paid to lawyers and attorneys, amount, in every court, to a much greater sum than the salaries of the judges. The circumstance of those salaries being paid by the crown, can nowhere much diminish the necessary expense of a lawsuit. . . .

A stamp-duty upon the law proceedings of each particular court, to be levied by that court, and applied towards the maintenance of the judges, and other officers belonging to it, might in the same manner, afford a revenue sufficient for defraying the expense of the administration of justice, without bringing any burden upon the general revenue of the society. The judges, indeed, might in this case, be under the temptation of multiplying unnecessarily the proceedings upon every cause, in order to increase, as much as possible, the produce of such a stamp-duty. It has been the custom in modern Europe to regulate, upon most occasions, the payment of the attorneys and clerks of court according to the number of pages which they had occasion to write; the court, however, requiring that each page should contain so many lines, and each line so many words. In order to increase their payment, the attorneys and clerks have contrived to multiply words beyond all necessity, to the corruption of the law language of, I believe, every court of justice in Europe. A like temptation might, perhaps, occasion a like corruption in the form of law proceedings.

## *Part Three*
# Of the Expense of Public Works and Public Institutions

The third and last duty of the sovereign or commonwealth, is that of erecting and maintaining those public institutions and those public works, which though they may be in the highest degree advantageous to a great society, are, however, of such a nature, that the profit could never repay the expense to any individual, or small number of individuals; and which it, therefore, cannot be expected that any individual, or small number of individuals, should erect or maintain. The performance of this duty requires, too, very different degrees of expense in the different periods of society.

After the public institutions and public works necessary for the defense of the society, and for the administration of justice, both of which have already been mentioned, the other works and institutions of this kind are chiefly for facilitating the commerce of the society, and those for promoting the instruction of the people. The institutions for instruction are of two kinds: those for the education of the youth, and those for the instruction of people of all ages. The consideration of the manner in which the expense of those different sorts of public works and institutions may be most properly defrayed will divide this third part of the present chapter into three different articles.

## Article One

### Of the Public Works and Institutions for Facilitating the Commerce of the Society

#### And, First, of Those Which Are Necessary for Facilitating Commerce in General

That the erection and maintenance of the public works which facilitate the commerce of any country, such as good roads, bridges, navigable canals, harbors, etc. must require very different degrees of expense in the different periods of society, is evident without any proof. The expense of making and maintaining the public roads of any country must evidently increase with the annual produce of the land and labor of that country, or with the quantity and weight of the goods which it becomes necessary to fetch and carry upon those roads. . . .

It does not seem necessary that the expense of those public works should be defrayed from that public revenue, as it is commonly called, of which the collection and application are in most countries, assigned to the executive power. The greater part of such public works may easily be so managed, as to afford a particular revenue, sufficient for defraying their own expense without bringing any burden upon the general revenue of the society.

A highway, a bridge, a navigable canal, for example, may, in most cases, be both made and maintained by a small toll upon the carriages which make use of them; a harbor, by a moderate port-duty upon the tonnage of the shipping which load or unload in it. The coinage, another institution for facilitating commerce, in many countries, not only defrays its own expense, but affords a small revenue or a seignorage to the sovereign. The post office, another institution for the same purpose, over and above defraying its own expense, affords, in almost all countries, a very considerable revenue to the sovereign.

When the carriages which pass over a highway or a bridge, and the lighters which sail upon a navigable canal, pay toll in proportion to their weight or their tonnage, they pay for the maintenance of those public works exactly in proportion to the wear and tear which they occasion of them. It seems scarce possible to invent a more equitable way of maintaining such works. This tax or toll, too, though it is advanced by the carrier, is finally paid by the consumer, to whom it must always be charged in the price of the goods. As the expense of carriage, however, is very much reduced by means of such public works, the goods, notwithstanding the toll, come cheaper to the consumer than they could otherwise have done, their price not being so much raised by the toll, as it is lowered by the cheapness of the carriage.

The person who finally pays this tax, therefore, gains by the application more than he loses by the payment of it. His payment is exactly in proportion to his gain. It is, in reality, no more than a part of that gain which he is obliged to give up, in order to get the rest. It seems impossible to imagine a more equitable method of raising a tax. . . .

When high roads, bridges, canals, etc. are in this manner made and supported by the commerce which is carried on by means of them, they can be made only where that commerce requires them, and, consequently, where it is proper to make them. Their expense, too, their grandeur and magnificence, must be suited to what that commerce can afford to pay. They must be made, consequently, as it is proper to make them. A magnificent high road cannot be made through a desert country, where there is little or no commerce, or merely because it happens to lead to the country villa of the intendant of the province, or to that of some great lord, to whom the intendant finds it convenient to make his court. A great bridge cannot be thrown over a river at a place where nobody passes, or merely to embellish the view from the windows of a neighboring palace; things which sometimes happen in countries, where works of this kind are carried on by any other revenue than that which they themselves are capable of affording.

In several different parts of Europe, the toll or lock-duty upon a canal is the property of private persons, whose private interest obliges them to keep up the canal. If it is not kept in tolerable order, the navigation necessarily ceases altogether, and, along with it, the whole profit which they can make by the tolls. If those tolls were put under the management of commissioners, who had themselves no interest in them, they might be less attentive to the maintenance of the works which produced them. . . .

The tolls for the maintenance of a high road cannot, with any safety, be made the property of private persons. A high road, though entirely neglected, does not become altogether impassable, though a canal does. The proprietors of the tolls upon a high road, therefore, might neglect altogether the repair of the road, and yet continue to levy very nearly the same tolls. It is proper, therefore, that the tolls for the maintenance of such a work should be put under the management of commissioners or trustees.

Even those public works, which are of such a nature that they cannot afford any revenue for maintaining themselves, but of which the conveniency is nearly confined to some particular place or district, are always better maintained by a local or provincial revenue, under the management of a local and provincial administration, than by the general revenue of the state, of which the executive power must always have the management. Were the streets of London to be lighted and paved at the expense of the treasury, is there any probability that they would be so well lighted and paved as they are at present, or even at so small an expense? . . .

The abuses which sometimes creep into the local and provincial administration of a local and provincial revenue, how enormous soever they may appear, are in reality, however, almost always very trifling in comparison of those which commonly take place in the administration and expenditure of the revenue of a great empire. They are, besides, much more easily corrected. . . .

### Of the Public Works and Institutions Which Are Necessary for Facilitating Particular Branches of Commerce

The object of the public works and institutions above mentioned is to facilitate commerce in general. But in order to facilitate some particular branches of it, particular institutions are necessary, which again require a particular and extraordinary expense.

Some particular branches of commerce which are carried on with barbarous and uncivilized nations require extraordinary protection. An ordinary store or counting house could give little security to the goods of the merchants who trade to the western coast of Africa. To defend them from the barbarous natives, it is necessary that the place where they are deposited should be in some measure fortified. . . . The interests of commerce have frequently made it necessary to maintain ministers in foreign countries, where the purposes either of war or alliance would not have required any.

The commerce of the Turkey Company first occasioned the establishment of an ordinary ambassador at Constantinople. The first English embassies to Russia arose altogether from commercial interests. . . .

It seems not unreasonable, that the extraordinary expense which the protection of any particular branch of commerce may occasion, should be defrayed by a moderate tax upon that particular branch; by a moderate fine, for example, to be paid by the traders when they first enter into it; or, what is more equal, by a particular duty of so much percent upon the goods which they either import into, or export out of, the particular countries with which it is carried on. The protection of trade, in general, from pirates and freebooters, is said to have given occasion to the first institution of the duties of customs. But, if it was thought reasonable to lay a general tax upon trade, in order to defray the expense of protecting trade in general, it should seem equally reasonable to lay a particular tax upon a particular branch of trade, in order to defray the extraordinary expense of protecting that branch.

The protection of trade, in general, has always been considered as essential to the defense of the commonwealth, and, upon that account, a necessary part of the duty of the executive power. The collection and application of the general duties of customs, therefore, have always been left to that power. But the protection of any particular branch of trade is a part of the general protection of trade; a part, therefore, of the duty of that power. . . .

When a company of merchants undertake, at their own risk and expense, to establish a new trade with some remote and barbarous nation, it may not be unreasonable to incorporate them into a joint-stock company, and to grant them, in case of their success, a monopoly of the trade for a certain number of years. It is the easiest and most natural way in which the state can recompense them for hazarding a dangerous and expensive experiment, of which the public is afterwards to reap the benefit. A temporary monopoly of this kind may be vindicated, upon the same principles upon which a like monopoly of a new machine is granted to its inventor, and that of a new book to its author. But upon the expiration of the term, the monopoly ought certainly to determine; the forts and garrisons, if it was found necessary to establish any, to be taken into the hands of government, their value to be paid to the company, and the trade to be laid open to all the subjects of the state.

By a perpetual monopoly, all the other subjects of the state are taxed very absurdly in two different ways: first, by the high price of goods, which, in the case of a free trade, they could buy much cheaper; and, secondly, by their total exclusion from a branch of business which it might be both convenient and profitable for many of them to carry on. It is for the most worthless of all purposes, too, that they are taxed in this manner. It is merely to enable the company to support the negligence, profusion, and malversation of their own servants, whose disorderly conduct seldom allows the dividend of the company to exceed the ordinary rate of profit in trades which are altogether free, and very frequently makes a fall even a good deal short of that rate. Without a monopoly, however, a joint-stock company, it would appear from experience, cannot long carry on any branch of foreign trade. . . . The East India Company, upon the redemption of their funds, and the expiration of their exclusive privilege, have a right, by act of parliament, to continue a corporation with a joint stock, and to trade in their corporate capacity to the East Indies, in common with the rest of their fellow subjects. But in this situation, the superior vigilance and attention of a private adventurer would, in all probability, soon make them weary of the trade. . . .

The only trades which it seems possible for a joint-stock company to carry on successfully, without an exclusive privilege, are those, of which all the operations are capable of being reduced to what is called a routine, or to such a uniformity of method as admits of little or no variation. Of this kind is, first, the banking trade; secondly, the trade of insurance from fire and from sea risk, and capture in time of war; thirdly, the trade of making and maintaining a navigable cut or canal; and, fourthly, the similar trade of bringing water for the supply of a great city.

Though the principles of the banking trade may appear somewhat abstruse, the practice is capable of being reduced to strict rules. To depart upon any occasion from those rules, in consequence of some flattering speculation of extraordinary gain, is almost always extremely dangerous and frequently fatal to the banking company which attempts it. But the constitution of joint-stock companies renders them in general, more tenacious of established rules than any private copartnery. Such companies, therefore, seem extremely well fitted for this trade. The principal banking companies in Europe, accordingly, are joint-stock companies, many of which manage their trade very successfully without any exclusive privilege. The bank of England has no other exclusive privilege, except that no other banking company in England shall consist of more than six persons. The two banks of Edinburgh are joint-stock companies, without any exclusive privilege. . . .

To establish a joint-stock company, however, for any undertaking, merely because such a company might be capable of managing it successfully; or, to exempt a particular set of dealers from some of the general laws which take place with regard to all their neighbors, merely because they might be capable of thriving, if they had such an exemption, would certainly not be reasonable. To render such an establishment perfectly reasonable, with the circumstance of being reducible to strict rule and method, two other circumstances ought to concur. First, it ought to appear with the clearest evidence, that the undertaking is of greater and more general utility than the greater part of common trades; and, secondly, that it requires a greater capital than can easily be collected into a private copartnery. . . .

The great and general utility of the banking trade, when prudently managed, has been fully explained in the second book of this Inquiry. But a public bank, which is to support public credit, and, upon particular emergencies, to advance to government the whole produce of a tax, to the amount, perhaps, of several millions, a year or two before it comes in, requires a greater capital than can easily be collected into any private copartnery.

The trade of insurance gives great security to the fortunes of private people, and, by dividing among a great many that loss which would ruin an individual, makes it fall light and easy upon the whole society. In order to give this security, however, it is necessary that the insurers should have a very large capital. Before the establishment of the two joint-stock companies for insurance in London, a list, it is said, was laid before the attorney-general, of one hundred and fifty private usurers, who had failed in the course of a few years. . . .

Except the four trades above mentioned, I have not been able to recollect any other, in which all the three circumstances requisite for rendering reasonable the establishment of a joint-stock company concur. . . . The joint-stock companies, which are established for the public-spirited purpose of promoting some particular manufacture, over and above managing their own affairs ill, to the diminution of the general stock of the society, can, in other respects, scarce ever fail to do more harm than good. . . .

# Article Two

## Of the Expense of the Institution for the Education of Youth

The institutions for the education of the youth may, in the same manner, furnish a revenue sufficient for defraying their own expense. The fee or honorary, which the scholar pays to the master, naturally constitutes a revenue of this kind.

Even where the reward of the master does not arise altogether from this natural revenue, it still is not necessary that it should be derived from that general revenue of the society, of which the collection and application are, in most countries, assigned to the executive power. Through the greater part of Europe, accordingly, the endowment of schools and colleges makes either no charge upon that general revenue, or but a very small one. It everywhere arises chiefly from some local or provincial revenue, from the rent of some landed estate, or from the interest of some sum of money, allotted and put under the management of trustees for this particular purpose, sometimes by the sovereign himself, and sometimes by some private donor.

# Article Three

## Of the Expense of the Institutions for the Instruction of People of All Ages

The institutions for the instruction of people of all ages, are chiefly those for religious instruction. This is a species of instruction, of which the object is not so much to render the people good citizens in this world, as to prepare them for another and a better world in the life to come. The teachers of the doctrine which contains this instruction, in the same manner as other teachers, may either depend altogether for their subsistence upon the voluntary contributions of their hearers; or they may derive it from some other fund, to which the law of their country may entitle them; such as a landed estate, a tithe or land tax, an established salary or stipend. Their exertion, their zeal and industry, are likely to be much greater in the former situation than in the latter. In this respect, the teachers of a new religion have always had a considerable advantage in attacking those ancient and established systems, of which the clergy, reposing themselves upon their benefices, had neglected to keep up the fervor of faith and devotion in the great body of the people.

## Part Four

# Of the Expense of Supporting the Dignity of the Sovereign

Over and above the expenses necessary for enabling the sovereign to perform his several duties, a certain expense is requisite for the support of his dignity. . . .

. . . We naturally expect more splendor in the court of a king, than in the mansion house of a doge or burgomaster.

# Chapter Two

## Of the Sources of the General or Public Revenue of the Society

THE REVENUE WHICH must defray, not only the expense of defending the society and of supporting the dignity of the chief magistrate, but all the other necessary expenses of government, for which the constitution of the state has not provided any particular revenue may be drawn, either, first, from some fund which peculiarly belongs to the sovereign or commonwealth, and which is independent of the revenue of the people; or, secondly, from the revenue of the people.

## *Part One*

# Of the Funds, or Sources, of Revenue Which May Peculiarly Belong to the Sovereign or Commonwealth

The republic of Hamburg is said to do so from the profits of a public wine cellar and apothecary's shop. That state cannot be very great, of which the sovereign has leisure to carry on the trade of a wine merchant or an apothecary. The profit of a public bank has been a source of revenue to more considerable states. It has been so, not only to Hamburg, but to Venice and –Amsterdam. A revenue of this kind has even by some people been thought not below the attention of so great an empire as that of Great Britain. Reckoning the ordinary dividend of the bank of England at five-and-a-half percent, and its capital at ten millions seven hundred and eighty thousand pounds, the neat annual profit, after paying the expense of management, must amount, it is said, to five hundred and ninety-two thousand nine hundred pounds. Government, it is pretended, could borrow this capital at three percent interest, and, by taking the management of the bank into its own hands, might make a clear profit of two hundred and sixty-nine thousand five hundred pounds a year. The orderly, vigilant, and parsimonious administration of such aristocracies as those of Venice and Amsterdam, is extremely proper, it appears from experience, for the management of a mercantile project of this kind. But whether such a government as that of England, which, whatever may be its virtues, has never been famous for good economy; which, in time of peace, has generally conducted itself with the slothful and negligent profusion that is, perhaps, natural to monarchies; and, in time of war, has constantly acted with all the thoughtless extravagance that democracies are apt to fall into, could be safely trusted with the management of such a project, must at least be a good deal more doubtful.

The post office is properly a mercantile project. The government advances the expense of establishing the different offices, and of buying or hiring the necessary horses or carriages, and is repaid, with a large profit, by the duties upon what is carried. It is, perhaps, the only mercantile project which has been successfully managed by, I believe, every sort of government. The capital to be advanced is not very considerable. There is no mystery in the business. The returns are not only certain but immediate.

Princes, however, have frequently engaged in many other mercantile projects, and have been willing, like private persons, to mend their fortunes, by becoming adventurers in the common branches of trade. They have scarce ever succeeded. The profusion, with which the affairs of princes are always managed, renders it almost impossible that they should. The agents of a prince regard the wealth of their master as inexhaustible; are careless at what price they buy, are careless at what price they sell, are careless at what expense they transport his goods from one place to another. Those agents frequently live with the profusion of princes; and sometimes, too, in spite of that profusion, and by a proper method of making up their accounts, acquire the fortunes of princes. . . .

No two characters seem more inconsistent than those of trader and sovereign. If the trading spirit of the English East India Company renders them very bad sovereigns, the spirit of sovereignty seems to have rendered them equally bad traders. While they were traders only, they managed their trade successfully, and were able to pay from their profits a moderate dividend to the proprietors of their stock. Since they became sovereigns, with a revenue which, it is said, was originally more than three millions sterling, they have been obliged to beg the ordinary assistance of government, in order to avoid immediate bankruptcy. In their former situation, their servants in India considered themselves as the clerks of merchants; in their present situation, those servants consider themselves as the ministers of sovereigns.

A state may sometimes derive some part of its public revenue from the interest of money, as well as from the profits of stock. If it has amassed a treasure, it may lend a part of that treasure, either to foreign states, or to its own subjects.

The canton of Berne derives a considerable revenue by lending a part of its treasure to foreign states, that is, by placing it in the public funds of the different indebted nations of Europe, chiefly in those of France and England. . . . This policy of lending money to foreign states is, so far as I know peculiar to the canton of Berne. . . .

The government of Pennsylvania, without amassing any treasure, invented a method of lending, not money, indeed, but what is equivalent to money, to its subjects. By advancing to private people, at interest, and upon land security to double the value, paper bills of credit, to be redeemed fifteen years after their date; and, in the meantime, made transferable from hand to hand, like banknotes, and declared by act of assembly to be a legal tender in all payments from one inhabitant of the province to another, it raised a moderate revenue, which went a considerable way towards defraying an annual expense of about 4,500*l*, the whole ordinary expense of that frugal and orderly government. The success of an expedient of this kind must have depended upon three different circumstances: first, upon the demand for some other instrument of commerce, besides gold and silver money, or upon the demand for such a quantity of consumable stock as could not be had without sending abroad the greater part of their gold and silver money, in order to purchase it; secondly, upon the good credit of the government which made use of this expedient; and, thirdly, upon the moderation with which it was used, the whole value of the paper bills of credit never exceeding that of the gold and silver money which would have been necessary for carrying on their circulation, had there been no paper bills of credit. The same expedient was, upon different occasions, adopted by several other American colonies; but, from want of this moderation, it produced, in the greater part of them, much more disorder than conveniency.

The unstable and perishable nature of stock and credit, however, renders them unfit to be trusted to as the principal funds of that sure, steady, and permanent revenue, which can alone give security and dignity to government. . . .

Land is a fund of more stable and permanent nature; and the rent of public lands, accordingly, has been the principal source of the public revenue of many a great nation that was much advanced beyond the shepherd state. . . . The rent of the crown lands constituted for a long time the greater part of the revenue of the ancient sovereigns of Europe. . . .

. . . The crown lands of Great Britain do not at present afford the fourth part of the rent which could probably be drawn from them if they were the property of private persons. If the crown lands were more extensive, it is probable, they would be still worse managed.

Though there is not at present in Europe, any civilized state of any kind which derives the greater part of its public revenue from the rent of lands which are the property of the state; yet, in all the great monarchies of

Europe, there are still many large tracts of land which belong to the crown. They are generally forest, and sometimes forests where, after traveling several miles, you will scarce find a single tree; a mere waste and loss of country, in respect both of produce and population. In every great monarchy of Europe, the sale of the crown lands would produce a very large sum of money, which, if applied to the payment of the public debts, would deliver from mortgage a much greater revenue than any which those lands have ever afforded to the crown....

Lands, for the purposes of pleasure and magnificence, parks, gardens, public walks, etc., possessions which are everywhere considered as causes of expense, not as sources of revenue, seem to be the only lands which, in a great and civilized monarchy, ought to belong to the crown.

Public stock and public lands, therefore, the two sources of revenue which may peculiarly belong to the sovereign or commonwealth, being both improper and insufficient funds for defraying the necessary expense of any great and civilized state; it remains that this expense must, the greater part of it, be defrayed by taxes of one kind or another; the people contributing a part of their own private revenue, in order to make up a public revenue to the sovereign or commonwealth.

## Part Two

# Of Taxes

The private revenue of individuals, it has been shown in the first book of this Inquiry, arises, ultimately from three different sources; rent, profit, and wages. Every tax must finally be paid from someone or other of those three different sources of revenue, or from all of them indifferently. . . .

Before I enter upon the examination of particular taxes, it is necessary to premise the four following maxims with regard to taxes in general.

1. The subjects of every state ought to contribute towards the support of the government, as nearly as possible, in proportion to their respective abilities; that is, in proportion to the revenue which they respectively enjoy under the protection of the state. . . . Every tax, it must be observed once for all, which falls finally upon one only of the three sorts of revenue above-mentioned, is necessarily unequal, in so far as it does not affect the other two. In the following examination of different taxes, I shall seldom take much farther notice of this sort of inequality; but shall, in most cases, confine my observations to that inequality which is occasioned

by a particular tax falling unequally upon that particular sort of private revenue which is affected by it.

2. The tax which each individual is bound to pay, ought to be certain and not arbitrary. The time of payment, the manner of payment, the quantity to be paid, ought all to be clear and plain to the contributor, and to every other person. Where it is otherwise, every person subject to the tax is put more or less in the power of the tax gatherer, who can either aggravate the tax upon any obnoxious contributor, or extort, by the terror of such aggravation, some present or perquisite to himself. The uncertainty of taxation encourages the insolence, and favors the corruption, of an order of men who are naturally unpopular, even where they are neither insolent nor corrupt. The certainty of what each individual ought to pay is, in taxation, a matter of so great importance, that a very considerable degree of inequality, it appears, I believe, from the experience of all nations, is not near so great an evil as a very small degree of uncertainty. . . .

3. Every tax ought to be so contrived, as both to take out and to keep out of the pockets of the people as little as possible, over and

above what it brings into the public treasury of the state. A tax may either take out or keep out of the pockets of the people a great deal more than it brings into the public treasury, in the four following ways. First, the levying of it may require a great number of officers, whose salaries may eat up the greater part of the produce of the tax, and whose perquisites may impose another additional tax upon the people. Secondly, it may obstruct the industry of the people, and discourage them from applying to certain branches of business which might give maintenance and employment to great multitudes. While it obliges the people to pay, it may thus diminish, or perhaps destroy, some of the funds which might enable them more easily to do so. Thirdly, by the forfeitures and other penalties which those unfortunate individuals incur, who attempt unsuccessfully to evade the tax, it may frequently ruin them, and thereby put an end to the benefit which the community might have received from the employment of their capitals.... Fourthly, by subjecting the people to the frequent visits and the odious examination of the tax gatherers, it may expose them to much unnecessary trouble, vexation, and oppression;

and though vexation is not, strictly speaking, expense, it is certainly equivalent to the expense at which every man would be willing to redeem himself from it. It is in some one or other of these four different ways, that taxes are frequently so much more burdensome to the people than they are beneficial to the sovereign. . . .

# Article One

## Taxes upon Rent—Taxes upon the Rent of Land

. . . A land tax which, like that of Great Britain, is assessed upon each district according to a certain invariable canon, though it should be equal at the time of its first establishment, necessarily becomes unequal in process of time, according to the unequal degrees of improvement or neglect in the cultivation of the different parts of the country. In England, the valuation, according to which the different counties and parishes were assessed to the land tax by the 4th of William and Mary, was very unequal even at its first establishment. This tax, therefore, so far offends against the first of the four maxims above mentioned. . . .

A land tax assessed according to a general survey and valuation, how equal soever it may be at first, must, in the course of a very moderate period of time, become unequal. To prevent its becoming so would require the continual and painful attention of government to all the variations in the state and produce of every different farm in the country. The governments of Prussia, of Bohemia, of Sardinia, and of the duchy of Milan, actually exert an attention of this kind; an attention so unsuitable to the nature of government, that it is not likely to be of long continuance, and which, if it is continued, will probably, in the long run, occasion much more trouble and vexation than it can possibly bring relief to the contributors. . . .

## Taxes Which Are Proportioned, Not in the Rent, but to the Produce of Land

Taxes upon the produce of land are, in reality, taxes upon the rent; and though they may be originally advanced by the farmer, are finally paid by the landlord. When a certain portion of the produce is to be paid away for a tax, the farmer computes as well as he can, what the value of this portion is, one year with another, likely to amount to, and he makes a proportional abatement in the rent which he agrees to pay to the landlord. There is no farmer who does not compute beforehand what the church tithe, which is a land tax of this kind, is, one year with another, likely to amount to. . . .

The tithe, as it is frequently a very unequal tax upon the rent, so it is always a great discouragement, both to the improvements of the landlord, and to the cultivation of the farmer. The one cannot venture to make the most important, which are generally the most expensive improvements; nor the other to raise the most valuable, which are generally, too, the most expensive crops; when the church, which lays out no part of the expense, is to share so very largely in the profit. . . .

As through the greater part of Europe, the church, so in many different countries of Asia, the state, is principally supported by a land tax, proportioned not to the rent, but to the produce of the land. In China, the principal revenue of the sovereign consists in a tenth part of the produce of all the lands of the empire. This tenth part, however, is estimated so very moderately, that, in many provinces, it is said not to exceed a thirtieth part of the ordinary produce. The land tax or land rent which used to be paid to the Mahometan government of Bengal, before that country fell into the hands of the English East India company, is said to have amounted to about a fifth part of the produce. The land tax of ancient Egypt is said likewise to have amounted to a fifth part. . . .

## Taxes upon the Rent of Houses

The rent of a house may be distinguished into two parts, of which the one may very properly be called the building-rent; the other is commonly called the ground-rent. . . .

The rent of houses, though it in some respects resembles the rent of land, is in one respect essentially different from it. The rent of land is paid for the use of a productive subject. The land which pays it produces it. The rent of houses is paid for the use of an unproductive subject. Neither the house, nor the ground which it stands upon, produce anything. The person who pays the rent, therefore, must draw it from some other source of revenue, distinct from and independent of this subject. . . . In general, there is not perhaps, any one article of expense or consumption by which the liberality or narrowness of a man's whole expense can be better judged of than by his house-rent. A proportional tax upon this particular article of expense might, perhaps, produce a more considerable revenue than any which has hitherto been drawn from it in any part of Europe. If the tax, indeed, was very high, the greater part of people would endeavor to evade it as much as they could, by contenting themselves with smaller houses, and by turning the greater part of their expense into some other channel.

The rent of houses might easily be ascertained with sufficient accuracy, by a policy of the same kind with that which would be necessary for ascertaining the ordinary rent of land. . . .

In Great Britain the rent of houses is supposed to be taxed in the same proportion as the rent of land, by what is called the annual land tax. The valuation, according to which each different parish and district is assessed to this tax, is always the same. It was originally extremely unequal, and it still continues to be so. . . .

In the province of Holland every house is taxed at two-and-a-half percent of its value, without any regard, either to the rent which it actually pays, or to the circumstance of its being tenanted or untenanted. . . . The valuation, indeed, according to which the houses are rated, though very unequal, is said to be always below the real value. When a house is rebuilt, improved, or enlarged, there is a new valuation, and the tax is rated accordingly.

The contrivers of the several taxes which in England have, at different times, been imposed upon houses, seem to have imagined that there was some great difficulty in ascertaining, with tolerable exactness, what was the real rent of every house. They have regulated their taxes, therefore, according to some more obvious circumstance, such as they had probably imagined would, in most cases, bear some proportion to the rent.

The first tax of this kind was hearth-money; or a tax of two shillings upon every hearth. In order to ascertain how many hearths were in the house, it was necessary that the tax gatherer should enter every room in it. This odious visit rendered the tax odious. Soon after the Revolution, therefore, it was abolished as a badge of slavery. . . .

This tax was afterwards repealed, and in the room of it was established the window-tax, which has undergone several alterations and augmentations.* The window tax, as it stands at present ( January 1775 ), over

---

* And presumably reduced the number of windows built. One wonders if later generations had a clue why their dwellings were dark.

and above the duty of three shillings upon every house in England, and of one shilling upon every house in Scotland, lays a duty upon every window, which in England augments gradually from two pence, the lowest rate upon houses with not more than seven windows, to two shillings, the highest rate upon houses with twenty-five windows and upwards.

The principal objection to all such taxes is their inequality; an inequality of the worst kind, as they must frequently fall much heavier upon the poor than upon the rich. A house of ten pounds rent in a country town, may sometimes have more windows than a house of five hundred pounds rent in London; and though the inhabitant of the former is likely to be a much poorer man than that of the latter. . . .

# Article Two

## Taxes upon Profit, or upon the Revenue Arising from Stock

The revenue or profit arising from stock naturally divides itself into two parts; that which pays the interest, and which belongs to the owner of the stock; and that surplus part which is over and above what is necessary for paying the interest.

This latter part of profit is evidently a subject not taxable directly. It is the compensation, and, in most cases, it is no more than a very moderate compensation for the risk and trouble of employing the stock. . . . If he employed it as a mercantile or manufacturing stock, he could raise the rate of his profit only by raising the price of his goods; in which case, the final payment of the tax would fall altogether upon the consumers of those goods. If he did not raise the rate of his profit, he would be obliged to charge the whole tax upon that part of it which was allotted for the interest of money. He could afford less interest for whatever stock he borrowed, and the whole weight of the tax would, in this case, fall ultimately upon the interest of money. So far as he could not relieve himself from the tax in the one way, he would be obliged to relieve himself in the other. . . .

There are . . . two [further] circumstances, which render [investment assets] a much less proper subject of direct taxation than the rent of land.

First, the quantity and value of the land which any man possesses, can never be a secret, and can always be ascertained with great exactness. But the whole amount of the capital stock which he possesses is almost always a secret, and can scarce ever be ascertained with tolerable exactness. It is liable, besides, to almost continual variations. A year seldom passes away, frequently not a month, sometimes scarce a single day, in which it does not rise or fall more or less. An inquisition into every man's private circumstances, and an inquisition which, in order to accommodate the tax to them, watched over all the fluctuations of his fortune, would be a source of such continual and endless vexation as no person could support.

Secondly, land is a subject which cannot be removed; whereas stock easily may. The proprietor of land is necessarily a citizen of the particular country in which his estate lies. The proprietor of stock is properly a citizen of the world, and is not necessarily attached to any particular country. He would be apt to abandon the country in which he was exposed to a vexatious inquisition, in order to be assessed to a burdensome tax; and would remove his stock to some other country, where he could either carry on his business, or enjoy his fortune more at his ease. By removing his stock, he would put an end to all the industry which it had maintained in the country which he left. Stock cultivates land; stock employs labor. A tax which tended to drive away stock from any particular country would so far tend to dry up every source of revenue, both to the sovereign and to the society. Not only the profits of stock, but the rent of land, and the wages of labor, would necessarily be more or less diminished by its removal.

The nations, accordingly, who have attempted to tax the revenue arising from stock, instead of any severe inquisition of this kind, have been obliged to content themselves with some very loose, and, therefore, more or less arbitrary estimation. The extreme inequality and uncertainty of a tax assessed in this manner, can be compensated only by its extreme moderation; in consequence of which, every man finds himself rated so very much below his real revenue, that he gives himself little disturbance though his neighbor should be rated somewhat lower.

By what is called the land tax in England, it was intended that the stock should be taxed in the same proportion as land. . . . [But] the greater part of it was laid upon the country; and of what was laid upon the towns, the greater part was assessed upon the houses. What remained to be assessed upon the stock or trade of the towns (for the stock upon the land was not meant to be taxed) was very much below the real value of that stock or trade. Whatever inequalities, therefore, there might be in the original assessment, gave little disturbance. Every parish and district still continues to be rated for its land, its houses, and its stock, according to the original assessment; and the almost universal prosperity of the country, which, in most places, has raised very much the value of all these, has rendered those inequalities of still less importance now. . . . If the greater part of the lands of England are not rated to the land tax at half their actual value, the greater part of the stock of England is, perhaps, scarce rated at the fiftieth part of its actual value. In some towns, the whole land tax is assessed upon houses; as in Westminster, where stock and trade are free. It is otherwise in London.

In all countries, a severe inquisition into the circumstances of private persons has been carefully avoided.

At Hamburg, every inhabitant is obliged to pay to the state one-fourth percent of all that he possesses;

and as the wealth of the people of Hamburg consists principally in stock, this tax may be considered as a tax upon stock. Every man assesses himself, and, in the presence of the magistrate, puts annually into the public coffer a certain sum of money, which he declares upon oath, to be one-fourth percent of all that he possesses, but without declaring what it amounts to, or being liable to any examination upon that subject. . . .

The canton of Underwald, in Switzerland, is frequently ravaged by storms and inundations, and it is thereby exposed to extraordinary expenses. Upon such occasions the people assemble, and everyone is said to declare with the greatest frankness what he is worth, in order to be taxed accordingly. . . .

To oblige every citizen to declare publicly upon oath, the amount of his fortune, must not, it seems, in those Swiss cantons, be reckoned a hardship. At Hamburg it would be reckoned the greatest. Merchants engaged in the hazardous projects of trade, all tremble at the thoughts of being obliged, at all times, to expose the real state of their circumstances. The ruin of their credit, and the miscarriage of their projects, they foresee, would too often be the consequence. A sober and parsimonious people, who are strangers to all such projects, do not feel that they have occasion for any such concealment. . . .

. . . The tax at Hamburg, and the still more moderate taxes of Underwald and Zurich, are meant, in the same manner, to be taxes, not upon the capital, but upon the interest or neat revenue of stock. . . .

## Taxes upon the Profit of Particular Employments

In some countries, extraordinary taxes are imposed upon the profits of stock; sometimes when employed in particular branches of trade, and sometimes when employed in agriculture.

Of the former kind, are in England, the tax upon hawkers and peddlers, that upon hackney coaches and chairs, and that which the keepers of alehouses pay for a license to retail ale and spirituous liquors. During the late war, another tax of the same kind was proposed upon shops. The war having been undertaken, it was said, in defense of the trade of the country, the merchants, who were to profit by it, ought to contribute towards the support of it.

A tax, however, upon the profits of stock employed in any particular branch of trade, can never fall finally upon the dealers (who must in all ordinary cases have their reasonable profit, and, where the competition is free, can seldom have more than that profit), but always upon the consumers, who must be obliged to pay in the price of the goods the tax which the dealer advances; and generally with some overcharge. . . .

. . . The tax of five shillings a week upon every hackney coach, and that of ten shillings a year upon every hackney chair, so far as it is advanced by the different keepers of such coaches and chairs, is exactly enough proportioned to the extent of their respective dealings. It neither favors the great, nor oppresses the smaller dealer. The tax of twenty shillings a year for a license to sell ale; of forty shillings for a license to sell spirituous liquors; and of forty shillings more for a license to sell wine, being the same upon all retailers, must necessarily give some advantage to the great, and occasion some oppression to the small dealers. The former must find it more easy to get back the tax in the price of their goods than the latter. The moderation of the tax, however, renders this inequality of less importance; and it may to many people appear not improper to give some discouragement to the multiplication of little alehouses.

The tax upon shops, it was intended, should be the same upon all shops. It could not well have been otherwise. It would have been impossible to proportion, with tolerable exactness, the tax upon a shop to the extent of the trade carried on in it, without such an inquisition as would have been altogether insupportable in a free country. If the tax had been considerable, it would have oppressed the small, and forced almost the whole retail trade into the hands of the great dealers. The competition of the former being taken away, the latter would have enjoyed a monopoly of the trade; and, like all other monopolists, would soon have combined to raise their profits much beyond what was necessary for the payment of the tax. The final payment, instead of falling upon the shopkeeper, would have fallen upon the consumer, with a considerable overcharge to the profit of the shopkeeper. For these reasons, the project of a tax upon shops was laid aside. . . .

The taxes which in Holland are imposed upon men and maidservants are taxes, not upon stock, but upon expense; and so far resemble the taxes upon consumable commodities. The tax of a guinea a head for every manservant, which has lately been imposed in Great Britain, is of the same kind. It falls heaviest upon the middling rank. A man of two hundred a year may keep a single manservant. A man of ten thousand a year will not keep fifty. It does not affect the poor. . . .

# Appendix to Articles One and Two

### Taxes upon the Capital Value of Lands, Houses, and Stock

While property remains in the possession of the same person, whatever permanent taxes may have been imposed upon it, they have never been intended to diminish or take away any part of its capital value, but only some part of the revenue arising from it. But when property changes hands, when it is transmitted either from the dead to the living or from the living to the living, such taxes have frequently been imposed upon it as necessarily take away some part of its capital value. . . .

By a feudal law, the vassal could not alienate without the consent of his superior, who generally extorted a fine or composition on granting it. This fine, which was at first arbitrary, came, in many countries, to be regulated at a certain portion of the price of the land. In some countries, where the greater part of the other feudal customs have gone into disuse, this tax upon the alienation of land still continues to make a very considerable branch of the revenue of the sovereign. In the canton of Berne it is so high as a sixth part of the price of all noble fiefs, and a tenth part of that of all ignoble ones. In the canton of Lucerne, the tax upon the sale of land is not universal, and takes place only in certain districts. But if any person sells his land in order to remove out of the territory, he pays ten percent upon the whole price of the sale. Taxes of the same kind, upon the sale either of all lands, or of lands held by certain tenures, take place in many other countries, and make a more or less considerable branch of the revenue of the sovereign.

Such transactions may be taxed indirectly, by means either of stamp duties, or of duties upon registration; and those duties either may, or may not, be proportioned to the value of the subject which is transferred. . . .

Those modes of taxation by stamp duties and by duties upon registration are of very modern invention. In the course of little more than a century, however, stamp duties have, in Europe, become almost universal, and duties upon registration extremely common. There is no art which one government sooner learns of another, than that of draining money from the pockets of the people. . . .

Such stamp duties as those in England upon cards and dice, upon newspapers and periodical pamphlets, etc. are properly taxes upon consumption; the final payment falls upon the persons who use or consume such commodities. . . .

# Article Three

### Taxes upon the Wages of Labor

The wages of the inferior classes of workmen, I have endeavored to show in the first book are everywhere necessarily regulated by two different circumstances; the demand for labor, and the ordinary or average price of provisions. The demand for labor, according as it happens to be either increasing, stationary, or declining; or to require an increasing, stationary, or declining population, regulates the subsistence of the laborer, and determines in what degree it shall be either liberal, moderate, or scanty. The ordinary average price of provisions determines the quantity of money which must be paid to the workman, in order to enable him, one year with another, to purchase this liberal, moderate, or scanty subsistence. While the demand for the labor and the price of provisions, therefore, remain the same, a direct tax upon the wages of labor can have no other effect than to raise them somewhat higher than the tax. Let us suppose, for example, that, in a particular place, the demand for labor and the price of provisions were such as to render ten shillings a week the ordinary wages of labor; and that a tax of one-fifth, or four shillings in the pound, was imposed upon wages. If the demand for labor and the price of provisions remained the same, it would still be necessary that the laborer should, in that place, earn such a subsistence as could be bought only for ten shillings a week; so that, after paying the tax, he should have ten shillings a week free wages. But, in order to leave him such free wages, after paying such a tax, the price of labor must, in that place, soon rise, not to twelve shillings a week only, but to twelve and six pence; that is, in order to enable him to pay a tax of one-fifth, his wages must necessarily soon rise, not one-fifth part only, but one-fourth. Whatever was the proportion of the tax, the wages of labor must, in all cases rise, not only in that proportion, but in a higher proportion. If the tax for example, was one-tenth, the wages of labor must necessarily soon rise, not one-tenth part only, but one-eighth. . . .

. . . In all such cases, not only the tax, but something more than the tax, would in reality be advanced by the person who immediately employed [the worker]. The final payment would, in different cases, fall upon different persons. The rise which such a tax might occasion in the wages of manufacturing labor would be advanced by the master manufacturer, who would both be entitled and obliged to charge it, with a profit, upon the price of his goods. The final payment of this rise of wages, therefore, together with the additional profit of the master manufacturer would fall upon the consumer. The rise which such a tax might occasion in the wages of country labor would be advanced by the farmer, who, in order to maintain the same number of laborers as before, would be obliged to employ a greater capital. In order to get back this greater capital, together with the ordinary profits of stock, it would be necessary that he should retain a larger portion, or, what comes to the same thing, the price of a larger portion, of the produce of the land, and, consequently, that he should pay less rent to the landlord. The final payment of this rise of wages, therefore, would, in this case, fall upon the landlord, together with the additional profit of the farmer who had advanced it. In all cases, a direct tax upon the wages of labor must, in the long run, occasion both a greater reduction in the rent of land, and a greater rise in the price of manufactured goods than would have followed from the proper assessment of a sum equal to the produce of the tax, partly upon the rent of land, and partly upon consumable commodities.

If direct taxes upon the wages of labor have not always occasioned a proportional rise in those wages, it is because they have generally occasioned a considerable fall in the demand of labor. The declension of industry, the decrease of employment for the poor, the diminution of the annual produce of the land and labor of the country, have generally been the effects of such taxes. In consequence of them, however, the price of labor must always be higher than it otherwise would have been in the actual state of the demand; and this enhancement of price, together with the profit of those who advance it, must always be finally paid by the landlords and consumers. . . .

Absurd and destructive as such taxes are, however, they take place in many countries. In France, that part of the taille which is charged upon the industry of workmen and day laborers in country villages is properly a tax of this kind. Their wages are computed according to the common rate of the district in which they reside; and, that they may be as little liable as possible to any overcharge, their yearly gains are estimated at no more than two hundred working days in the year. The tax of each individual is varied from year to year, according to different circumstances, of which the collector or the commissary, whom intendant appoints to assist him, are the judges. In Bohemia, in consequence of the alteration in the system of finances which was begun in 1748, a very heavy tax is imposed upon the industry of artificers. . . .

The recompense of ingenious artists, and of men of liberal professions, I have endeavored to show in the first book, necessarily keeps a certain proportion to the emoluments of inferior trades. A tax upon this recompense, therefore, could have no other effect than to raise it somewhat higher than in proportion to the tax. If it did not rise in this manner, the ingenious arts and the liberal professions, being no longer upon a level with other trades, would be so much deserted, that they would soon return to that level.

The emoluments of offices are not, like those of trades and professions, regulated by the free competition of the market, and do not, therefore, always bear a just proportion to what the nature of the employment requires. They are, perhaps, in most countries, higher than it requires; the persons who have the administration of government being generally disposed to regard both themselves and their immediate dependents, rather more than enough. The emoluments of offices, therefore, can, in most cases, very well bear to be taxed. The persons, besides, who enjoy public offices, especially the more lucrative, are, in all countries, the objects of general envy; and a tax upon their emoluments, even though it should be somewhat higher than upon any other sort of revenue, is always a very popular tax. In England, for example, when, by the land tax, every other sort of revenue was supposed to be assessed at four shillings in the pound, it was very popular to lay a real tax of five shillings and six pence in the pound upon the salaries of offices which exceeded a hundred pounds a year; the pensions of the younger branches of the royal family, the pay of the officers of the army and navy, and a few others less obnoxious to envy, excepted. There are in England no other direct taxes upon the wages of labor.

# Article Four

## Taxes Which It Is Intended Should Fall Indifferently upon Every Different Species of Revenue

### *Capitation Taxes*

. . . Capitation taxes, if it is attempted to proportion them to the fortune or revenue of each contributor, become altogether arbitrary. The state of a man's fortune varies from day to day; and, without an inquisition, more intolerable than any tax, and renewed at least once every year, can only be guessed at. His assessment, therefore, must, in most cases, depend upon the good or bad humor of his assessors, and must, therefore, be altogether arbitrary and uncertain. . . .*

In the different poll-taxes which took place in England during the reign of William III the contributors were, the greater part of them, assessed according to the degree of their rank; as dukes, marquises, earls, viscounts, barons, esquires, gentlemen, the eldest and youngest sons of peers, etc. All shopkeepers and tradesmen worth more than three hundred pounds, that is the better sort of them, were subject to the same assessment, how great soever might be the difference in their fortunes. Their rank was more considered than their fortune. . . .

---

\* Per person or per household.

### Taxes upon Consumable Commodities

The impossibility of taxing the people, in proportion to their revenue, by any capitation, seems to have given occasion to the invention of taxes upon consumable commodities. The state not knowing how to tax, directly and proportionally, the revenue of its subjects, endeavors to tax it indirectly by taxing their expense, which, it is supposed, will, in most cases, be nearly in proportion to their revenue. Their expense is taxed, by taxing the consumable commodities upon which it is laid out.

### Consumable commodities are either necessaries or luxuries.

By necessaries I understand, not only the commodities which are indispensably necessary for the support of life, but whatever the custom of the country renders it indecent for creditable people, even of the lowest order, to be without. A linen shirt, for example, is, strictly speaking, not a necessary of life. The Greeks and Romans lived, I suppose, very comfortably, though they had no linen. But in the present times, through the greater part of Europe, a creditable day laborer would be ashamed to appear in public without a linen shirt, the want of which would be supposed to denote that disgraceful degree of poverty, which, it is presumed, nobody can well fall into without extreme bad conduct. Custom, in the same manner, has rendered leather shoes a necessary of life in England. The poorest creditable person, of either sex, would be ashamed to appear in public without them. In Scotland, custom has rendered them a necessary of life to the lowest order of men; but not to the same order of women, who may, without any discredit, walk about barefooted. In France, they are necessaries neither to men nor to women; the lowest rank of both sexes appearing there publicly, without any discredit, sometimes in wooden shoes, and sometimes barefooted. Under necessaries, therefore, I comprehend, not only those things which nature, but those things which the established rules of decency have rendered necessary to the lowest rank of people. All other things I call luxuries, without meaning, by this appellation, to throw the smallest degree of reproach upon the temperate use of them. Beer and ale, for example, in Great Britain, and wine, even in the wine countries, I call luxuries. A man of any rank may, without any reproach, abstain totally from tasting such liquors. Nature does not render them necessary for the support of life; and custom nowhere renders it indecent to live without them. . . .

. . . A tax upon the necessaries of life operates exactly in the same manner as a direct tax upon the wages of labor. The laborer, though he may pay it out of his hand, cannot, for any considerable time at least, be properly said even to advance it. It must always, in the long run, be advanced to him by his immediate employer, in the advanced state of wages. His employer, if he is a manufacturer, will charge upon the price of his goods the rise of wages, together with a profit, so that the final payment of the tax, together with this overcharge, will fall upon the consumer. If his employer is a farmer, the final payment, together with a like overcharge, will fall upon the rent of the landlord.

It is otherwise with taxes upon what I call luxuries, even upon those of the poor. The rise in the price of the taxed commodities, will not necessarily occasion any rise in the wages of labor. A tax upon tobacco, for example, though a luxury of the poor, as well as of the rich, will not raise wages. Though it is taxed in England at three times and in France at fifteen times its original price, those high duties seem to have no effect upon the wages of labor. The same thing may be said of the taxes upon tea and sugar, which, in England and Holland, have become luxuries of the lowest ranks of people; and of those upon chocolate, which, in Spain, is said to have become so. . . .

The high price of such commodities does not necessarily diminish the ability of the inferior ranks of people to bring up families. Upon the sober and industrious poor, taxes upon such commodities act as sumptuary laws, and dispose them either to moderate, or to refrain altogether from the use of superfluities which they can no longer easily afford. . . . All the poor, indeed, are not sober and industrious; and the dissolute and disorderly might continue to indulge themselves in the use of such commodities, after this rise of price, in the same manner as before, without regarding the distress which this indulgence might bring upon their families. Such disorderly persons, however, seldom rear up numerous families, their children generally perishing from neglect, mismanagement, and the scantiness or unwholesomeness of their food. If by the strength of their constitution, they survive the hardships to which the bad conduct of their parents exposes them, yet the example of that bad conduct commonly corrupts their morals; so that, instead of being useful to society by their industry, they become public nuisances by their vices and disorders. Through the advanced price of the luxuries of the poor, therefore, might increase somewhat the distress of such disorderly families, and thereby diminish somewhat their ability to bring up children, it would not probably diminish much the useful population of the country. . . .

Taxes upon luxuries have no tendency to raise the price of any other commodities, except that of the commodities taxed. Taxes upon necessaries, by raising the wages of labor, necessarily tend to raise the price of all manufactures, and consequently to diminish the extent of their sale and consumption. Taxes upon luxuries are finally paid by the consumers of the commodities taxed, without any retribution. They fall indifferently upon every species of revenue, the wages of labor, the profits of stock, and the rent of land. Taxes upon necessaries, so far as they affect the laboring poor, are finally paid, partly by landlords, in the diminished rent of their lands, and partly by rich consumers, whether landlords or others, in the advanced price of manufactured goods; and always with a considerable overcharge. The advanced price of such manufactures as are real necessaries of life, and are destined for the consumption of the poor, of coarse woolens, for example, must be compensated to the poor by a farther advancement of their wages.

The middling and superior ranks of people, if they understood their own interest, ought always to oppose all taxes upon the necessaries of life, as well as all direct taxes upon the wages of labor. The final payment of both the one and the other falls altogether upon themselves, and always with a considerable overcharge.* They fall heaviest upon the landlords, who always pay in a double capacity; in that of landlords, by the reduction, of their rent; and in that of rich consumers, by the increase of their expense. The observation of Sir Matthew Decker, that certain taxes are, in the price of certain goods, sometimes repeated and accumulated four or five times, is perfectly just with regard to taxes upon the necessaries of life. In the price of leather, for example, you must pay not only for the tax upon the leather of your own shoes, but for a part of that upon those of the shoemaker and the tanner. You must pay, too, for the tax upon the salt, upon the soap, and upon the candles which those workmen consume while employed in your service; and for the tax upon the leather, which

---

* Note: This applies to all consumers today.

the salt maker, the soap maker, and the candle maker consume, while employed in their service.

In Great Britain, the principal taxes upon the necessaries of life are those upon the four commodities just now mentioned, salt, leather, soap, and candles. . . .

As all those four commodities are real necessaries of life, such heavy taxes upon them must increase somewhat the expense of the sober and industrious poor, and must consequently raise more or less the wages of their labor.

In a country where the winters are so cold as in Great Britain, fuel is, during that season, in the strictest sense of the word, a necessary of life, not only for the purpose of dressing victuals, but for the comfortable subsistence of many different sorts of workmen who work within doors; and coals are the cheapest of all fuel. The price of fuel has so important an influence upon that of labor, that all over Great Britain, manufactures have confined themselves principally to the coal counties; other parts of the country, on account of the high price of this necessary article, not being able to work so cheap. In some manufactures, besides, coal is a necessary instrument of trade; as in those of glass, iron, and all other metals. If a bounty could in any case be reasonable, it might perhaps be so upon the transportation of coals from those parts of the country in which they abound, to those in which they are wanted. But the legislature, instead of a bounty, has imposed a tax of three shillings and three pence a ton upon coals carried coast-ways; which, upon most sorts of coal, is more than sixty percent of the original price at the coal pit. Coals carried, either by land or by inland navigation, pay no duty. Where they are naturally cheap, they are consumed duty-free; where they are naturally dear, they are loaded with a heavy duty.

Such taxes, though they raise the price of subsistence, and consequently the wages of labor, yet they afford a considerable revenue to government, which it might not be easy to find in any other way. There may, therefore, be good reasons for continuing them. The bounty upon the exportation of corn, so far us it tends, in the actual state of tillage, to raise the price of that necessary article, produces all the like bad effects; and instead of affording any revenue, frequently occasions a very great expense to government. The high duties upon the importation of foreign corn, which, in years of moderate plenty, amount to a prohibition; and the absolute prohibition of the importation, either of live cattle, or of salt provisions, which takes place in the ordinary state of the law, and which, on account of the scarcity, is at present suspended for a limited time with regard to Ireland and the British plantations, have all had the bad effects of taxes upon the necessaries of life, and produce no revenue to government. Nothing seems necessary for the repeal of such regulations, but to convince the public of the futility of that system in consequence of which they have been established.

Taxes upon the necessaries of life are much higher in many other countries than in Great Britain. Duties upon flour and meal when ground at the mill, and upon bread when baked at the oven, take place in many countries. In Holland the money-price of the bread consumed in towns is supposed to be doubled by means of such taxes. In lieu of a part of them, the people who live in the country pay every year so much a head, according to the sort of bread they are supposed to consume. Those who consume wheaten bread pay three guilders fifteen stivers; about six shillings and nine pence half-penny. Those, and some other taxes of the same kind, by raising the price of labor, are said to have ruined the greater part of the manufactures of Holland. . . .

Consumable commodities, whether necessaries or luxuries, may be taxed in two different ways. The consumer may either pay an annual sum on account of his using or consuming goods of a certain kind; or the goods may be taxed while they remain in the hands of the dealer, and before they are delivered to the consumer. The consumable goods which last a considerable time before they are consumed altogether, are most properly taxed in the one way; those of which the consumption is either immediate or more speedy in the other. The coach tax and plate tax are examples of the former method of imposing; the greater part of the other duties of excise and customs, of the latter.

The duties of excise are imposed chiefly upon goods of home produce, destined for home consumption. . . .

They fall almost altogether upon what I call luxuries, excepting always the four duties above mentioned, upon salt, soap, leather, candles, and perhaps that upon green glass.

The duties of customs are much more ancient than those of excise. They seem to have been called customs, as denoting customary payments, which had been in use for time immemorial. They appear to have been originally considered as taxes upon the profits of merchants. . . . In those ignorant times, it was not understood, that the profits of merchants are a subject not taxable directly; or that the final payment of all such taxes must fall, with a considerable overcharge, upon the consumers. . . .

. . . The ancient duties of customs were imposed equally upon all sorts of goods, necessaries as well its luxuries, goods exported as well as goods imported. . . .

. . . In the forty-seventh year of Edward III, a duty of six pence in the pound was imposed upon all goods exported and imported, except wools, wool-felts, leather, and wines which were subject to particular duties. . . . A great variety of other duties have occasionally been imposed upon particular sorts of goods, in order sometimes to relieve the exigencies of the state, and sometimes to regulate the trade of the country, according to the principles of the mercantile system.

That system has come gradually more and more into fashion. . . . The greater part of the ancient duties which had been imposed upon the exportation of the goods of home produce and manufacture, have either been lightened or taken away altogether. In most cases, they have been taken away. Bounties have even been given upon the exportation of some of them. Drawbacks, too, sometimes of the whole, and, in most cases, of a part of the duties which are paid upon the importation of foreign goods, have been granted upon their exportation.... This growing favor of exportation, and discouragement of importation, have suffered only a few exceptions, which chiefly concern the materials of some manufactures. These our merchants and manufacturers are willing should come as cheap as possible to themselves, and as dear as possible to their rivals and competitors in other countries. Foreign materials are, upon this account, sometimes allowed to be imported duty-free; Spanish wool, for example, flax, and raw linen yarn. The exportation of the materials of home produce, and of those which are the particular produce of our colonies has sometimes been prohibited, and sometimes subjected to higher duties. The exportation of English wool has been prohibited. That of beaver skins, of beaver wool, and of gum-senega, has been subjected to higher duties; Great Britain, by the conquests of Canada and Senegal, having got almost the monopoly of those commodities.

That the mercantile system has not been very favorable to the revenue of the great body of the people, to the annual produce of the land and labor of the country, I have endeavored to show in the fourth book of this Inquiry. It seems not to have been more favorable to the revenue of the sovereign; so far, at least, as that revenue depends upon the duties of customs.

In consequence of that system, the importation of several sorts of goods has been prohibited altogether. This prohibition has, in some cases, entirely prevented, and in others has very much diminished, the importation of those commodities, by reducing the importers to the necessity of smuggling. It has entirely prevented the importation of foreign woolens; and it has very much diminished that of foreign silks and velvets. In both cases, it has entirely annihilated the revenue of customs which might have been levied upon such importation.

The high duties which have been imposed upon the importation of many different sorts of foreign goods in order to discourage their consumption in Great Britain, have, in many cases, served only to encourage smuggling, and, in all cases, have reduced the revenues of the customs below what more moderate duties would have afforded. The saying of Dr. Swift, that in the arithmetic of the customs, two and two, instead of making four, make sometimes only one, holds perfectly true with regard to such heavy duties, which never could have been imposed, had not the mercantile system taught us, in many cases, to employ taxation as an instrument, not of revenue, but of monopoly. . . .

. . . It has been the opinion of many people, that, by proper management, the duties of customs might . . . without any loss to the public revenue, and with great advantage to foreign trade, be confined to a few articles only.

The foreign articles, of the most general use and consumption in Great Britain, seem at present to consist chiefly in foreign wines and brandies; in some of the productions of America and the West Indies, sugar, rum, tobacco, cocoa-nuts, etc. and in some of those of the East Indies, tea, coffee, chinaware, spiceries of all kinds, several sorts of piece goods, etc. These different articles afford, the greater part of the perhaps, at present, revenue which is drawn from the duties of customs. The taxes which at present subsist upon foreign manufactures, if you except those upon the few contained in the foregoing enumeration, have, the greater part of them, been imposed for the purpose, not of revenue, but of monopoly, or to give our own merchants an advantage in the home market. By removing all prohibitions, and by subjecting all foreign manufactures to such moderate taxes, as it was found from experience, afforded upon each article the greatest revenue to the public, our own workmen might still have a considerable advantage in the home market; and many articles, some of which at present afford no revenue to government, and others a very inconsiderable one, might afford a very great one.

High taxes, sometimes by diminishing the consumption of the taxed commodities, and sometimes by encouraging smuggling frequently afford a smaller revenue to government than what might be drawn from more moderate taxes. . . .

. . . If every duty was occasionally either heightened or lowered according as it was most likely, either the one way or the other, to afford the greatest revenue to the state; taxation being always employed as an instrument of revenue, and never of monopoly; it seems not improbable that a revenue, at least equal to the present neat revenue of the customs, might be drawn from duties upon the importation of only a few sorts of goods of the most general use and consumption; and that the duties of customs might thus be brought to the same degree of simplicity, certainty, and precision, as those of excise. . . .

If, by such a change of system, the public revenue suffered no loss, the trade and manufactures of the country would certainly gain a very considerable advantage. The trade in the commodities not taxed, by far the greatest number would be perfectly free, and might be carried on to and from all parts of the world with every possible advantage. Among those commodities would be comprehended all the necessaries of life, and all the materials of manufacture. So far as the free importation of the necessaries of life reduced their average money price in the home market, it would reduce the money price of labor, but without reducing in any respect its real recompense. The value of money is in proportion to the quantity of the necessaries of life which it will purchase. That of the necessaries of life is altogether independent of the quantity of money which can be had for them. The reduction in the money price of labor would necessarily be attended with a proportional one in that of all home manufactures, which would thereby gain some advantage in all foreign markets.

The price of some manufactures would be reduced, in a still greater proportion, by the free importation of the raw materials. If raw silk could be imported from China and Indostan, duty-free, the silk manufacturers in England could greatly undersell those of both France and Italy. There would be no occasion to prohibit the importation of foreign silks and velvets. The cheapness of their goods would secure to our own workmen, not only the possession of a home, but a very great command of the foreign market. Even the trade in the commodities taxed, would be carried on with much more advantage than at present. If those commodities were delivered out of the public warehouse for foreign exportation, being in this case exempted from all taxes, the trade in them would be perfectly free. The carrying trade, in all sorts of goods, would, under this system, enjoy every possible advantage. If these commodities were delivered out for home consumption, the importer not being obliged to advance the tax till he had an opportunity of selling his goods, either to some dealer, or to some consumer, he could always afford to sell them cheaper than if he had been obliged to advance it at the moment of importation. . . .

The duties upon foreign luxuries, imported for home consumption, though they sometimes fall upon the poor, fall principally upon people of middling or more than middling fortune. Such are, for example, the duties upon foreign wines, upon coffee, chocolate, tea, sugar, etc.

The duties upon the cheaper luxuries of home produce, destined for home consumption, fall pretty equally upon people of all ranks, in proportion to their respective expense. The poor pay the duties upon malt, hops, beer, and ale, upon their own consumption; the rich, upon both their own consumption and that of their servants.

The whole consumption of the inferior ranks of people, or of those below the middling rank, it must be observed, is, in every country, much greater, not only in quantity, but in value, than that of the middling, and of those above the middling rank. The whole expense of the inferior is much greater than that of the superior ranks. In the first place, almost the whole capital of every country is annually distributed among the inferior ranks of people, as the wages of productive labor. Secondly, a great part of the revenue, arising from both the rent of land and the profits of stock, is annually distributed among the same rank, in the wages and maintenance of menial servants, and other unproductive laborers. Thirdly, some part of the profits of stock belongs to the same rank, as a revenue arising from the employment of their small capitals. The amount of the profits annually made by small shopkeepers, tradesmen, and retailers of all kinds, is everywhere very considerable, and makes a very considerable portion of the annual produce. Fourthly and lastly, some part even of the rent of land belongs to the same rank; a considerable part to those who are somewhat below the middling rank, and a small part even to the lowest rank; common laborers sometimes possessing in property an acre or two of land.

Though the expense of those inferior ranks of people, therefore, taking them individually, is very small, yet the whole mass of it, taking them collectively, amounts always to by much the largest portion of the whole expense of the society; what remains of the annual produce of the land and labor of the country, for the consumption of the superior ranks, being always much less, not only in quantity, but in value. The taxes upon expense, therefore, which fall chiefly upon that of the superior ranks of people, upon the smaller portion of the annual produce, are likely to be much less productive than either those which fall indifferently upon the expense of all ranks, or even those which fall chiefly upon that of the inferior ranks, than either those which fall indifferently upon the whole annual produce, or those which fall chiefly upon the larger portion of it. The excise upon the materials and manufacture of homemade fermented and spirituous liquors is, accordingly, of all the different taxes upon expense, by far the most productive; and this branch of the excise falls very much, perhaps principally, upon the expense of the common people. In the year which ended on the 5th of July 1775, the gross produce of this branch of the excise amounted to 3,341,837*l*. 9*s*. 9*d*.

It must always be remembered, however, that it is the luxuries, and not the necessary expense of the inferior ranks of people, that ought ever to be taxed. The final payment of any tax upon their necessary expense would fall altogether upon the superior ranks of people; upon the smaller portion of the annual produce, and not upon the greater. Such a tax must, in all cases, either raise the wages of labor, or lessen the demand for it. It could not raise the wages of labor, without throwing the final payment of the tax upon the superior ranks of people. It could not lessen the demand for labor, without lessening the annual produce of the land and labor of the country, the fund upon which all taxes must be finally paid. Whatever might be the state to which a tax of this kind reduced the demand for labor, it must always raise wages higher than they otherwise would be in that state; and the final payment of this enhancement of wages must, in all cases, fall upon the superior ranks of people.

Fermented liquors brewed, and spirituous liquors distilled, not for sale, but for private use, are not in Great Britain liable to any duties of excise. This exemption, of which the object is to save private families from the odious visit and examination of the tax gatherer, occasions the burden of those duties to fall frequently much lighter upon the rich than upon the poor. It is not, indeed, very common to distill for private use, though it is done sometimes. But in the country, many middling and almost all rich and great families brew their own beer. . . .

In consequence of the notion, that duties upon consumable goods were taxes upon the profits of merchants, those duties have, in some countries, been repeated upon every successive sale of the goods. If the profits of the merchant-importer or merchant-manufacturer were taxed, equality seemed to require that those of all the middle buyers, who intervened between either of them and the consumer, should likewise be taxed. The famous alcavala of Spain seems to have been established upon this principle. It was at first a tax of ten percent afterwards of fourteen percent and it is at present only six percent upon the sale of every sort of property whether moveable or immoveable; and it is repeated every time the property is sold. The levying of this tax requires a multitude of revenue officers, sufficient to guard the transportation of goods, not only from one province to another, but from one shop to another. It subjects, not only the dealers in some sorts of goods, but those in all sorts, every farmer, every manufacturer, every merchant and shopkeeper, to the continual visit and examination of the tax gatherers. Through the greater part of the country in which a tax of this kind is established, nothing can be produced for distant sale. The produce of every part of the country must be proportioned to the consumption of the neighborhood. It is to the alcavala, accordingly, that

Ustaritz imputes the ruin of the manufactures of Spain. He might have imputed to it, likewise, the declension of agriculture, it being imposed not only upon manufactures, but upon the rude produce of the land. . . .

The uniform system of taxation, which, with a few exceptions of no great consequence, takes place in all the different parts of the united kingdom of Great Britain, leaves the interior commerce of the country, the inland and coasting trade, almost entirely free. The inland trade is almost perfectly free; and the greater part of goods may be carried from one end of the kingdom to the other, without requiring any permit or let-pass, without being subject to question, visit, or examination, from the revenue officers. There are a few exceptions, but they are such as can give no interruption to any important branch of inland commerce of the country. Goods carried coastwise, indeed, require certificates or coast-cockets. If you except coals, however, the rest are almost all duty-free. This freedom of interior commerce, the effect of the uniformity of the system of taxation, is perhaps one of the principal causes of the prosperity of Great Britain; every great country being necessarily the best and most extensive market for the greater part of the productions of its own industry. If the same freedom in consequence of the same uniformity could be extended to Ireland and the plantations, both the grandeur of the state, and the prosperity of every part of the empire, would probably be still greater than at present.

In France, the different revenue laws which take place in the different provinces, require a multitude of revenue officers to surround, not only the frontiers of the kingdom, but those of almost each particular province, in order either to prevent the importation of certain goods, or to subject it to the payment of certain duties, to the no small interruption of the interior commerce of the country. . . . There are many local duties which do not extend beyond a particular town or district. . . . It is unnecessary to observe how much both the restraints upon the interior commerce of the country, and the number of the revenue officers, must be multiplied, in order to guard the frontiers of those different provinces and districts which are subject to such different systems of taxation. . . .

Such various and complicated revenue laws are not peculiar to France. The little dutchy of Milan is divided into six provinces, in each of which there is a different system of taxation, with regard to several different sorts of consumable goods. The still smaller territories of the duke of Parma are divided into three or four, each of which has, in the same manner, a system of its own. Under such absurd management, nothing but the great fertility of the soil, and happiness of the climate, could preserve such countries from soon relapsing into the lowest state of poverty and barbarism.

Taxes upon consumable commodities may either be levied by an administration, of which the officers are appointed by government, and are immediately accountable to government, of which the revenue must, in this case, vary from year to year, according to the occasional variations in the produce of the tax; or they may be let in farm for a rent certain, the tax farmer being allowed to appoint his own officers, who, though obliged to levy the tax in the manner directed by the law, are under his immediate inspection, and are immediately accountable to him. The best and most frugal way of levying a tax can never be by farm.... In countries where the public revenues are in farm, the [tax] farmers are generally the most opulent people. Their wealth would alone excite the public indignation; and the vanity which almost always accompanies such upstart fortunes, the foolish ostentation with which they commonly display that wealth, excite that indignation still more.

The farmers of the public revenue never find the laws too severe, which punish any attempt to evade the payment of a tax.... In the greatest exigencies of the state, when the anxiety of the sovereign for the exact payment of his revenue is necessarily the greatest, they seldom fail to complain, that without laws more rigorous than those which actually took place, it will be impossible for them to pay even the usual rent. In those moments of public distress, their commands cannot be disputed. The revenue laws, therefore, become gradually more and more severe. The most sanguinary are always to be found in countries where the greater part of the public revenue is in farm; the mildest, in countries where it is levied under the immediate inspection of the sovereign. Even a bad sovereign feels more compassion for his people than can ever be expected from the farmers of his revenue. He knows that the permanent grandeur of his family depends upon the prosperity of his people, and he will never knowingly ruin that prosperity for the sake of any momentary interest of his own. It is otherwise with the farmers of his revenue, whose grandeur may frequently be the effect of the ruin, and not of the prosperity, of his people.

A tax is sometimes not only farmed for a certain rent, but the farmer has, besides, the monopoly of the commodity taxed. In France, the duties upon tobacco and salt are levied in this manner. In such cases, the farmer, instead of one, levies two exorbitant profits upon the people; the profit of the farmer, and the still more exorbitant one of the monopolist. Tobacco being a luxury, every man is allowed to buy or not to buy as he chooses; but salt being a necessary, every man is obliged to buy of the farmer a certain quantity of it; because, if he did not buy this quantity of the farmer, he would, it is presumed, buy it of some smuggler. The taxes upon both commodities are exorbitant. The temptation to smuggle, consequently, is to many people irresistible; while, at the same time, the rigor of the law, and the vigilance of the farmer's officers, render the yielding to the temptation almost certainly ruinous. The smuggling of salt and tobacco sends every year several hundred people to the galleys, besides a very considerable number whom it sends to the gibbet.... Similar taxes and monopolies of salt and tobacco have been established in many other countries, particularly in the Austrian and Prussian dominions, and in the greater part of the states of Italy....

The French system of taxation seems, in every respect, inferior to the British. In Great Britain, ten millions sterling are annually levied upon less than eight millions of people, without its being possible to say that any particular order is oppressed. From the Collections of the Abbé Expilly, and the observations of the author of the Essay upon the Legislation and Commerce of Corn, it appears probable that France, including the provinces of Lorraine and Bar, contains about twenty-three or twenty-four millions of people; three times the number, perhaps, contained in Great Britain. The soil and climate of France are better than those of Great Britain. The country has been much longer in a state of improvement and cultivation, and is, upon that account, better stocked with all those things which it requires a long time to raise up and accumulate; such as great towns, and convenient and well-built houses, both in town and country. With these advantages, it might be expected, that in France a revenue of thirty millions might be levied for the support of the state, with as little inconvenience as a revenue of ten millions is in Great Britain. In 1765 and 1766, the whole revenue paid into the treasury of France, according to the best, though, I acknowledge, very imperfect accounts which I could get of it, usually run between 308 and 325 millions of livres; that is, it did not amount to fifteen millions sterling; not the half of what might have been expected, had the people contributed in the same proportion to their numbers as the people of Great Britain. The people of France, however, it is generally acknowledged, are much more oppressed by taxes than the people of Great Britain. France, however, is certainly the great empire in Europe, which, after that of Great Britain, enjoys the mildest and most indulgent government.

In Holland, the heavy taxes upon the necessaries of life have ruined, it is said, their principal manufacturers, and are likely to discourage, gradually, even their fisheries and their trade in shipbuilding. The taxes upon the necessaries of life are inconsiderable in Great Britain, and no manufacture has hitherto been ruined by them. The British taxes which bear hardest on manufactures are some duties upon the importation of raw materials, particularly upon that of raw silk. The revenue of the States-General and of the different cities [of Holland], however, is said to amount to more than five millions two hundred and fifty thousand pounds sterling; and as the inhabitants of the United Provinces cannot well be supposed to amount to more than a third part of those of Great Britain, they must, in proportion to their number, be much more heavily taxed....

... The republican form of government seems to be the principal support of the present grandeur of Holland. The owners of great capitals, the great mercantile families, have generally either some direct share, or some indirect influence, in the administration of that government. For the sake of the respect and authority which they derive from this situation, they are willing to live in a country where their capital, if they employ it themselves, will bring them less profit, and if they lend it to another, less interest; and where the very moderate revenue which they can draw from it will purchase less of the necessaries and conveniences of life than in any other part of Europe. The residence of such wealthy people necessarily keeps alive, in spite of all disadvantages, a certain degree of industry in the country. Any public calamity which should destroy the republican form of government, which should throw the whole administration into the hands of nobles and of soldiers, which should annihilate altogether the importance of those wealthy merchants, would soon render it disagreeable to them to live in a country where they were no longer likely to be much respected. They would remove both their residence and their capital to some other country, and the industry and commerce of Holland would soon follow the capitals which supported them.

## Chapter Three

# Of Public Debts

IN THAT RUDE state of society which precedes the extension of commerce and the improvement of manufactures . . . the person who possesses a large revenue . . . could not well, indeed, do anything else but hoard whatever money they saved. To trade, was disgraceful to a gentleman; and to lend money at interest, which at that time was considered as usury, and prohibited by law, would have been still more so. In those times of violence and disorder, besides, it was convenient to have a hoard of money at hand, that in case they should be driven from their own home, they might have something of known value to carry with them to some place of safety. The same violence which made it convenient to hoard, made it equally convenient to conceal the hoard. . . .

The same disposition, to save and to hoard, prevailed in the sovereign, as well as in the subjects. Among nations, to whom commerce and manufacture are little known, the sovereign, it has already been observed in the Fourth book, is in a situation which naturally disposes him to the parsimony requisite for accumulation. In that situation, the expense, even of a sovereign, cannot be directed by that vanity which delights in the gaudy finery of a court. The ignorance of the times affords but few of the trinkets in which that finery consists. Standing armies are not then necessary; so that the expense, even of a sovereign, like that of any other great lord can be employed in scarce anything but bounty to his tenants, and hospitality to his retainers. But bounty and hospitality very seldom lead to extravagance; though vanity almost always does. All the ancient sovereigns of Europe, accordingly, it has already been observed, had treasures. Every Tartar chief, in the present times, is said to have one.

In a commercial country abounding with every sort of expensive luxury, the sovereign, in the same manner as almost all the great proprietors in his dominions, naturally spends a great part of his revenue in purchasing those luxuries. . . . If he does not . . . spend upon those pleasures so great a part of his revenue as to debilitate very much the defensive power of the state, it cannot well be expected that he should not spend upon them all that part of it which is over and above what is necessary for supporting that defensive power. His ordinary expense becomes equal to his ordinary revenue, and it is well if it does not frequently exceed it. . . . The present and the late King of Prussia are the only great princes of Europe, who, since the death of Henry IV of France, in 1610, are supposed to have amassed any considerable treasure. The parsimony which leads to accumulation has become almost as rare in republican as in monarchical governments. The Italian republics, the United Provinces of the Netherlands, are all in debt. The canton of Berne is the single republic in Europe which has amassed any considerable treasure. The other Swiss republics have not. The taste for some sort of pageantry, for splendid buildings, at least, and other public ornaments, frequently prevails as much in the apparently sober senate house of a little republic, as in the dissipated court of the greatest king.

The want of parsimony, in time of peace, imposes the necessity of contracting debt in time of war. When war comes, there is no money in the treasury, but what is necessary for carrying on the ordinary expense of the peace establishment. . . . In this exigency, government can have no other resource but in borrowing.

The same commercial state of society which, by the operation of moral causes, brings government in this manner into the necessity of borrowing, produces in the subjects both an ability and an inclination to lend. . . .

Commerce and manufactures can seldom flourish long in any state which does not enjoy a regular administration of justice; in which the people do not feel themselves secure in the possession of their property; in which the faith of contracts is not supported by law; and in which the authority of the state is not supposed to be regularly employed in enforcing the payment of debts from all those who are able to pay. Commerce and manufactures, in short, can seldom flourish in any state, in which there is not a certain degree of confidence in the justice of government. The same confidence which disposes great merchants and manufacturers upon ordinary occasions, to trust their property to the protection of a particular government, disposes them, upon extraordinary occasions, to trust that government with the use of their property. By lending money to government, they do not even for a moment diminish their ability to carry on their trade and manufactures; on the contrary, they commonly augment it. The necessities of the state render government, upon most occasions willing to borrow upon terms extremely advantageous to the lender. The security which it grants to the original creditor is made transferable to any other creditor; and from the universal confidence in the justice of the state, generally sells in the market for more than was originally paid for it. The merchant or moneyed man makes money by lending money to government, and instead of diminishing, increases his trading capital. . . .

The government of such a state is very apt to repose itself upon this ability and willingness of its subjects to lend it their money on extraordinary occasions. It foresees the facility of borrowing, and therefore dispenses itself from the duty of saving.

In a rude state of society, there are no great mercantile or manufacturing capitals. The individuals, who hoard whatever money they can save, and who conceal their hoard, do so from a distrust of the justice of government; from a fear, that if it was known that they had a hoard, and where that hoard was to be found, they would quickly be plundered. In such a state of things, few people would be able, and nobody would be willing to lend their money to government on extraordinary exigencies. The sovereign feels that he must provide for such exigencies by saving, because he foresees the absolute impossibility of borrowing. This foresight increases still further his natural disposition to save.

The progress of the enormous debts which at present oppress, and will in the long run probably ruin, all the great nations of Europe, has been pretty uniform. Nations, like private men, have generally begun to borrow upon what may be called personal credit, without assigning or mortgaging any particular fund for the payment of the debt; and when this resource has failed them, they have gone on to borrow upon assignments or mortgages of particular funds. . . .

The ordinary expense of the greater part of modern governments, in time of peace, being equal, or nearly equal, to their ordinary revenue, when war comes, they are both unwilling and unable to increase their revenue in proportion to the increase of their expense. They are unwilling, for fear of offending the people, who, by so great and so sudden an increase of taxes, would soon be disgusted with the war; and they are unable, from not well knowing what taxes would be sufficient to produce the revenue wanted. The facility of borrowing delivers them from the embarrassment which this fear and inability would otherwise occasion. By means of borrowing, they are enabled, with a very moderate increase of taxes, to raise, from year to year, money sufficient for carrying on the war; and by the practice of perpetual funding, they are enabled, with the smallest possible increase of taxes, to raise annually the largest possible sum of money. In great empires, the people who live in the capital, and in the provinces remote from the scene of action, feel, many of them, scarce any inconveniency from the war, but enjoy, at their ease, the amusement of reading in the newspapers the exploits of their own fleets and armies. To them this amusement compensates the small difference between the taxes which they pay on account of the war, and those which they had been accustomed to pay in time of peace. They are commonly dissatisfied with the return of peace, which puts an end to their amusement, and to a thousand visionary hopes of conquest and national glory, from a longer continuance of the war.

The return of peace, indeed, seldom relieves them from the greater part of the taxes imposed during the war. These are mortgaged for the interest of the debt contracted, in order to carry it on. If, over and above paying the interest of this debt, and defraying the ordinary expense of government, the old revenue, together with the new taxes, produce some surplus revenue, it may, perhaps, be converted into a sinking fund for paying off the debt. But, in the first place, this sinking fund, even supposing it should be applied to no other purpose, is generally altogether inadequate for paying, in the course of any period during which it can reasonably be expected that peace should continue, the whole debt contracted during the war; and, in the second place, this fund is almost always applied to other purposes.

The new taxes were imposed for the sole purpose of paying the interest of the money borrowed upon them. If they produce more, it is generally something which was neither intended nor expected, and is, therefore, seldom very considerable. Sinking funds have generally arisen, not so much from any surplus of the taxes which was over and above what was necessary for paying the interest or annuity originally charged upon them, as from a subsequent reduction of that interest. . . .

During the most profound peace, various events occur, which require an extraordinary expense; and government finds it always more convenient to defray this expense by misapplying the sinking fund, than by imposing a new tax. Every new tax is immediately felt more or less by the people. It occasions always some murmur, and meets with some opposition. The more taxes may have been multiplied, the higher they may have been raised upon every different subject of taxation; the more loudly the people complain of every new tax, the more difficult it becomes, too, either to find out new subjects of taxation, or to raise much higher the taxes already imposed upon the old. A momentary suspension of the payment of debt is not immediately felt by the people, and occasions neither murmur nor complaint. To borrow of the sinking fund is always an obvious and easy expedient for getting out of the present difficulty. The more the public debts may have been accumulated, the more necessary it may have become to study to reduce them; the more dangerous, the more ruinous it may be to misapply any part of the sinking fund; the less likely is the public debt to be reduced to any considerable degree, the more likely, the more certainly, is the sinking fund to be misapplied towards defraying all the extraordinary expenses which occur in time of peace. When a nation is already overburdened with taxes, nothing but the necessities of a new war, nothing but either the animosity of national vengeance, or the anxiety for national security, can induce the people to submit, with tolerable patience, to a new tax. Hence the usual misapplication of the sinking fund. . . .

. . . Were the expense of war to be defrayed always by a revenue raised within the year, the taxes from which that extraordinary revenue was drawn would last no longer than the war. The ability of private people to accumulate, though less during the war, would have been greater during the peace, than under the system of funding. War would not necessarily have occasioned the destruction of any old capitals, and peace would have occasioned the accumulation of many more new. Wars would, in general, be more speedily concluded, and less wantonly undertaken. The people feeling, during continuance of war, the complete burden of it, would soon grow weary of it; and government, in order to humor them, would not be under the necessity of carrying it on longer than it was necessary to do so. The foresight of the heavy and unavoidable burdens of war would hinder the people from wantonly calling for it when there was no real or solid interest to fight for. The seasons during which the ability of private people to accumulate was somewhat impaired, would occur more rarely, and be of shorter continuance. Those, on the contrary, during which that ability was in the highest vigor would be of much longer duration than they can well be under the system of funding.

When funding, besides, has made a certain progress, the multiplication of taxes which it brings along with it, sometimes impairs as much the ability of private people to accumulate, even in time of peace, as the other system would in time of war. The peace revenue of Great Britain amounts at present to more than ten millions a year. If free and unmortgaged, it might be sufficient, with proper management, and without contracting a shilling of new debt, to carry on the most vigorous war. The private revenue of the inhabitants of Great Britain is at present as much encumbered in time of peace, their ability to accumulate is as much impaired, as it would have been in the time of the most expensive war. . . .

In the payment of the interest of the public debt, it has been said, it is the right hand which pays the left. The money does not go out of the country. It is only a part of the revenue of one set of the inhabitants which is transferred to another; and the nation is not a farthing the poorer.* This apology is founded altogether in the sophistry of the mercantile system; and, after the long examination which I have already bestowed upon that system, it may, perhaps, be unnecessary to say anything further about it. It supposes, besides, that the whole public debt is owing to the inhabitants of the country, which happens not to be true; the Dutch, as well as several other foreign nations, having a very considerable share in our public funds. But though the whole debt were owing to the inhabitants of the country, it would not, upon that account, be less pernicious. . . .

The proprietor of land is interested, for the sake of his own revenue, to keep his estate in as good condition as he can, by building and repairing his tenants' houses, by making and maintaining the necessary drains and enclosures, and all those other expensive improvements which it properly belongs to the landlord to make and maintain. But, by different land taxes, the revenue of the landlord may be so much diminished, and, by different duties upon the necessaries and

---

* This is much less true now, when so much borrowing is international.

conveniences of life, that diminished revenue may be rendered of so little real value, that he may find himself altogether unable to make or maintain those expensive improvements. When the landlord, however, ceases to do his part, it is altogether impossible that the tenant should continue to do his. As the distress of the landlord increases, the agriculture of the country must necessarily decline.

When, by different taxes upon the necessaries and conveniences of life, the owners and employers of capital stock find, that whatever revenue they derive from it, will not, in a particular country, purchase the same quantity of those necessaries and conveniences which an equal revenue would in almost any other, they will be disposed to remove to some other. And when, in order to raise those taxes, all or the greater part of merchants and manufacturers, that is, all or the greater part of the employers of great capitals, come to be continually exposed to the mortifying and vexatious visits of the tax gatherers, this disposition to remove will soon be changed into an actual removing. The industry of the country will necessarily fall with the removal of the capital which supported it, and the ruin of trade and manufactures will follow the declension of agriculture. . . .

The practice of funding has gradually enfeebled every state which has adopted it. The Italian republics seem to have begun it. Genoa and Venice, the only two remaining which can pretend to an independent existence, have both been enfeebled by it. Spain seems to have learned the practice from the Italian republics, and (its taxes being probably less judicious than theirs) it has, in proportion to its natural strength, been still more enfeebled. The debts of Spain are of very old standing. It was deeply in debt before the end of the sixteenth century, about a hundred years before England owed a shilling. France, notwithstanding all its natural resources, languishes under an oppressive load of the same kind. The republic of the United Provinces is as much enfeebled by its debts as either Genoa or Venice. Is it likely that, in Great Britain alone, a practice, which has brought either weakness or dissolution into every other country, should prove altogether innocent?

The system of taxation established in those different countries, it may be said, is inferior to that of England. I believe it is so. . . . To the honor of our present system of taxation, indeed, it has hitherto given so little embarrassment to industry, that, during the course even of the most expensive wars, the frugality and good conduct of individuals seem to have been able, by saving and accumulation, to repair all the breaches which the waste and extravagance of government had made in the general capital of the society. At the conclusion of the late war, the most expensive that Great Britain ever waged, her agriculture was as flourishing, her manufacturers as numerous and as fully employed, and her commerce as extensive, as they had ever been before. The capital, therefore, which supported all those different branches of industry, must

have been equal to what it had ever been before. Since
the peace . . . Great Britain seems to support with ease,
a burden which, half a century ago, nobody believed
her capable of supporting, Let us not, however, upon
this account, rashly conclude that she is capable of supporting any burden; nor even be too confident that she
could support, without great distress, a burden a little
greater than what has already been laid upon her.*

When national debts have once been accumulated
to a certain degree, there is scarce, I believe, a single
instance of their having been fairly and completely
paid. The liberation of the public revenue, if it has ever
been brought about at all, has always been brought
about by a bankruptcy; sometimes by an avowed one,
though frequently by a pretended payment.

The raising of the denomination of the coin has
been the most usual expedient by which a real public
bankruptcy has been disguised under the appearance
of a pretended payment. If a six pence, for example,
should, either by act of parliament or royal proclamation, be raised to the denomination of a shilling, and
twenty sixpences to that of a pound sterling, the person who, under the old denomination, had borrowed
twenty shillings, or near four ounces of silver, would,

---

* It must be acknowledged that the United Kingdom did survive these
  debts, and even greater ones incurred during the wars with Napoleon.
  But Smith is right to pose the question and to suggest that there is a
  limit to debt and especially to the growth of debt in excess of that of
  the overall economy.

under the new, pay with twenty sixpences, or with something less than two ounces. A national debt of about a hundred and twenty-eight millions, near the capital of the funded and unfunded debt of Great Britain, might, in this manner, be paid with about sixty-four millions of our present money. It would, indeed, be a pretended payment only,* and the creditors of the public would really be defrauded of ten shillings in the pound of what was due to them. The calamity, too, would extend much further than to the creditors of the public, and those of every private person would suffer a proportional loss; and this without any advantage, but in most cases with a great additional loss, to the creditors of the public.

If the creditors of the public, indeed, were generally much in debt to other people, they might in some measure compensate their loss by paying their creditors in the same coin in which the public had paid them. But in most countries, the creditors of the public are, the greater part of them, wealthy people, who stand more in the relation of creditors than in that of debtors, towards the rest of their fellow citizens. A pretended payment of this kind, therefore, instead of alleviating, aggravates, in most cases, the loss of the creditors of the public; and, without any advantage to the public, extends the calamity to a great number of other

---

* The usual method today would be for government to issue new paper money to pay its debt, which is another, and easier, form of pretended payment.

innocent people. It occasions a general and most pernicious subversion of the fortunes of private people; enriching, in most cases, the idle and profuse debtor, at the expense of the industrious and frugal creditor; and transporting a great part of the national capital from the hands which were likely to increase and improve it, to those who are likely to dissipate and destroy it.

When it becomes necessary for a state to declare itself bankrupt, in the same manner as when it becomes necessary for an individual to do so, a fair, open, and avowed bankruptcy, is always the measure which is both least dishonorable to the debtor, and least hurtful to the creditor. The honor of a state is surely very poorly provided for, when, in order to cover the disgrace of a real bankruptcy, it has recourse to a juggling trick of this kind, so easily seen through, and at the same time so extremely pernicious.

# Endnotes

1. John Kenneth Galbraith, *The Age of Uncertainty* (Boston: Houghton Mifflin Co., 1977), 13.

2. *Essay on the Nature of Commerce in General*, written in French in 1730s (1755).

3. Anne-Robert-Jacques Turgot, *Reflections on The Formation and The Distribution of Wealth* (1770).

4. David Hume, *Essays, Moral and Political* (1748).

5. François Quesnay, *Tableau économique* (1758).

6. Joseph Schumpeter, *History of Economic Analysis* (Oxford: Oxford University Press, 1954), 184.

7. *Journal of Libertarian Studies* (1990).

8. David Gordon, http://www.mises.org (September 21, 2009).

9. Hunter Lewis, ed., *The Essence of Adam Smith's* Wealth of Nations (Mt. Jackson, VA: Axios Press, 2011), 106.

10. Ibid., 342–343.

11. Ibid., 338.

12. Ibid., 327.

13. Ibid., 107.

14. Ibid., 133.

15. Ibid., 410.

16. Hunter Lewis, *Are The Rich Necessary? Great Economic Arguments and How They Reflect Our Personal Values*, Updated & Expanded Edition, (Mt. Jackson, VA: Axios Press, 2009), 310–311.

17. Lecture in 1775, quoted in Dugald Stewart, *Account of the Life and Writings of Adam Smith LLD*, Section IV, 25.

18. Lewis, ed., *The Essence of Adam Smith's* Wealth of Nations, 316.

19. Adam Smith, *The Theory of Moral Sentiments* (1759), Part IV, chapter 1, 184, para 10.

20. Henry Hazlitt, *The Conquest of Poverty*, (Irvington-on-Hudson, NY: Foundation for Economic Education, 1994), 51.

21. Arthur Okun, *Fortune* (November 1975): 199.

22. *Business Week* (August 12, 1985): 10.

23. Lewis, *Are The Rich Necessary?*, 102–105.

24. Paul Johnson, *Forbes Magazine* (April 26, 2010), 17.

25. Lewis, ed., *The Essence of Adam Smith's* Wealth of Nations, 177.

26. Ibid., 245.

27. Ludwig von Mises, *Human Action: A Treatise on Economics*, (Chicago: Henry Regnery Co., 1966), 422.

28. Lewis, ed., *The Essence of Adam Smith's* Wealth of Nations, 245.

29. Ibid., 273.

30. P. J. O'Rourke, *On the Wealth of Nations: Books that Changed the World* (New York: Atlantic Monthly Press, 2006).

31. Karl Marx, Friedrich Engels, *Critique of the Gotha Program* (1875).

32. *Encyclopedia Britannica* (1911), Article on Adam Smith, http://www.1911encyclopedia.org/Adam_Smith.

# Index